PASTURES OF PLENTY

A SELF-PORTRAIT

(For more information about Woody Guthrie, write to Woody Guthrie Publications, 250 West 57th St., New York, NY 10107.)

PASTURES OF PLENTY

A SELF-PORTRAIT

WOODY GUTHRIE

EDITED BY

**DAVE MARSH
AND HAROLD LEVENTHAL**

HarperCollins*Publishers*

PASTURES OF PLENTY

FIRST EDITION

Art Director: Sandra Choron
Managing Editor: Bob Oskam
Designer: Stanley S. Drate/Folio Graphics Company, Inc.

Packaged by Rapid Transcript, a division of March Tenth, Inc.

LIBRARY OF CONGRESS CATALOG NUMBER 89-46547

ISBN 0-06-016342-9

90 91 92 93 94 MPC 10 9 8 7 6 5 4 3 2 1

CONTENTS

ACKNOWLEDGMENTS

In Woody Guthrie's view of the world, nobody operates alone. That's never been more true than in this project. We owe thanks to several people for their assistance. Robert Santelli did much of the retyping of Woody's original material, aided with identifications of many of the more obscure people and events in the text, and lent us valuable perspective with an early reading of much of the material. Kristen Carr also assisted in the retyping. Fred Hellerman and Pete Seeger lent us irreplaceable insight about the man and the times. Woody's children—Arlo, Joady, and Nora—graciously allowed us to roam through the still-fertile fields of their father's creativity. Nora deserves a special accolade for tracking down and printing the cover photograph.

We also want to thank Irene Allong, Joy Graeme, and Natalie Leventhal from Harold Leventhal's office for their help. Also Toshi Seeger, Mary Jo Edgmon, and Larry Richmond.

The Office of Folklife Programs of the Smithsonian Institution made available to us the Woody Guthrie papers and drawings that are part of the Moses and Frances Asch Collection, and we thank Anthony Seeger, Lori Taylor, and Jeff Place for their cooperation.

Sandra Choron, our agent, brought us to Harper & Row and Tom Miller, our editor. We thank both of them for their belief and dedication. Bob Oskam made an extraordinarily involved copy-editing job as painless as it could be.

Dave Marsh would also like to thank Daniel Wolff, Jon Landau, Lee Ballinger, Barbara Carr (as always) . . . and especially Harold Leventhal, for giving me the opportunity and making it fun—not to mention an education.

Woody and Leadbelly, Chicago ca. 1941. For some reason, every time this photo has been printed until now, it has always been cropped to show only Leadbelly. (Courtesy of Stephen Deutch)

You elected me to this office
Of a poet and a singer
And I think I know
What you want me to do here
Things are said in history
And they are said again
And these of today
Have got to be said
Said again
Because today is our first time
To say
What we are today—
And I will say
And sing of these things
These things
That you fight for today.

FOREWORD

BY HAROLD LEVENTHAL

I first met Woody in 1947 when I began to attend the folk music "hootennannies" in New York. He was performing along with Huddie Leadbelly, Pete Seeger, Josh White, and many others who were later to make folk music history. I was then working as a "song-plugger" for a popular music publisher on Broadway's Tin-Pan Alley but was attracted to the political-topical songs sung by Woody and his friends.

It wasn't until 1950, when I became the personal manager of the Weavers, that I got to know him better and spend more time with him. In the early fifties, Woody would show up at places the Weavers performed, and I would have to take care of him and get him to his next appointment.

By late 1952 it was obvious that something was wrong with Woody's behavior. He was inconsistent in his singing, he'd fluff lines, his guitar picking was erratic, and his stance always seemed wobbly. We berated him for "getting drunk," but when he finally went to Brooklyn State Hospital, examination revealed the early stages of Huntington's disease as the cause of his unstable condition.

His family and friends were concerned about Woody's deteriorating condition, about the need to get him proper medical treatment, and to have all his writings and songs under proper control and management. I was given the responsibility to take care of these financial and organizational matters. Woody was delighted that someone was "taking care of me" and promptly asked me for an "advance of a couple of dollars."

As the years went by I regularly visited Woody at the various hospitals where he was confined. I would report to him on the progress of his songs, many of which were widely recorded for the first time in the early sixties. Woody was pleased that his songs were now reaching a wide public via radio, records, and television. All during the years of his hospitalization I was able, with Woody's encouragement, to arrange the reissuance of his early recordings and books. Woody's condition deteriorated, and after thirteen years in the hospital, he died on October 3, 1967.

This collection of writings, drawings, photos, and memorabilia is a very small part of the files of the Woody Guthrie Archives.

The Archives would not have existed but for the determination of the late Marjorie Guthrie. She encouraged Woody and was very supportive of his work and his struggling career as a songwriter-performer. She kept Woody's original notebooks, drawings, letters, songs, scrapbooks, and his voluminous correspondence.

At the 1956 benefit held at New York City's Pythian Temple. Harold Leventhal is third from left, Woody next to him.

In 1957, after Woody had already been hospitalized, Marjorie conceived the idea of the Archives and began the effort, which continues today, to assemble and catalog all extant Woody Guthrie material. That same year a young researcher was hired to contact a long list of friends, relatives, coworkers, record and radio associates, and especially people who had known and worked with Woody as early as the Dust Bowl days.

The initial letter that was sent explained: "The first phase of this project, as you can see, is to collect all the material that we can, from wherever it may come, no small task considering the extent of Mr. Guthrie's travels and writings . . . We ask your help in bringing to light any letters, stories, articles, etc. that you may have or know the whereabouts of, so we may thoroughly go over all his writings. . . ."

Since then the Archives have been greatly expanded, and material has come from all parts of the country. Friends, relatives, and coworkers all responded, and continue to do so.

Woody was a prodigious writer. Hardly a day passed without his pouring out songs (especially topical songs inspired by newspaper items), letters, notes, all written on whatever paper was available. In 1941, while working with the Almanac Singers when they had a booking in Chicago, Woody stayed at Studs Terkel's apartment. "I remember the summer of '41. Woody and three singing colleagues were in transit and spent a few days and nights in our jam-packed flat," writes Studs. "At four in the morning my dream was interrupted by the click-clack of my Royal portable. It was Woody, who had just ambled home, touch-typing like crazy. I turned over and slept dreamlessly. A few hours later, as Woody snored softly and innocently in the adjoining room, I was picking sheets of paper from our waste basket. There must have been at least thirty pages, single spaced. Verse and prose, wild and vivid images of his night at a South Side tavern. They danced off the pages!"

In 1961, as the Archives expanded, Marjorie "temporarily" moved the many file cabinets from their Howard Beach home to my office on West 57th Street. It has "temporarily" been there for twenty-nine years, and the number of file cabinets has more than doubled from the original. Somewhere along the way I joined with Marjorie as a coarchivist in seeking out more of Woody's material, which continually surfaced as people wrote to us offering a letter, some old photos, a postcard, even old government employment records from the Bonneville Dam.

Fortunately, much of the creative work of Woody is not resting unexamined in the files, awaiting researchers. From the files have come several books already, among them *Born to Win*, edited by Robert Shelton (1965); *Woody Sez*, a collection from Woody's column in the *People's World* newspaper (1975); and Woody's last autobiographical novel, *Seeds of Man* (1976). Biographer Joe Klein, author of *Woody Guthrie: A Life*, spent long hours for almost a year perusing the files of the Archives.

Woody's songs are now an indelible part of our American culture; they have stood the test of time through three generations. His songs are sung so often in schools over the United States that "This Land Is Your Land" has become virtually a second national anthem. Contemporary singers continue to perform and record his songs, and his writings are an acknowledged part of the nation's literary legacy.

The Smithsonian Institution has agreed to house the Woody Guthrie Archives in Washington, D.C., as part of its American Folklore collections. In the very near future, Woody's works will finally take their place among the best of our American heritage, as the Archives are transferred to the nation's capital.

NOTICE!

All Songs in this book are filed in <u>alphabetical</u> <u>Order</u>

Put them back the same way.

And be sure you put them back.

signed
a desperate man,
Woody Guthrie

INTRODUCTION

BY DAVE MARSH

Well, it's always we rambled, that river and I
All along your green valley I'll work 'til I die
My land I'll defend, with my life if it be
'Cause my pastures of plenty must always be free

Pastures of Plenty isn't a book about Woody Guthrie. It's a book by him. So its introduction had to begin with Woody's own words. On the other hand, Woody is long gone. This material took its shape from two years of editorial interaction with old notebooks, clippings, journals, meticulously penned lyrics, and messy typescripts. Some explication is in order.

When Harold Leventhal asked if I'd be interested in editing what he called "the Woody Guthrie scrapbook," a collection of previously unpublished material, my reaction was cool. Woody's words had already been collected so many times over that it seemed unlikely the leftovers would add anything new to our picture of him. And it was the end of the eighties: Who needed more agitprop? I said I'd take a look at what Leventhal had mainly because Harold himself seemed like a good person to get to know.

When I walked into his office that afternoon in the winter of '88, the first thing that struck my eye was a framed 8″ × 10″ photograph on his desk. It was a picture of Woody unlike any I'd ever seen. He was precisely groomed, his shirt neatly buttoned to the very collar, and he stared straight into the camera with a glint in his eye. I knew that look; it was the gaze of a man seeing the Main Chance. He could have been a movie star—or a rock and roller. The picture told me something about Woody Guthrie, his ambition and his determination, that I'd learned from none of his records or books or any of the books about him.

Harold explained that the picture was a snapshot from one of those automated four-for-a-quarter booths. It was taken in a Times Square arcade sometime around 1940, just after Woody first hit New York. Sometime in late '87, Nora Guthrie found it and had it blown up as a Christmas present. Leventhal didn't seem especially impressed by it, although he never demurred when I said, "Well, I don't know if you've got a book. But you've sure got a cover."

I wondered why Leventhal was so matter-of-fact about such a powerful photograph. Then he showed me the "scrapbook" material he had in mind: It filled half a dozen filing cabinet drawers and spilled over into scrapbooks and portfolios and boxes. There were, I guessed later, perhaps three-quarters of a million words of manuscript there. He'd made a preliminary selection from it, just enough previously uncollected Guthrie stories and articles and lyrics (or poems) and other memorabilia to whet my appetite.

Over the next eighteen months, I periodically found myself sated and saturated, going through those cabinets folder by folder, item by item, page by page. But the full flavor always returned. Occasionally, I'd get it back by coming across some landmark treasure: The original manuscript of "This Land Is Your Land" (entitled "God Blessed America") was simply sitting in one of the cabinets, encased in an acetate folder. (It's since been given a more properly archival abode.) But more often, I stumbled across a totally unexpected trove: entire notebooks of "letters" Woody'd written to his unborn child; huge lists of songs he knew (or alternately, songs he meant to make up). Sometimes the gold came in combination, as with a parody of the Beatitudes done as a kind of appendix to "Jesus Christ," his rewrite of "Jesse James."

Woody wrote in diary-style journals or in lined hardboard notebooks or, once in a while, in green, ruled stenographer's notebooks, the kind you can still buy in any dimestore. No one knows what percentage of those notebooks actually survived, and there are sporadic gaps, but with the addition of his published work in *The Sunday Worker* and *Dance* magazine and the like, they offer a fairly complete chronology of the period from Woody's first arrival in New York through the early fifties, when his creative capacities deteriorated as a result of the Huntington's chorea that finally killed him.

Pastures of Plenty! Words must literally have poured out of Guthrie's typewriter and fountain pen and pencil stubs. He wrote with an elegant hand, the result of training in Palmer method handwriting and as a sign painter (an occupation he practiced peripatetically), and it continues to mystify me how Woody could have put down so many pages, so neatly, day after day, and still find time to be husband, parent, folk singer, conversationalist, raconteur, songwriter, recording artist, sketch artist, and general vagabond. So, intermittently for better than a year, I dug through those files with a sense of awe and delight.

Like anybody familiar with the American folk music movement, I knew that Woody created many songs that are still beloved and still sung forty years and more after their creation: "This Land," "So Long (It's Been Good to Know You)," "Do Re Mi," "Grand Coulee Dam," "Pretty Boy Floyd," "Put Your Finger in the Air," "Deportees," "I Ain't Got No Home," and "Roll On Columbia," to name a few. In addition, I knew that his writings and performances established an artistic persona—almost a school for a certain kind of persona of which Bob Dylan, Tracy Chapman, Ramblin' Jack Elliott, and, for that matter, U2's Bono are all examples—still vital and influential after half a century. But it wasn't until I'd rummaged through those files that it hit me that Woody had achieved everything he did in less than twenty years. His creative lifespan basically extended only from the mid-thirties, when he left Texas for California, to the early fifties, when disease robbed him of his artistic coherence. He was only in his late thirties then. Had Woody had a more normal lifespan, Harold Leventhal might have needed as many file cabinets as the Pentagon.

In any event, none of the canonical Guthrie masterworks appear in the text of *Pastures of Plenty*. Everything in it is new material; very little of it has ever been published in any form, and almost all of what has been previously seen (usually in newspapers or magazines) has been out of print for decades. But these aren't leftovers, either. Part of what makes this new assortment of Woody's writings so fascinating is the frequency with which the words here conflict with his image as it has been passed down over the three decades since Huntington's chorea stilled his public voice. This book doesn't just give us Woody the invincible natural creative force, the politically correct songwriting machine, the incorrigible optimist, or even, for that matter, the perennially irresponsible hobo and perpetual big city hayseed. Every quality in that list assumes vivid existence in these pages, but so does another, equally complex Woody Guthrie: a man who had to struggle for personal and political responsibility and felt troubled and sometimes even defeated when he couldn't get a handle on it; a man who doubted in the dead of night; a man who matched unquenchable faith and optimism with an intimate knowledge of the near impossibility of living up to expectations.

These aspects of Woody's personality have been kept concealed by hagiographers or overlooked by debunkers. Yet these sides of his life and thinking don't diminish his artistry or his majestic personal integrity. They enlarge it, by giving us a more human Guthrie, more of a striver and, nevertheless, a man to whom many things come naturally, most of all doubts and questions. In that first batch that Leventhal showed me were these lines, unlike any Woody Guthrie I'd ever encountered:

> You've found something
> Something I missed
> You found a gladness being here
> And how to stand up proud to laugh with everybody else
> You found your work
> And your notch
> And where you belong
> In a chain of others that can't be broken and a stone
>   foundation that can't be shook down.
> So far, I haven't found that
> I found a drifting wind and a blowing rain
> And a coward and a stranger to people's pain
> And people never will show you their laugh
> Till you find it out through their pain
> Maybe I'm learning
> That secret of all secrets, (and it ain't even no secret).

I won't call the Woody Guthrie we encounter here an existentialist (though to what other school of philosophy do those lines belong?), but I will say that this comes closer to explaining Woody's famous hatred of songs that "leave you feeling low-down" than anything that assumes that he was nothing but a nativist hick or radical bumpkin.

In these pages, we see Woody Guthrie in intimate contact with a society from which those lines exhibit a profound estrangement. At its best, *Pastures of Plenty* is an account by a doomed outsider of his discovery of and nurture by an almost sacred community, a world in the process of being born in a spirit of grace (if not perfection). *Pastures of Plenty* is, among other things, a document of an important corner of that society, proof that it actually existed and that it was created out of a deep and abiding faith in nothing more (or less) mystical than a future in which socialism would order men's affairs.

For Woody, Dust Bowl denizen though he truly was, this pursuit of socialism may well begin in the search for a solution to a dilemma more existential than economic or political. "To be lonesome is one of the first mistakes you can make and lots of fellers make a

The worst thing that can happen to you is to cut yourself loose from people. And the best thing is to sort of vaccinate yourself right into the the big streams and blood of the people.

To feel like you know the best and the worst of folks that you see everywhere and never to feel weak, or lost, or even lonesome anywhere.

There is just one thing that can cut you to drifting from the people, and that's any brand or style of greed.

There is just one way to save yourself, and that's to get together and work and fight for everybody.

— WOODY GUTHRIE

business out of it and claim that it's a good thing. No, it's a bad one," he writes. Within the cadence of those sentences, you can feel him arguing with himself. But once he's persuaded, he can't resist extending the point: "The main trouble with the rich folks is they're so lonesome. . . . and the sorriest reason why they're lonesome is because amongst the rich folks it's every man for his self—in spite of their big clubs and organizations it's still every man for his self—that's the religion they believe in and it will cause them a lot of trouble, and not only cause them trouble but will really make times so hard that the poor folks will get together and take things over. It won't be because the rich folks are lonesome that they'll lose out but because they think too much of their own self and not enough about what other folks want to do."

Such a voice sounds odd to our ears, and not because the possibility of such a revolution has withered. (There are places in the world where that last sentence might articulate nothing more than conventional wisdom.) What's strange about Guthrie's sentences is that they consider current activity in light of a certain future, and what is most true today about all the people in the land that nurtured Woody Guthrie is that none of us can with certainty imagine any future, let alone such a hopeful one.

This is the story *Pastures of Plenty* told me as we compiled it, wading through prose and stories and drawings, old red-baiting newspaper clippings, and jocular diary entries. It's told mostly between the lines, as great stories are so often told, but it's unmistakable as we watch Woody try to build a life for himself, and then for himself and Marjorie, and then for himself and his wife and their children, all the while maintaining contact with that larger family beyond their doorstep, a family that embraces shopkeepers and folk-singing associates, "goofs on the Bowery" and elegant modern dancers, and reaches out and out to include the entire crewmen's mess of the Merchant Marine and every impover-ished infant in liberated Sicily. You get the flavor of it from Woody's casual references to day care—in the late forties, in Brooklyn, where day care is *today* a precious, hard-to-find service.

I tried to explain my amazement at this aspect of Woody's writings to a friend who'd grown up a red diaper baby in Brooklyn a few years later, when that community was unravelling. "These were people with an incredible sense of The Future!" I enthused, and he said, more dourly, that yes, those people had believed in a future because they believed that in one nation, the Soviet Union, the future was already being enacted.

But it's not that simple, either. American socialists, like socialists all over the world in those years, didn't just believe in the enactment of their cause in Mother Russia. In fact, Woody was engaged with particular socialists, the ones grouped around the large and powerful New York wing of the U.S. Communist Party, which was then certainly the most important such enterprise in this country. Confronted with a fascist reality that threatened to drag all of humanity into a long, permanent night (and another thing we tend to forget, and which *Pastures of Plenty* reminds us, is how immediate and imminent the fascist threat was), such stalwarts surely required an anchor for their hopes.

But if they used the Soviet Union as a model of the future that worked, it was in order to begin building one of their own. For these communists (and their associates—for there's no record that Woody ever belonged to the party, and lots of circumstantial evidence that he didn't), activism wasn't just a matter of rallies and speeches and theoretical jargon. It was a way to build a new world. New from the ground up—new rhythm, new words, virtually new air to breathe. That's why Woody continually finds himself competing with "Whitman, Pushkin and Sandburg"; they were poets who claimed to have found the voice of the common man.

God knows, you can learn absolutely nothing of political theory from Woody's writings (though of poetical theory he has a thing or two to tell), and he certainly never behaved in the Sunday-go-to-meeting manner associated with left orthodoxy, from that day unto this. Meetings were never his metier; the few he attended, he did his utmost to turn into parties of the opposite kind. But Guthrie lived in a community suffused with socialism, in which whatever of its principles could be enacted without state power were put into practice. Most important, Woody Guthrie wrote his greatest songs and stories while living among people who believed in and worked toward a high and mighty goal outside themselves. In many ways, that goal and such work is the subject of all his writing.

We, who not only don't live in such a world but are so totally estranged from any long-term vision of the future, can barely imagine what it would mean to live as though such principles and goals were realistic and attainable. We're inclined to deny the possibility that it existed, and *Pastures of Plenty* gave me my greatest reward with these bits of evidence that it really did. Duped by nothing, the men and women in these pages are vital and funny, the most dangerous kind of characters you can carry away from literature, because they will haunt and inspire the rest of your days. If their greatest dreams didn't come true, well, whose have?

Needless to say, the greatest character of them all is Woody himself. He knows it, too, even says it of himself flat out once or twice. "I feel like my work in this field will someday be seen as the most radical, the most militant, and the most topical of them all," Woody writes to Moe Asch in 1946. It was this firm conviction of his own importance to posterity that prompted Woody Guthrie to sit down to write every living day, and it was out of her conviction that he was right that Marjorie Guthrie strove to save everything he recorded or created.

Marjorie Guthrie's faith in Woody and his work was legendary—and really ought to be more so. With his health disintegrating even as McCarthyism dispatched the remnants of the world in which his work had been done, what he'd accomplished would almost certainly have been forgotten if not lost altogether but for her efforts—and, collaterally, those of Harold Leventhal. If it is true that without Woody Guthrie, there would have been no Bob Dylan, and without Bob Dylan, no popular music as we understand it today, we owe her an incalculable debt.

That, even among friends and associates who recognized Woody as something special, Marjorie's devotion was extraordinary is borne out by the fact that the great bulk of his legacy comes from the years of their marriage. Only fragments exist from the years before that; the record again becomes spotty in the later years when Woody ran off from his family obligations and the specter of his disease. But from the time when Woody and Marjorie lived together, we have a tremendous volume of material, which includes the books *Bound for Glory, Born to Win, Woody Sez,* and this one. (Several others could, and perhaps will be, compiled—for instance, the journal of "Letters to Railroad Pete," of which this volume presents only a fragment, is book length.)

One reason *Pastures of Plenty* offers such a different perspective on Woody's life and thinking is that it is very much a book centered in New York, rather than in the Southwest, where his famous Okie writings are set. And though Woody came to New York because of Will Geer and the chance to work in the nation's media capital, he stuck around because he'd found Marjorie and the chance to build together a life shaped by their common dreams.

Like all great dreams, this one is unending. *Pastures of Plenty* steps out from its shadows and shows it to us anew. So, as this introduction began with Woody's own words, it can do no better than to end with more of them, written in 1954, when he was nearly at the end of his creative life. They were scrawled in a journal, written in a hand so shaky that it took a full page to contain just those few lines. But they prove that there were things about Woody—his humor and his humanity, his sense of worth and history—that Huntington's chorea never touched. Like the rest of this book, they're mostly about hope:

> I want you to pay a lot more attention to all my words longer and deeper and quieter and louder than I ever could. You'll get more out of them than I did around here.

EDITORS' NOTE

The materials in this book were compiled from a variety of sources, ranging from handwritten scraps of paper to published newspaper and magazine articles, with a heavy lean toward the former. As a result, there are lots of unknown threads hanging around. Generally, we've been able to date (as to year, at least) everything presented, although sometimes the evidence is fairly circumstantial. Where the provenance of a piece is known or relevant, we've cited it. But often determining the source and even the purpose or intended form of something that Woody wrote would be guesswork. We've asked around, among Woody's friends and family. But in general, rather than worry about what it is, we've let what it says determine whether the material here belonged. You're welcome to your own best guess, now that we've had ours.

Any of Woody's writings that appear as rhymed verse are songs—but the melodies are unknown. The lyrics we've chosen for publication (out of several hundred available) are all meant to be read, anyhow, though knowledgeable folk song enthusiasts won't have any trouble fitting tunes to the ones they like best.

This is a book of Woody Guthrie's writings, not ours. Therefore, we've tried to keep our comments and notes to a minimum. We've intervened only where we deemed it absolutely necessary. Many of the more obscure places and characters to which Woody refers are identified in an appendix. (The rest of 'em, we couldn't figure out ourselves.)

All the words are just what Woody wrote. We've cut nothing out (that's censorship) and added nothing (that's worse). Woody often misspelled words—sometimes for effect, sometimes because in the heat of battle, the last thing he was going to do was stop and look it up. We've kept most of those, too.

God Blessed America

This Land ~~Was made~~ For You + me

This land is your land, this land is my land
From ~~the~~ California to the ~~Staten~~ Island,
From the Redwood Forest, to the Gulf stream waters,
God blessed America for me.

As I went walking that ribbon of highway
And saw above me that endless skyway,
And saw below me the golden valley, I said:
~~God blessed America for me.~~

I roamed and rambled, and followed my footsteps
To the sparkling sands of her diamond deserts,
And all around me, a voice was sounding:
~~God blessed America for me~~

there
Was a big high wall ^ that tried to stop me
A sign was painted said: Private Property.
But on the back side it didn't say nothing —
~~God blessed America for me.~~

When the sun come shining, then I was strolling
In wheat fields waving, and dust clouds rolling;
The voice was chanting as the fog was lifting:
~~God blessed America for me.~~

One bright sunny morning ~~in~~ the shadow ~~of the~~ steeple
By the Relief office I ~~saw~~ my people —
As they stood hungry, I ~~stood there~~ wondering if
~~God blessed~~ America for me.

* all you can write is
what you see.

Original copy
of this song

Woody G.
N.Y., N.Y., N.Y.
Feb. 23, 1940
43rd st + 6th ave,
Hanover House

Original manuscript for "This Land Is Your Land."

VOICE

I don't know how far I'm going to have to go
To see my own self or to hear my own voice
I tuned in on the radio and for hours never heard it
And then I went to the moving pictures show
And never heard it there
I put handsful of coins into machines and watched records turn
But the voice there was no voice of mine
I mean it was not my voice
The words not my words that I hear in my own ears
When I walk along and look at your faces
I set here in a Jewish delicattassen, I order a hot pastrami
Sandwitch on rye bread and I hear the lady ask me
Would you like to have a portion of cole slaw on the side
And I knew when I heard her speak that
She spoke my voice
And I told her I would take my slaw on a side dish
And would like to have a glass of tea with lemon
And she knew that I was speaking her words
And a fellow sat across at a table near my wall
And spoke while he ate his salami and drank his beer
And somehow I had the feeling
As I heard him speak, and he spoke a long time,
But not one word was in my personal language,
And I could tell by the deep sound, by the full tone
Of his voice that he spoke my language
I suppose you may wonder just how he could speak
In a dialect that I could not savvy nor understand
And yet understand every sound that he made
I learned to do this a long time ago
Walking up and down the sideroads and the main stems
Of this land here
I learned to listen this way when I washed dishes on the ships
I had to learn how to do it when I walked ashore in Africa
And in Scotland and in Ireland and in Britain,
London, Liverpool, Glasgow, Scots towns and Anglo's farms,
Irish canals and railroad bridges, Highlander's cows and
    horses
And here I knew the speech was the same as mine but
It was the dialect again, nasal, throatsy, deep chesty,
From the stomach, lungs, high in the head, pitched up and
    down,
And here I had to learn again
To say this is my language and part of my voice

Oh but I have not even heard this voice, these voices,
On the stages, screens, radios, records, juke boxes,
In magazines nor not in newspapers, seldom in courtrooms,
And more seldom when students and policemen study the faces
Behind the voices
And I thought as I saw a drunken streetwalking man mutter
And spit and curse into the wind out of the cafe's plate glass,
That maybe, if I looked close enough, I might hear
Some more of my voice
And I ate as quiet as I could, so as to keep my eyes
And my ears and my feelings wide open
And did hear
Heard all that I came to hear here in Coney Island's Jewish air
Heard reflections, recollections, seen faces in memory,
Heard voices untangle their words before me
And I knew by the feeling I felt that here was my voice.

Woody Guthrie

MY LIFE

My mother prayed that I would be
A man of some renown
But I am just a refugee, boys
As I go ramblin' round

—"Ramblin' Round"

Woody wrote this autobiographical sketch as part of the introduction to the American Folk Song *songbook, published in 1947. It's considerably less mythologized than* Bound for Glory, *Woody's book-length autobiography. (For the whole story from a more distanced perspective, read Joe Klein's* Woody Guthrie: A Life.)

MY MOTHER'S NAME was Nora Belle Tanner, and then she changed it to NORA BELLE GUTHRIE. Her mother was Mrs. Lee Tanner, one of the earliest log cabin school teachers in Okfuskee County, Oklahoma. The tales of the river bottom school house on the Deep Fork were full of the wild cat, the panther, the coyote, the overgrown wolf, the mountain lion, and the fights between man and beast to settle Okfuskee County. It was in the quicksands and muds of the river's rising, the wind that blew and whipped from east to west in a spit second, the lightning that splintered the barn loft, the snakey tailed cyclone, prairie cloudbursts, the months of fiery drouth that crippled the leaves, in the timber fires, prairie fires that took more than it could build back, in the fights of the men against all of these, that I was born, the third child in our family, and heard my mother sing to my brother, Roy, and to my sister, Clara.

MY FATHER'S NAME WAS CHARLES EDWARD GUTHRIE, born down in Bell County, Texas, in the scruboak and short cotton country. They called him Charlie, and he had almost as much of the singing blood in him as Mama had.

I am pretty positive that my mother's father, Lee Tanner, was an Irishman, and that my grandmother, Mrs. Lee Tanner, was Scottish. My mother learned all of the songs and ballads that her parents knew, and there were lots that were neither Scotch nor Irish, but Mexican, Spanish, and many made up by the Negroes in the South. This was not all that melted into the songs that I heard around me, because my Father, Charlie, was always out talking, dancing, drinking and trading with the Indians. He could speak several Creek words, taught me how to count in Chickasaw or Choctaw, Cherokee, Sioux, Osage, or Seminole dialect. From a shirt tearing boy papa had grown up to a straight talking man, a trained fist fighter in the days when Jess Willard and Jack Dempsey were sung like songs. Charlie grew up to be as clever a trader as he was a singer. He stepped out from back of his store counter and hung out his sign as a Real Estate Dealer. Land Leases. Royalties. Deeds and Titles. He was a Clerk of the County Court for several years and our house was full of the smells of big leather law books, and the poems of pomp and high dignity that he memorized and performed over for us with the same wild pioneer outdoor chant as he sang his Negro and Indian square-dances and Blueses. He was a guitar and banjo picker with a Cowboy Band or two, then hung up his deviled strings for domestic reasons.

At the new seven room house that Lee and Mary Tanner built on their farm, everything was nice, new and pretty. My mama was given a piano, her other sisters and brothers had one of the first phonographs in that county. The first notes of so-called civilized music echoed in the holler trees along Buckeye Creek and in the leaves of the sumac and the green June corn from out the screen door of the Tanner house. The Negroes made up songs and sung around the new Tanner place every day of its building up. Indians walked the backtrails and rooty rut roads, sang, cursed, chanted blessings and poison words out at the white man. This and the shirt staining fist fights that broke out around the house parties and dances, the foamy ponied outlaws, and the screaks of greasy wheeled buggies and wagons, newly-oiled trigger springs, the first oil scouting crowds that had commenced to drift out from back East, South, West and up North, their hurts, greeds, fears, this was the big song I heard all around me.

The Okemah, Oklahoma, house in which Guthrie grew up. It has now fallen down from neglect. (Courtesy of Mary Jo Guthrie Edgmon)

THE SOFT COAL mines, the lead and zinc mines around Henryetta, were only seventeen miles from my home town, Okemah, and I heard their songs. We drove the seven miles from Grandma's farm into town to do our trading and I stood down on the buggy floorboards and heard both papa's voice and mama's sing apart and together on hymns, spiritual songs, songs about how to save your lost and homeless soul and self. The color of the songs was the Red Man, Black Man, and the White folks.

OKEMAH WAS ONE OF THE SINGINGEST, square danc-ingest, drinkingest, yellingest, preachingest, walkingest, talk-ingest, laughingest, cryingest, shootingest, fist fightingest, bleedingest, gamblingest, gun, club, and razor carryingest of our ranch and farm towns, because it blossomed out into one of our first Oil Boom Towns. Here came the Lawyer Man, Doctor Man, Merchant Man, Royalty Man, Lease Man, Tong Bucker Man, Pipe Liner Man, Greasy Gloves Man, Big Wrench Man, the Cowboy and the Cowman, the Spirit and the Hoodoo Man, the ladies for all of these, the girls, and the Mistresses for the Pool Stick and Domino Sharker, the Red Light Pimper and Sidewalk Barker. I sold newspapers, sang all of the songs I picked up. I learned to jig dance along the sidewalks to things called porta-ble phonographs and sung for my first cancered pennies the "Dream of the Miner's Child," "Sinking of the Titanic," "Drun-kard's Dream," "Sailor's Plea," "Soldier's Sweetheart," "It Was Sad When That Great Ship Went Down," "Hindenburgh Disas-ter," "Marie Fagin," "Barbara Allen." My dad met the new comer, talked, traded, and built us a new six room house. But the speed and hurry, all of this pound and churn, roar and spin, this staggering yell and nervous scream of our little farm town turning into an Oil and Money Rush, it was too much of a load on my Mother's quieter nerves. She commenced to sing the sadder songs in a loster voice, to gaze out our window and to follow her songs out and up and over and away from it all, away over yonder in the minor keys.

Then our new built six room house burned down. We lived in several other houses and I heard all of the hurt songs over in a wilder way. These were the plainest days that I remember and the songs were made deepest in me along in these seasons. This was the time that our singing got the saddest. Mama asked papa to pull out of the land trading game.

I can hear him now as he sung in his Indian and Negro half chant as he rode down our road and into our barbed wire gate. I heard him call his horses and it sounded like a song to me. When he would call the purebred pigs, sows, shoats and boars, his voice was as much of a song in the air as ever was. And when the mare was led into the lot gate the neigh and nicker of the stud was a song as soft as a mating pigeon. I heard the work hands make songs about their work as they kept care of the prize animals, and I heard the song that is in a man's voice when he builds up all of these things by close trading, then loses them by some mistake, some crazy something in a ticker tape machine. My dad told me that he was the only man in the world that lost a farm a day for thirty days. The loss of these things hurt mama because she knew they hurt papa.

I will skip a few years and a few songs, and will just say that it did not get any better. My sister, Clara died in the explosion of a coal oil stove. Later on, worried from this and things that added as they went, my mother's nerves gave away like an overloaded bridge. Papa tried to get back into the trading and the swapping game, but never got a new toehold. I heard

Drawing of sharecropper shack.
Drawn in a notebook, July 1944.

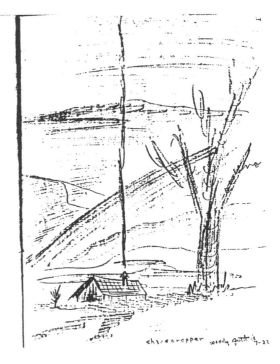

WRITE SHARECROPPER SONGS
— SHARECROPPER ALBUM —
Old by Bed of Hay
Cumberland mountain Farms

sharecropper woody guthrie 7-22

him sing as he held me on his lap in our older and rottener houses and I could tell by the sounds of his voice that he was not singing to make his own self feel good but to try to make us kids feel better. The time and seasons passed and we saw the car and the Doctor come and take mama away to the State Asylum at Norman, Oklahoma. Then our shack house caught on fire. Dad was hurt in it and they sent him to Texas on a wheat farm where he laid in bed close to eighteen months under the care of his sister.

I hit the road south to Houston, Galveston, the Gulf, and back, doing all kinds of odd jobs, hoeing figs, orchards, picking grapes, hauling wood, helping carpenters and cement men, working with water well drillers. I was thirteen or fourteen. I carried my harmonica and played in barbershops, at shine stands, in front of shows, around the pool halls, and rattled the bones, done jig dances, sang and played with Negroes, Indians, whites, farmers, town folks, truck drivers, and with every kind of a singer you can think of. I learned all of the tricks of string and music and all of the songs that I could remember and learn by ear. I struck back up across Texas to the wheat farm where my dad was.

If there was anybody around there that did not play some instrument I did not see them. I heard Jeff, my dad's half brother, play his squawling panther fiddle, and his other fiddle that he called just a wild cat in a Lost Canyon.

I went into the oil town of Pampa and got a store job, and the boss had an old busted guitar. Jeff got a deputy job and taught me how to chord on the guitar. After a while I was rattling around with him playing my way at the ranch and farm house dances. We worked our way up to playing inside of the city limits, and then for the banquet thrown by the Chamber of Commerce. We played for rodeos, centennials, carnivals, parades, fairs, just bustdown parties, and played several nights and days a week just to hear our own boards rattle and our strings roar around in the wind. It was along in these days I commenced singing, I guess it was singing.

Jeff and Allene decked themselves out in real show clothes and got a magic show together. We done this for several years around at country school houses till the mud on the upper plains clogged in our wheels and caught us with an empty gas tank and a flat pocketbook with a high norther blowing up bringing dust storms down across the oil fields where the big tall derricks waved above the wheat's oceans and where the cattle stood and chewed and tried to figure out how the poor families got stripped of everything and had to hit the old crooked road going west of nowhere. I married a fine Irish girl

Woody's first family (left to right): older daughter Gwen; wife, Mary, holding son, Bill; and Woody holding younger daughter Sue. Manhattan, ca. 1940.

Jack Guthrie (left) and Woody Guthrie, in Beverly Hillbillies wagon, California, ca. 1935.

by the name of Mary Jennings and we lived in the ricketiest of the oil town shacks long enough to have no clothes, no money, no groceries and two children, both girls, Sue and Teeny.

I hit the highway to look around for a place for us to go. I carried my pockets full of paint brushes and my guitar slung across my back. I painted all kinds of window signs, posters, show cards, banners, car and truck signs, in the daylight and played with my hat down on the old saloon floor after night had set in. Got to California and went up and down the west coast a few times, found a cousin of mine, Jack, and we took a fifteen minute radio program in order to collect give us enough prestige around at the saloons to ask for a two dollar guarantee for six hours.

It was not too long till I met the Crissman family out on some street of car smoke in Glendale. Roy and the Mrs. Crissman had two daughters, Mary Ruth and "Lefty Lou" from Old Mizoo. She was a tall thin-faced corn-fed Missouri farm girl with a voice rough and husky and I played my southern E chord guitar in back of our voices while we sung as "WOODY AND LEFTY LOU" and got twenty thousand letters during the almost two years that we sung over the mikes of KFVD. KFVD belonged to J. Franke Burke and he was the campaign manager the year Olsen was elected governor. Lefty Lou and me took quite a hand in politics and sung some of our first political and religious songs of our own making right then and there. A big Agent hired Lefty Lou and me to go down below the border to XELO, Tia Juana. I saw the home-made music boxes of the Mexican peons that played around the streets, and we picked up lots of good genuine Mexican folk songs from them.

Woody in cotton field, 1939. (Courtesy of Will Geer)

Back in L.A., I got back on KFVD again, this time by my own lonesome. I rented a house and my younger brother, George, hitched out from Oklahoma and got a clerk job in a big market. He paid the rent and I paid the bills and we saved up money and sent for Mary and the two daughters. I sung songs for the cotton pickers and cotton strikers, and for migratory workers, packers, canning house workers, fruit pickers, and all sorts of other country and city workers. I wrote a daily article for the People's Daily World, called Woody Says. I always read the radical papers over my program and took sides with the workers all I knew how.

I drew pen sketches for the Peoples World and learned all I could from the speeches and debates, forums, picnics, where famous labor leaders spoke. I heard William Z. Foster, Mother Bloor, Gurley Flynn, Blackie Myers, I heard most all of them and played my songs on their platforms.

I hated the false front decay and rot of California's fascistic oil and gas deals, the ptomaine poison and brass knucks in the jails and prisons, the dumped oranges and peaches and grapes and cherries rotting and running down into little streams of creosote poisoned juices.

I saw the hundreds of thousands of stranded, broke, hungry, idle, miserable people that lined the highways all out through the leaves and underbrush. I heard these people sing in their jungle camps and in their Federal Work Camps and sang songs I made up for them over the air waves.

I went to fancy Hollywood drinking parties and rubbed my elbows with the darkling glasses that they wore over their eyes to keep down everything. I met up with an actor named Will Geer and while we drove my '31 Chevvery around the sad canyons to play for migrant strikers, Mary gave birth on the side of a Glendale mountain to a fine big son which we named Bill Rogers Guthrie.

Labor in general, at that time, was in the nickel and the penny stages, very few strong and well run unions but lots of tear gas and guns being used by hired thugs and all kinds of vigilantes. The movement could not pay me enough money to keep up my eats, gas, oil, travel expenses, except Five Dollars here and Three there, Two and a Quarter yonder, at places where I sung. I thought that if I could drift back towards New York and get myself a fresh new start, things might run smoother. So Mary, Sue, Teeny, Bill and me took off across the rims and ledges of the Two Thousand Mile Desert to crawl and sweat and ache and pound back again to our little shack house in Texas. In the oil and farming town of Konawa, Oklahoma, I took my brother Roy's $35 (Thirty Five Dollars), and thanked him, told him I was whipping her up on towards New York City, and showed him an old letter that Will Geer had written to me back in Texas.

I stayed with Will and Herta Geer in a fancy apartment up on 59th and Fifth Avenue, which rented for A Hundred and Fifty a month. I thought at first that was for a whole year. I sang at a hundred IWO lodges and met every color and kind of a human being you can imagine. I moved from

With Matt Jennings (left) and a third musician, Pampa, Texas, ca. 1930.

Will and Herta's and lived down along the Bowery for a few months. I wrote an article every day for the Daily Worker, called Woody Sez. I met Alan Lomax and he carried me down to Washington to the Library of Congress where they recorded several hours of questions and answers and all of the songs I could remember on a pint of pretty cheap whiskey. I made twelve records called "Dust Bowl Ballads" for Victor after I seen *Grapes of Wrath* a couple or three times in a row. I met up with Peter Seeger, a long tall string bean kid from up in New England and we worked together putting a book of several hundred songs together. We bought us a Plymouth and drove down through the South and then crossed over into Oklahoma to sing for the Hooversville Camptowners "Community Camp" on the rim of Oklahoma's worst garbage dump. I made up my song "Union Maid" on the typewriter of Bob and Ina Wood, the organizers of the Communist Party in Oklahoma. They gave me as good a feeling as I ever got from being around anybody in my whole life. They made me see why I had to keep going around and around with my guitar making up songs and singing. I never did know that the human race was this big before. I never did really know that the fight had been going on so long and so bad. I never had been able to look out over and across the slum section nor a sharecropper farm and connect it up with the owner and the landlord and the guards and the police and the dicks and the bulls and the vigilante men with their black sedans and sawed off shot guns. Mussolini had already bombed and strafed the Ethiopians to death, and Hitler was waving his arms and doing little jig dances toward Poland.

Woody skinnydips, ca. 1939.
(Courtesy of Will Geer)

Then I sent for Mary and the kids in Oklahoma and I got jobs on the big New York radio shows, Pursuit of Happiness, Cavalcade of America, Back Where I Come From, Pipe Smoking Time, WNYC's Music Festivals, and bought a new forty-one Pontiac. I got disgusted with the whole sissified and nervous rules of censorship on all of my songs and ballads, and drove off down the road across the southern states again.

In the mountains of north California later we got a registered letter that told us to come up to the Columbia River to the Bonneville and the Grand Coulee dam, to the office of the Bonneville Power Administration. Well, I talked to people, I got my job, it was to read some books about the Coulee and Bonneville dams, to walk around up and down the rivers, and to see what I could find to make up songs about. I made up twenty-six. They played them over the loud speakers at meetings to sell bonds to carry the high lines from the dams to the little towns. The private power dams hated to see these two babies born to stand up out there across those rockwall canyons, and they pulled every trick possible to hold up the deal, saying that the materials would be wasted and could be used to build a big war machine to beat Hitler with. Our argument was that we could run a thousand towns and factories, farms, with these two power dams, and turn out aluminum bombers to beat Hitler a lot quicker with. And our side won out on top.

Well, then what? I got a letter after a couple of months from the Almanac Singers, Lee Hays, Pete Seeger, Mill Lampell, back in New York. Come back to us and let's make a cross country tour singing in union halls. We made Two albums of Records for the General Record Co., Sod Buster Ballads, and Deep Sea Chanteys. We rolled the gasoline hose down into our tank and left it there to suck and blow till we hit our first union hall stopoff. We made up songs. From the Alleghaney to the Ohio she's all gonna melt up CIO, Pittsburgh! Lord God! Pittsburgh!

We went into union halls and sang before, during and after the speakers had spoke, and took up a collection to buy gas, oil, and to grease the breezes. We sang: Union Maid. Talking Union. I Don't Want Your Millions Mister. Get Thee Behind Me Satan. Union Train a'Comin'. And made up dozens and dozens as we rolled along or as we stayed over the night at a friendly house. We rolled on out to Denver, then onto Frisco and sang for five thousand longshoremen at the Harry Bridges Local. We sang for the Ladies Auxiliary. We sang for the farm and factory workers around lower California, and then back to Frisco.

Pete and me drove on down into Mexico and sung. We drove back up along the coast to Seattle and sang for the Commonwealth Federation of Washington, the Old Age Pensioners, the Unemployed Unions, the Farmers Unions, and the office and factory workers unions.

Pete and me drifted back into New York. We sang together again as the Almanacs. We made up war songs against Hitlerism and fascism homemade and imported. We sang songs about our Allies and made up songs to pay honor and tribute to the story of the trade union workers around the world. We got jobs singing on overseas broadcasts for the Office of War Information for direct beaming to front line fighters. Pete was drafted into the Army. I had gotten a divorce from Mary, and had shipped out in the Merchant

OLD GRAY TEAM HOSSES

I was in a buckboard wagon
   going down the old plank
   road
When I spied a Ford a-coming down my way.
I will tell you just what happened, how I lost my
   wagon load
When that old gray team of
   hosses run away.

When at first they heard the
   rattle and the clatter of the
   car,
Me and Lindy Lou was a-setting side by side.
Well, she throwed her arms
   around me when the hosses
   jumped the tongue,
And here is what my sweet
   Malindy cried:

"Ain't there somethin' you can
   do to keep these hosses
   standin' still?
What makes you set and
   stare the way you do?"
Well, I put my arms around
   her and I took her by the
   hand
And I says, "Now don't you
   fret, Malindy Lou!"

Marines. She was right from her side and I was right from my side.

I shipped out with my guitar, and two seaman buddies, both good NMU men, Cisco Houston, a guitar player and high tenor singer, and Jimmy Longhi, an Italian boy with as good an anti-fascist head on him as I have ever seen. We played our guitars, and I took along a fiddle and a mandolin. Our first boat was torpedoed off the coast of Sicily, pulled into Lake Bizerte, but we got to visit the old bombed town of four hundred thousand souls, Palermo, Sicily, where Jimmy walked us up a mountainside singing underground songs to prisoners of war, and the people laughed and cried and shook our hands.

We caught an empty Liberty ship back to the States, sailed out again to North Africa, at the time that the Fascists' police would not let the NMU president, Joe Curran, come ashore there. We walked around to several of the most pitiful Arab Villages that I have ever seen. We saw whole swarms of people race out of their rock and mud huts to fight like cats and dogs over a hunk of soap, and then to run away again when the soap was torn into a hundred pieces. We heard these people pound on their native skin drums and sing some of the saddest and prettiest music that I have ever heard anywhere.

BACK IN THE STATES after this trip Cisco Houston, Blind Sonny Terry, and myself went up to the Asch studios. Moe Asch, son of Sholem Asch, took us in, cranked up his machinery and told us to fire away with everything that we had. We yelled and whooped and beat and pounded till Asch had taken down One Hundred and Twenty Some Odd Master sides (sides that might do to release to the public). We tried hilltop and sunny mountain harmonies and wilder yells and whoops of the dead sea deserts, and all of the swampy southland and buggy mud bottom sounds that we could make. We sung to the mossy trees and to the standing moon, and Moe Asch and Marian Distler worked through their plate glass there in the recording studio.

Sonny Terry blew and whipped, beat, fanned and petted his harmonica, cooed to it like a weed hill turtle dove, cried to it like some worried woman come to ease his worried mind. He blew it down two to one and let it down easy, flipped his lip over and across and his tongue sending all of his wind into one hole, straining the reed with too much pressure and making it sound like it had several side tones

Well, them hosses was a-running and they fairly split the breeze.
I was a-hugging sweet Malindy with a smile.
I had always wanted to hug her, so I bowed my head and prayed
They would run a hundred thousand million miles.

At a standstill there I kissed her when at last the hosses fell,
Quite exhausted from the run that they had made,
And I married sweet Malindy, so I'm happy in my soul
That the old gray team of hosses run away.

THIS IS THE FIRST SONG I EVER WROTE—W.G.

and tones that dance between. He put the tobacco sheds of North and South Carolina in it and all of the blistered and hurt and hardened hands cheated and left empty, hurt and left crying, robbed and left hungry, pilfered and left starving, beaten and left dreaming. He rolled down the trains that the colored hand cannot drive only clean and wash down. He blew into the wood holes and the brassy reeds the tale and the wails of Lost John running away from the dogs of the chain gang guards, and the chain gang is the landlord that is never around anywhere.

I talked to Sonny about these things in his art and he tells me that he is blind and that he still knows that his people can see a world where we all vote, eat, work, talk, plan and think together and with all of our smokes and wheels rolling and all of our selves well dressed and well housed and well fed. These are the things that the artist in Blind Sonny Terry knows and sees in his blindness. These are the upland echoes of the things that stir and sing along his big muddies. These are the plans and visions seen in the kiss and whisper of tall tree jack pines falling into the chutes to make your papery pulps. These are the freedoms. These are the samples of the kinds of soul art that the Negro, Indian, Mexican, the Irish, the Jew, the Russian, the Greek, Italian, all of us, have to bring to be seen and heard. These are the thoughts that Asch and Marian and me and Cisco and everybody felt when we made those hundred and twenty some odd record sides. I don't know where there is a more progressive atmosphere amongst artists, performers, and engineers, packers, shippers, owners, and pressers and stampers.

I have made twelve albums of records for Asch and had time to be in three invasions in the Merchant Marines, to get torpedoed twice, to walk all over the British Isles, Canada, Mexico, to see forty-six of our forty-eight States, to get a divorce from one woman and turn right around and marry myself off to another one. My second wife is a dancer and a teacher with the Martha Graham Company, her name is Marjorie Mazia Guthrie and she is twenty-nine, and our daughter is Cathy Ann, I call her Stacky-bones and she goes to Nursery School and is just past the Three Year line. She sings and laughs and dances to all of the records Asch makes, and says, How did they get you inside the music box, daddy?

After my second torpedo, off the coast of Normandy, Cherbourg, I got pulled back to the port of Southampton, and then spent several weeks ashore on the British Isles, still with my two singing pardners, Cisco Houston and Jimmy Longhi. I got a good look at the real England.

I came back to the States again and got drafted into the Army on the same day, May eighth, that Hitler surrendered. I don't know if it was me or that big Red Army or those few million Yanks there acrost his fence that caused him to give in. I was sent down to Texas and went through a cloudburst, windstorm that broke the speedometers at a hundred miles an Hour. I sung at the barracks, Px's. My next camp was down along the mudflow of the Mississippi. Then out to a desert camp in Las Vegas, (Lost Wages), Nevada, the rambling gambling town where the big shots go to toss off your dough on the prettiest lit up neon wheels and green tables that you nearly ever seen. They counted my kids and found out that I had a big army of my own, sent me back to this New York place.

Went down to a meeting of a new union of progressive songwriters that call themselves "Peoples Songs," found Peter Seeger and his banjo, the president and Lee Hays (Arkansaw Hard Luck Lee), the vice president. I found Betty Sanders, Leadbelly, Bernie Asbel, Alan Lomax, Bess Lomax, Tom Glazer, Charlotte Anthony, Lou Kleinman, Mildred Linsley, and Shaemas O'Sheel, Bob Russell, there, almost every songwriter pitching in their efforts to make out of all of their little works one big union called "Peoples Songs."

The reason for Peoples Songs is to shoot your union the kind of a song or songs when you want it and fast. To help you to make a songbook, a program, a throwaway songsheet, a whole evening. Or maybe your problem is just about how to make a song and get it copyrighted, printed, circulated around, how to set a fee, and what to do with your works after you create them. I am one of the fifteen now on the Executive Committee of Peoples Songs, 130 West 42nd Street, New York City, New York. I think all of us that are members of Peoples Songs can pat ourselves on the backs that we have at our hands here a broadminded recording and distributing company with the imagination and hindsight and foresight in social pastures, Moe Asch's Union Records and his Disc Company of America. I don't think that any better luck could have come to these artists nor to this firm. I have never in my life seen a better blend and unity. I would like for you to check this list of record albums, this list of single records, and to take notice of who is here, who is spoken for here, and more, the way they are spoken for. Each one of these speak in music for a people. It is through such music firms as this that your people will know my people, know each others plans and hopes and our past struggles and fights. Unless we do hear the work songs, war songs, and love songs, dance songs, of all the people everywhere we are most apt to lose the peace and this world along with it. I know more about those Arab Villages, those Sicilian bombed towns, those British Cities knocked to their knees, those North African dust and rock piles, I know more about these people because of the songs I heard them sing than of any words I heard them speak in their own native tongues.

This is my letter. This is my letter that I could keep on writing on all night and ten nights. I find that there is almost no place for me to stop once I commence writing such a letter as this, and I can't believe hardly that I am writing such a letter as this to a recording company to be printed by them to tell you what is eating at just one of their many expert performers. It is a story that is not complete, and could not be in such a few pages. It is a story enough, though, maybe, to give you a little taste, a sample feeling, of the roads from back down which we come. I think every artist recorded by Asch has got quite a road to tell you about.

2

HARD TRAVELIN'
1936–1940

I've been having some hard travelin'
I thought you knowed
I've been having some hard travelin'
Way down the road

—"Hard Travelin' "

Because Woody spent most of the thirties moving around—from Oklahoma to Texas to California, on the bum or with his first wife, Mary Jennings, and their three kids—relatively little of his unpublished work from those years has been found. There is, however, much documentation of his work at KFVD, the Los Angeles radio station where he began appearing in July 1937, first as part of a duo with his cousin Jack Guthrie, and later with Maxine "Lefty Lou" Crissman. The songs, brief comments, and stories included here are characteristic of the self-consciously country postures the performers adopted for those shows.

Additionally, some parts of Woody's always voluminous correspondence survived. The two letters presented here frame his developing attitudes as the thirties—and the Depression and his career—progressed. The 1936 letter to Ann Guthrie, who had recently married

Lee Roy, the most respectable of Woody's brothers, shows his cornpone at its most raucous. The letter to his sister, Mary Jo, is actually from 1940, just after he'd recorded the "Dust Bowl Ballads" for RCA Victor—it shows how far from cornpone Woody had come, without abandoning country allegiances.

The following lyrics and short humorous commentaries are from 1937–1938 transcriptions of the "Lefty and Lou" KFVD radio program. Their half-hour show, aimed at southern California's increasingly large population of Southwest—and particularly Oklahoma/Texas—natives, eventually aired as many as three times a day, at 8 A.M., noon, and 11 P.M.

WOODY'S AND LEFTY LOU'S THEME SONG

Drop whatever you are doing,
Stop your work and worry, too;
Sit right down and take it easy,
Here comes Woody and Lefty Lou.

You just drop a card or letter,
We will sing a song for you,
We're easy goin' country people
Plain ole Woody and Lefty Lou

(That's what we sing when we're cranking up and a-fixin' to come onto the air waves, then after we have throughly wrecked the studio, here's what we sing):

So long! We'll see you in the morning,
We'll be singing when we do,
If you've got a favorite number,
Write to Woody and Lefty Lou

If you like our kind of singing,
I'm gonna tell you what to do,
Get your pencil and your paper
Write to Woody and Lefty Lou

If you're ever sad and lonely,
Bring your folks and chilluns too,
Hitch your bay mare to your buggy
Come see Woody and Lefty Lou

Woody and Lefty Lou, KFVD, Los Angeles, ca. 1935.

Don't forget us in the morning,
We won't be forgettin' you,
We ain't never seen a stranger,
Plain ole Woody and Lefty Lou.

————————

I ain't got this here song memorized yit. Jest wrote it up last summer. Write us a letter, 'cause we shore git a big kick out of you writin'.

I have always believed Lefty Lou could lead and I'd foller her, but sometimes she gits her voorce box throwed over her tonsil, and I caint hear what she's a sayin. In sech cases we both jest hum till we come 'round agin.

The first night you aint got nuthin to do, set down and write us and let us know how you're a gettin along. We like to hear from you. We call you our Unseen Friend. But course we got a pitcher of you sorta in our minds—jest like you got one about us.

CONVICT AND THE ROSE

Within my Prison cell so dreary
Alone I sit with Aching Heart
I'm thinking of my Lonely Darling
From her forever I must Part!

A rose she sent me as a Token
She sent it just to Light my Gloom;
To tell me that her Heart was broken,
To cheer me 'fore I meet my Doom

She wrote: I took it from the Garden
Where once we wandered side by side!
But now you hold no hope of Pardon,
And I can never be your Bride!

The judge would not believe my story!
The jury said I'd have to pay.
And to the Rose in all its Glory,
Not Guilty is all I have to say.

Goodbye Sweetheart, for in the Morning
I meet my Maker and Repose!
And when I go at Daylight's Dawning
Against my Heart you'll find your Rose!

———————————

Cyclones happened so often down on Possum Holler that Leonard Blake got wise to it. One used to come up out of the holler there about four o'clock every evenin', and Leonard made good use of it. He set a fifteen gallon keg of white likker on a cottonwood stump, and the cyclone delivered it every day to Jim Wilkinson four mile up the river.

Cyclones used to be continually a puttin th' wrong cattle in the right pasture.

One cyclone brought Paw a bay mare with a game leg, and took nine dollars out of his tobaccer sack to pay fer it. Purty soon here come a little prairie whirlwind, and got 27 cents fer Sales Tax.

Photo taken at radio station XELO, Mexico. Front to back: unidentified, Lefty Lou, Woody, ca. 1935.

KISS MY MOTHER AGAIN

Dear Mother you're gone to your heavenly home
Where heartaches can't enter in . . . .
Tonite all alone in spirit I've flown
To kiss my mother again.

    Mother, your love was more precious than jewels
    And lasts till eternity's end . . . .
    I'd give all I own in this hard wicked world
    To kiss my mother again.

O kiss my mother again . . . again
O kiss my mother again . . . .
I'll follow my saviour to heaven and then
I'll kiss my mother again.

Dear mother was sweet as an angel's smile
Her voice with the angels did blend . . . .
She carried her cross with a smile every mile
With Christ to eternity spend

I see mother now and I hope that somehow
Her heavenly blessing I'll win. . . .
And if death come a sneakin' upon me
I'd kiss my mother again

(One of my old stand-bys. Sung a lot on KFVD. Women squalled. Kids bawled. Men folks hauled.)

—Original song words-tune
Woody Guthrie & KFVD 2-25-39

Woody with Margaret Johnson, a fellow performer on his 1940 CBS radio program.

Most of my education come from the picture shows. I figgered that was all right cause I didn't have a chance when I was young to learn much. I was always penned up in the school house while the more intelligent kids stayed with Mama Nature on the banks of some creek. I've went to skule as high as five days right in a row. Then I'd spend five days over on Rock Creek a catchin Sun Perch. Then five days over on Greenleaf Creek catchin mudcat on bank hooks set way down in the mud. Then five over on Nuyaka Creek tryin' out new bait on a trot line a fishin fer Channel Cat and Bullhead Cat that swum about three feet off th' bottom in deep water. They was lots of Rock Bass around there, too, but them big Bullhead Cat and Channel Cat was the legal tender of Ohfuskee County, they attracted attention when booze news even failed. I guess I didn't git so much in my head, but I've had less headaches a gittin by on an empty one. All a feller knows is what he does, and this Life is just a Fishin Hole anyhow. Everybody's fishin fer Suckers to Skin and when they squeak, they Fry.

(Attached to original song, "Country Boy")

———— ▬ ————

Pampa, Texas
Box #1351   4/16/'36

Dear Ann:

I feel it my soulful duty to give you sort of a character analysis of my brother, Roy, lately your other half (for better or for worse). Now, I have known this young man for a long time, and am in position to give you a few pointers that will be worth many dollars and several cents before your lifetime is over. I trust that you will excuse the abnormalcy of this letter, and will go on with the analysis.

Roy has a curious complex. He thinks he walks funny. And when he was a few years younger this was amazingly true. At the age of sixteen, he used to have a lot of trouble that way because his right foot did not match his left one. They were certainly out of shape. He would slip off to town thru the snow leaving footprints. But his pa couldn't tell by the tracks whether he had come or gone.

When he visited me not long ago, my big police dog drug one of his shoes out near the alley and commenced using it for a doghouse. Roy was forced to buy a new pair of shoes.

Here's a letter
    Wrote with rum
  All stirred up
    With chewing gum
Glue you up
and lick you down
and
Mail You over
To some big town

He asked the clerk for friendly fives and the clerk said, "You'll need neighborly tens."

Roy fell in love down in Arkansaw when we toured down thru there. The girl lived in a log house and was pining for love. Roy was sappy about her and barked about it continually. We were walking down the road and Roy got awful tired, and took off his left hind shoe. Pretty soon a farmer came along in a wagon and said, "I'd let yez ride, son, but I ain't got room for that pianner crate in th' waggin.'"

As far as drinking is concerned, Roy never touches a drop unless he is by himself or with somebody, and he never uses anything stronger than water—for a chaser. He has never fermented any brew; he just sits it in the woodshed and lets nature take its course. But he always pours it out as fast as he makes it. About ten years ago I tried to offer him a drink and he threw it in my face. Last year I offered him another one and he threw it in his own.

You will find a nervous tendency in Roy. He always acts automatically once he gets a thing memorized. Somedays he gets up on the wrong side of the house and things go backwards all day. I saw him one night in Okemah with some white girl—going to a movie. When he saw that I was looking at him, he got all tangled up. He handed the ticket taker his popcorn, ate the tickets, and walked his girl out in the street and sat down to see the show. Of course he isn't this way all the time, but I am simply telling you what 'might' happen.

I assume it true that you are a lady of noble temperament. In order to hold down your present task you will have to fall back on your good points a lot of times. I think that you will find my brotherly quite a brother. Having never had him for a husband, I cannot give you many valuable pointers there. You will know him better than I do, but I will own the distinction of having known him the longer.

I studied phrenology for a long time. I was going to analyze Roy's character for him on his last trip up here—according to his profile. But when he got here he had left it in Konawa and we never did get the [phrenologist] to read it and weep. Now she reads them and moans. And I've even forgotten how to write: can't think of anything anymore.

Walking is a good exercise. At Roy's present salary, you will get plenty of exercise. I would suggest that you make him save his money. You could send it to me each week and I shall save it for you. From what I know of Roy—he can't save a cent. Just as quick as he gets ten saved-up, why he lends it to me and is broke again. I don't know why he is so everlast-

HIGH BALLADREE

I was born in the hungriest
   richest of states
In old Oklahoma in the Creek
   Indian nation
Okemah is my town, Okfus-
   kee's my county
In Nineteen and Twelve while
   a world war was on.

Okemah was a farmer and a
   cowman's town
Cowpokes and hoppers go-
   ing broke up and down
Ramblers and gamblers and
   lawyers and molls
Hit town on the day that Okemah struck oil.

I run to my hill and I looked to
   my skies
And a jillion oil derricks
   jumped up in my eyes
I seen wagons, seen buggies,
   seen trucks, I seen cars,
I seen settlers and Indians with
   big black cigars.

I saw lawyers in new hats with
   fast walking canes
Smelt Blue Bell Hair Tonic on
   farmer's wild hairs
Seen Negro and Indian with
   Leppher (?) bootshine
Dogs barking, cars honking,
   the kids all a crying.

ingly unable to write. That is—I didn't know. But you see I see now that he was wrapped in the harms of sweet romance. There is a boy who is continually getting all wrapped in something. It used to be the army blanket when I was sleeping with him, but we sold that, and he turned right around and commenced using my pajamas for the same purpose. I trust that your fortune here will far surpass mine—for I know the run you are risking when you attempt sleeping with him without an army blanket. You see, he got his odd neurosis while sleeping with an army mule in the navy. The mule died. It stunted my growth. And now the die points to you. You will tell me someday for thanking you this—you will shank me—shell—you will glee bad I told you—(skip it).

Now as to Roy's temper. There is the viper we want to analyze. You will have to help me with it. I've been knowing him twenty four year, and ain't been able to find one yet. But by working together, we can no doubt discover it after three or four generations have passed. Roy used to fly off the handle right smart—before I was borned. But one day he was cranking an old Chalmers automobile, and it wouldn't crank. Makes me mad to think about it. Anyway, Roy's handle flew off—and he ain't never had no temper since.

As far as support is concerned—you will have plenty of that if you can get the right people back of you. Roy always did bring home the backbone.

He used to bring home the neighbors chickens too. He sought a number of chickens. When his tooth gave him trouble he would pullet. In his early romances anything fowl was barred, however. He roosted in the drug stores up till midnight when they closed and drove him home. He sometimes got mixed up with some bad eggs.

Since he was twenty, he has been more or less of a long wolf. I mean, a *lone wolf*. He generally runs around by himself with four other guys. He goes to bed when there aint nowhere else to go and comes to work when its time to get off and go home. If you ever want him and cant find him just locate him and then you'll know where he is. I used to lose track of him when he was giving me nickels and this was a distressing period in my life. So in my childish way I'd just start a conversation with some good looking girl, and Roy would show up pretty soon.

If you don't buy a car pretty quick you will find your life unhappy. Roy walks so ##""!'**%&& fast that nobody can keep up with him. I used to go barefooted when we lived a mile north of town, and I'd try to go to school in the morning

An airplane flew over and the
   teams run away
I seen F. Flat Dozen get
   knocked down that day
Wild horses tore down the
   fronts of our stores
The cars and trucks run in and
   out all our doors.

I grabbed a guitar and I
   plunked on the side
At a drunk barber shop where
   your boots I did shine
I heard about cotton and cattle and booze
I heard of Gyp leases and
   ragged you new shoes.

Your new high deputy in his
   buzzerd brim hat
Told off where your big copper dripworm was at.
Old Jinko the Barber sung
   bass with Ed Moore
That laughing lone song of
   your syphbelly whore.

Clap John the horse trader
   rode on a sore bay
He yelled out the farmers sold
   at auction today
The three Beaver Sisters, Rose,
   Agnes, and Blanche,
Rolled drunks on the sidewalk
   without a dark chance.

(continued)

with him. The sand was hot and I'd get burrs in my feet if I walked off the path—and I'd have to stand in the shade of a sunflower about two minutes so's to cool them. Roy would gain half a mile on me in those 2 minutes. I don't want your happiness to be wrecked on account of his fast walking. I should say that I have no fear of his out stepping on you— you know, stepping in on you with other wimmen. (Anyway, you get the drift of my meaning). I am simply sowing the seeds in this letter which will sprout later on in ideas of your original design. I trust you wont let Roy get ahold of this here letter. I dont care so much for him getting hold of the letter, but I don't want him to get hold of my neck. My neck is designed for my own personal use and I have no inclination to put on any help in wringing it. So you just keep these secrets secret. Secrets is secrets, you know.

I've been trying to figure out what you'd be to me if I was Roy's ½ brother. You would be my—ah—half neighbor. No, I'd be your half husband—by law . . . half sister by force. Sister in law and a half. That's it! Sister in law and a half. But I'm gaining half a sister in law somewhere in the deal.

I never was no hand to figure out kinfolks. I simply write their name on my borrowing list and call them by their first name. I'm gonna call you Ann. No—here's a better nickname: 'Annie doesn't live here iny more'. I guess that's what your Oklahoma City folks are thinking about now. Since the barbarious young credit manager from the south galloped up and awayed with you. It all goes back to Helen of Troy. But in this kidnap case it is Annie of Roy. (pause for applause).

Your new husband isn't impulsive and high strung like his brother me. He takes everything orderly, decently, and in polished order. He is making his life, and I am letting my life make me. He reminds me of a sailing vessel that is always under control no matter the storm at sea. He plies sensibly and safe, though sometimes slowly, into and out of the various highwaters that foam foam all over we who attempt to ride this tight rigged ship of Life.

Well, Ann, you must write to us. We have (Mary and I) a perfect little six months old particle of enlightenment whose name we call Gwendolyn Gail. Mary compliments you both and she hopes that your tour through this span of existence is blessed as wondrously as can be. She is sewing something for the baby—and wants to tell old Roy that she is glad he has made the matrimonial step. Gwen says, 'gloo-oo' (translated it means, "May your life be as beautiful as the coming ice cream season"). As for me, all I can think of to say has

Chickymorg Jerry wild-
  hawked our new busses
To Sand Spring, Slick City,
  Smackover and Studs
A good easy rider and a
  whiskey head driver
Through buffalo wallers and
  bog holes of mud.

I see you walk into my court
  room and stand
And yell, stomp and clap
  while my land changes
  hands
My Negro, my Indian, my settler in here
Has got the same chance as
  a mouse with a bear.

My Indian I seen by the thousands and more
Eating bad cheese and
  crackers at my sodie pop
  store
Family stands talking and
  pointing out the door
While the flies eat my kid's ice
  cream cone on my floor

My black folks I watch by
  more thousands and more
Eating dry Nelly Wafers in your
  old grocery store
Family sings talking and nod-
  ding out doors
Kids crawl in the spittoon sawdust on my floor.

already been said by others who knew the knack of saying things. I am putting mine into a bit of low grade prose herewith. Read it and weep.

> Your brother and a half
> In law and a half,
>
> Woody Guthrie

Woody changed radically in California, and in this letter to his sister he explains just how he saw the world in the late thirties. These thoughts and ideas were the ones that led him to socialism, not through ideology but as a way of explaining the poverty, neglect, and ignorance of the people he'd met on the road from Okemah to Los Angeles and back again to New York and Washington, D.C., from the farm and oil territory to the lands of false promise. If there are elements of cant in what he tells his sister here (and as regards the coming war, blinkered cant at that), they are always softened by Woody's indomitable and unfailingly romantic vision of intimate human relationships—his awareness that what his sister will really care about is his visit to New York City. This is where this letter, and all his work, finds its poetry.

Hello Mary Jo:

I remember when I was through there not so awful long ago, you asked me if I would write you a copy of a certain thing that I wrote and gave to you when you were living with Betty Jean. I think of this often and think of you often also, and I wonder how you're getting along, and what is running through your mind.

When I saw you last, you said that your ambition in life was to be a cashier or teller in a bank, or at least somebody that stands in the window in a nice clean dress and handles money, and goes to church and has lots of nice friends around over town. I believe this is pretty close to what you described to me that night when I was thawing out from a 2 day ride in the old broke-down Chevvy. I didn't say much of anything right then, because I wanted to do it some other time, and some other way.

Well, Mary Jo, you're getting grown now. You're a lady, and lots of things will come across your path. I suppose right

A nickel post card I buy off
  your rack
To show you what happens if
  you're black and fight back
A lady and two boys hanging
  down by their necks
From the rusty iron rigs of my
  Canadian Bridge.

I quit my shoe shining and
  grabbed my guitar
To play in old restaurants and
  hotels and bars
I combed your dead alley filling sacks full of junk
I counted your Bay Rum and
  bellyrub drunks.

Did you lose your man in my
  alley some place?
Did you see the hope fire go
  dead on his face?
Did you see the dogs and
  cats sniffle his skin?
This is what I seen with my oil
  coming in.

TO ALL EMPLOYEES OF THE DEPARTMENT OF THE INTERIOR.

The Hatch Act of August 2, 1939 included the following provisions:

"Sec. 9A. (1) It shall be unlawful for any person employed in any capacity by any agency of the Federal Government, whose compensation, or any part thereof, is paid from funds authorized or appropriated by any Act of Congress, to have membership in any political party or organization which advocates the overthrow of our constitutional form of government in the United States.

(a) Any person violating the provisions of this section shall be immediately removed from the position or office held by him, and thereafter no part of the funds appropriated by any Act of Congress for such position or office shall be used to pay the compensation of such person."

In accordance with the spirit and the requirement of this legislation, I desire an answer from every employee of this Department to the question appearing below. This sheet after execution should be returned to me through official channels.

Harold L. Ickes

Secretary of the Interior.

Do you have membership in any political party or organization which advocates the overthrow of our constitutional form of government in the United States? (Answer "Yes" or "No") *No* .

I, the undersigned, DO SOLEMNLY SWEAR (OR AFFIRM) that the above statement by me in answer to the foregoing question is true. SO HELP ME GOD.

Woodrow W Guthrie
(Signature)

BONNEVILLE POWER ADMINISTRATION
(Bureau or Office)

now, the main thing you're thinking about is love and sweet-hearts, and marriage, and family life, which is all right, but is not everything. There is all of this to think about, and plenty more. And since you have been born and raised in so much hard luck and suffering and misery and hunger, I'm going to tell you a few things in this letter which later on will dawn in your mind, and you'll understand better than you do now.

In this old world there are 2 bunches of people, the one's that are rich and the ones that are poor. The ones that do the work and the ones that get the money. The ones that make the big money dont do much work, and some of them dont do any at all. They are the ones that get to be millionaires, and multi-millionaires, and billionaires. The people, like you and me, that have always been poor and always had very little, and have lived a life of hard times and tough spots, well, we just sort of do the work in this old world, and after a bite to eat, a shot of liquor, a movie or 2, and a little fun, we're broke again, and we got to go back out and do some work for somebody to get a little bit more money in our pocket to go spend again, for some clothes, some groceries, some fun, or house rent.

Right at this time, you're thinking what kind of work you can take up, that will feed you and clothe you and give you a house to live in, and a car to drive, and all of that, plus the business of falling head over heels in love, as I said before, with some good looking boy with a big chance to get high in the world, and a happy home with many days and nights of pure and sweet and simple love, you know, with babies, and dresses, and little clothes and all that goes with having children around.

I know you better, I believe, than anybody else in the world. If that's stretching things a little, I will say that I know you, at least, as good, and have watched you grow up ever since the time when you laid on the bed in the little room out at grandma Tanners, when you was about 3 months old and I watched you grow on up to the time when you went to Texas to be with Aunt Maude and Uncle Robert, and then when you got up to where you started to school, and then when you moved in with Betty Jean, and papa, and of course you remember as well as I do, the many, many times that hard times and trouble came along and how it caused a lot of sorrow and a lot of tears to all of us, especially papa.

I'm writing this letter to recall to you the things that we have come through together, because it will be those things that will make us what we are today, and make us think like

THIS MORNING I
AM BORN AGAIN

This morning I am born again
And light shines thru the land
And I do not seek a heaven
In some deathly distant land;
No longer desire a pearly
    gate
Nor want a street of gold.
I do not want a mansion
For my heart is never cold.

This morning I am born again
I am whole, new, complete—
I am o'ercome all my sins
I stand on my own feet—
I am life unlimited
My body as the sky
I am at home in the universe
Where yonder planets fly.

This morning I am born again
My past is dead and gone—
This great eternal moment
Is my great eternal dawn;
I give myself, my heart, my
    soul
To give some friend a hand.
This morning I am born again
I am in the promised land.

—3-11-'39

PERSONAL HISTORY STATEMENT
(To be prepared by person or persons in handwriting)

Date 5-13-41

Department or Establishment _____

1. Name in full (Mr., Mrs., or Miss) ~~Woodrow Guthrie~~ Woodrow Wilson
2. Present address #42 Ireland Gate Court, Portland, Oregon — Los Angeles, Calif.
3. Legal (voting) residence — Los Angeles — When born 7-14-12 (Month Day Year)
4. Where born Okemah Oklahoma
5. If foreign-born, state whether naturalized or alien
6. Indicate sex, marital condition, and race by check thus ✓

SEX	RACE	MARITAL CONDITION
Male	White	Married

7. Number and ages of dependents domiciled with you other than military or naval: 4, Wife 23, Girl 5, Girl 3, Boy 1½

8. A complete record of your past service for the United States Government:

BRANCH OF SERVICE	PLACE OF EMPLOYMENT	POSITION	SALARY	DATE APPOINTED	DATE SEPARATED
None	None	None	None		

9. Are any members of your family, who are domiciled with you, in the U.S. Government service? If so, state below:

NAME	POSITION AND DEPARTMENT OR OFFICE IN WHICH EMPLOYED	RELATIONSHIP
none	none	

10. Do you now hold any State or __ none
11. Are you the wife of a disabled __ none
12. Military and naval record:

None	Army	Navy
Enlisted		
Rank		
Organization		

Page 3

(a) Grammar school: Attended from Sept. 1918 June 1926 Highest grade completed 8th
(b) High school: Name and location Okemah High School, Okemah, Oklahoma Attended from Sept. 1928 June 1929 Highest grade completed 10th
Were you graduated? No

(c) College or university:

NAME	LOCATION	Dates of attendance	Major subject	Degree
None				

18. Furnish in blanks below a complete, comprehensive statement, showing every employment you have had since you first began to work.

Places and dates of employment	NAME AND ADDRESS OF EMPLOYER AND DEPARTMENT IN WHICH EMPLOYED	NATURE OF YOUR DUTIES	Monthly salary	REASON FOR LEAVING
Okemah, Okla. 9-28 to 6-29	George Meadors, Meadors Hotel	Night clerk & porter	$30	Called to Texas by illness in family.
Pampa, Texas 7-29 to 8-29	Marvin Johnson, Root Beer Stand	Clerk	$90	Employer moved his business.
Pampa, Texas 8-29 to 32	C. T. Harris, Harris Drug	Clerk and sign painter. Drove delivery truck.	$45	Discharged because of decrease in business.
Pampa, Texas 32 to 34	Chas. Boosikee, Home Supply Market	Clerk, stocker, sign painter, & drove delivery truck.	$30	Terminated relations with business.
Pampa, Texas 34 to	Unemployed 408 S. Russell St.	Played in a cowboy band.		
Los Ang., Cal. 6-37 to 38	Frank Burke, Radio Station KFVD, Los Angeles, Calif.	30-minute program collecting &	$30	Left to tour northern California.
Calif. 38 to	Unemployed			To New York to work for Tobacco Road Co.

---

12. State any special qualifications not involved in your present position (for instance, lawyer, physician, civil engineer, knowledge of foreign languages, etc.) Good painter, signs, pictures, commercial posters, the cards, window signs, banners, and so forth.

14. Statement of principal employment other than with the United States Government:

NAME AND ADDRESS OF EMPLOYER	POSITION AND CHARACTER OF WORK	LENGTH OF SERVICE
C.T. Harris Drug Store, Pampa, Texas	Clerk, stocker, painter	3½ years
Home Supply Market, Pampa, Texas	Clerk, sign painter, delivery truck	2 years
Radio Station KFVD, Los Angeles, Calif.	Presenting cowboy songs	2 years
Will Geer, Forrest Theater, N.Y. City	Back stage hand and errand boy	4 months
Columbia Broadcasting Co., N.Y. City	Singer & actor	6 months
485 Madison Ave., N.Y. City		Temporary Position
Victor Record Co., N.Y. City	Recording songs	

15. Education. Indicate by circling the number of years:

16. In case of emergency, notify Matt Jennings
Address 2408 Texas St., El Paso, Texas.
Relationship Wife's Bro. Post office address

I certify that the foregoing answers are correct to the best of my knowledge and belief.

Woodrow W. Guthrie

Subscribed and sworn to before me this 13th day of May A.D. 19__

at Portland, Oregon

Elva Brown
NOTARY PUBLIC FOR OREGON
MY COMMISSION EXPIRES DEC 27 19-

APPLICATION FOR EMPLOYMENT

UNITED STATES
DEPARTMENT OF THE INTERIOR

No. 112349

Woodrow K. Guthrie
General Delivery
Columbia, California

Date: May 13, 1941

1. Are you a citizen of the United States?	Yes
In what State or Territory (or District of Columbia) is your legal actual or voting residence established?	Oklahoma
In what county have your legal or voting residence?	Okemah, Oklahoma
2. Where do you live?	California
3. Are you physically sound?	Yes
4. Height 5 feet 7 inches, Weight 145 pounds	
5. Are you now in the employ of the U.S. Government?	No

9. State kind of employment for which you believe yourself to be particularly qualified: I can qualify as a singer, actor and narrator on radio programs and for motion pictures. I am also experienced in writing narration or dialogues, with musical accompaniment.

1.	Nos. 6 & 8.	My work with Station KFVD as singer and actor, for over 2 years (30 minute programs each day)
2.	No. 1.	The fact that I have a voice and style of delivery suitable for recording, and my experience in making records for the RCA Victor Record Co.
3.	No. 11 & Nos. 15 to 17, Inc.	My experience as script writer, actor and singer on various programs over the Columbia Broadcasting System.
4.	No. 19	My experience in the motion picture "The Fight for Life", directed by Pare Lorenz of the U.S. Film Service.

No.	Place	Employer	Position	Salary	Remarks
9.	Gulf Coast, Texas, Nov.,1939 to Jan.,1940	Unemployed	Occasional entertaining with folk songs.		
10.	New York City Jan.,1940 to Apr.,1940	Will Geer, Tobacco Road Co., W. 48th St., Forrest Theater	Backstage hand & errand boy	$48	Picked up radio and recording jobs.
11.	New York City Apr.,1940 to May,1940	Columbia Broadcasting System, 485 Madison Avenue	Script writer, actor & singer	$50	One program
12.	New York City May,1940	RCA Victor Record Co, 155 E. 24th St.	Recording songs	$300	12 records
13.	New York City May,1940 to	Columbia Broadcasting System, 485 Madison Avenue	Singer & actor	$50	Two programs
14.	New York City	Columbia Broadcasting System, 485 Madison Avenue	Appeared on "American school of the Air"	$50 per program	Temporary position
15.	New York City	Columbia Broadcasting System	Script writer & actor on "Back There I Come From" program	$228	"
16.	New York City to Sept.,1940	Columbia Broadcasting System	Wrote & sang "Ballad of Wild Bill Hickock on DuPont's Cavalcade of America	$250	"
17.	New York City Nov.,1940 to Jan.,1941	Columbia Broadcasting System	Actor, singer and narrator	$600	The entire show was recast.
18.	California Jan.,1941 to present	Unemployed (Columbia,Calif.)			

19. Note: In the summer of 1939 I worked in the picture, "The Fight for Life" directed by Pare Lorenz of the U.S. Film Service.

we do today, and make us think and do what we do tomorrow, and every day afterwards. I have never known or met a single person in the world that I felt like I do towards you, and yet I have said very little to you, because I thought your past life would naturally lead you into a very wonderful, great, and useful life in the days to come. I know it has been my hard luck in the past that has caused me to do what little I've done, and I know it will be your past experiences that will lead you into the life that is before you, and make you a very wonderful person, doing good work, helping people, and living a good, useful, life.

The main thing that I want you to think about is this: The two bunches of people in the world, the ones that are rich without working, and the ones that work all of the time and are never rich, and the ones that are standing around never rich, and the ones that are standing around with their hands in their pockets waiting for some rich man to give them a job so they can eat and drink, and pay their house-rent, and have a little fun.

Now it looks like there are some wars breaking out around over the world. This is between the rich people. Us poor folks have nothing in the world to do with these wars, because, win, lose, or draw, we are poor to commence with, and will be poor to end with. So it is plain that these wars are between the rich people, for more lands, more fields, more mines, more oil fields, more factories, more colonies, more folks to work for them, and more profits in their pockets to buy Lincoln Zephyrs, Cadillacs, Silk Dresses, Good Whiskey, Pretty Women, and Streamlined Houses. This is the way the idle rich spend their time and money, and I will add Poodle Dogs, because it looks like Poodle Dogs are another very big thing in the lives of our rich rulers. Now, it looks like this is true about these wars. And now I see, as you see, that our country is dickering around with these European troubles, and getting up big armies and navies to take up guns and go fight for the rich men. But worst of all, in a way, was when I got the news that our George had joined the gun-carriers, to go running out shooting and killing and torpedo-ing, and bombing, other young boys of other countries, whom he had never seen in his life before, nor—that is, they were all rank strangers to one another, the boys on Our side, and the boys on the Other side. That is the business of Murder, that is the art of War, that is the business of Killing. But—all of this for what? I'll tell you for what: All of this Blood must flow because the rich men had an argument, and because one of them was stealing something off of the other one, and they got into a fight about it, but were too big a cowards to go and fight their own battles, so they hire boys like George to take up a gun and go and kill or get killed for an argument that he dont know a dam thing about, all because he wanted a job to learn radio, or television, all because he wanted to make something out of himself, all because he was a good boy, wanting a job, wanting to work, wanting to do some good for everybody. And our big politicians and rich men give him a gun and say, Go and Fight Shoot and Kill—That's what they call Religion, That's what they call God, That's what they call Progress, and if you get out and speak or talk against them, they throw you in Jail and leave you there . . . just like they nailed Jesus on a cross and left him there to die. The rich folks still do the same thing, they always did, they always will.

garden of Eden

woody Guthrie

Now, when you look around you, see how this battle is taking shape all around you, and how it is a fight between the rich folks and the poor folks every day. The question I want to ask you is this: What side are you on from Day to Day? Rich folks who own the newspapers, the banks, the radio, the picture shows, the stores, the land, the houses, the pretty cars, the silk clothes, the sissy boys, and the silly daughters, the wax preachers, and the superstitious monks and nuns, and the clerks in all of the business houses, and the policemen that walk the streets, and the boys in the army and navy, and in the National Guards and Armories around over the country. I know that the other side is my side.

The poor folks dont own anything. They are scattered, wandering, broke, hungry, dirty, ragged, hungry-looking, and all of that, but one good thing, they are workers, hard workers, and they are ten times more honest than the upper crust people, and I like them fifty times more, because they're Real People, Real Honest To Goodness People, going all over Hell's Half Acre looking for work, to California, to the Rio Grande, to the Gulf of Mexico, to New York, to the Great Lakes, and back South again when the sun gets warm enough to walk down the road. There are ten times more of these people than the rich kind, because, as you know, there always have been more rich than poor. Since this is True, the Rich folks must have someway of making us poor folks believe their way, so they put out radio programs, sermons, moving pictures, books, magazines, and all sorts of silly advertising. This junk is piled around every house in the world like a big pile of trash, but most folks believe it, and are sunk in it, and never try to get out of it, but just take some sort of a little job at a little pay, and work all of the time and never get ahead, and never have any vacations or fun or big cars, and they just sort of get scared, and stay in this same old 'rut.' I call it a 'rut' because that's exactly what it is.

You'll have plenty of chances in your life to read some books on the things I've said in this letter, about Work, Hours, Wages, Factories, Farms, Mills, Mines, Money, Rich People, Religion, Freedom, Fun, and Marriage, and the job of Loving Everybody.

It may be that you will bump your head around in Life till all of this dawns in your mind. I know you have been raised just exactly right to see the Truth and know It when you see it, and to go over and work on the right side when the time comes. I dont know exactly what you're thinking now, but for God's Sake dont get to be a Pansie or a Sissy, or be afraid, or be too Superstitious, or afraid of Religion, or

These
are
my pals

ROEKER   FIELDS   Did you say 10¢?   HALL   GUTHRIE

Promo flyer for "Pipe Smoking Time" show on CBS Radio, ca. 1940.

afraid to think what you want to and say what you please. Someday when I see you in person, we'll take a drive together and I'll tell you lots more things, and—by the way you'd get a big kick out of driving with me, 'cause I just bought a new Plymouth, and it really splits the breeze.

I've made 14 Victor Records and been in about 100 shows since I got to New York. I'm in Washington D.C, this afternoon writing a book, and am coming to Oklahoma right away as soon as I get a check due me from the Columbia Broadcasting Co., by the way I was on a coast to coast broadcast last week with Burgess Meredith, and Franchot Tone. Tone is a swell guy, and I got $50 for about 6 minutes work. Not bad, if the 6 minutes was everyday, or is that being a Hog? Well, Columbia's got lots of money, and I dont mind taking it from them. I got $400 cash in advance, and 5% Royalties from Victor for the Records. I wish you could have seen New York City with me. I learned a lot, and had a lot of fun. And I know you would get a hell of a big kick out of something like that.

Remember you are my favorite sister. Have a good time, and tell all of the folks I said Howdy. Might see you pretty soon . . .

Love,
Woody

3

HARD TIMES IN NEW YORK TOWN

1940–1941

Well, it's always we ramble, that river and I
All along your green valley, I'll work till I die
My land I'll defend with my life, if it be
'Cause my pastures of plenty must always be free

—"Pastures of Plenty"

I n 1940 Woody came to New York at the behest of the radical actor Will Geer, then *appearing on Broadway. Geer, who was among Woody's first associates on the Hollywood left, not only brought Guthrie to town, he helped him find work and a place to live.*

Immediately noticeable here, both in the songs and annotations and in the correspondence, is Woody's increasing political commitment and involvement.

Judging from the date, "The New York Trains" must have been one of the first songs that Woody wrote after arriving in Manhattan.

THE NEW YORK TRAINS

My wife come in this morning from Texas down the line
In the big Grand Central Station the clock was striking nine
She rode the Southwest Limited on the New York Central Road
She chartered sixteen coaches and she brought the kids along.

We rode the bus and subways all over New York town
To rent us an apartment and try to settle down
The trains run through the buildings and also underground
And you spend another nickel ever time you turn around.

The subway trains are crowded and when they make a stop
You're at the wrong dern station when the crowds they push
    you off
They heave and push and squeeze and squirm, they slip and
    slide and crowd
And when your station comes along, well then you caint get out

We hooked a train and rode an hour to see the Bronx Park Zoo
And landed out in Brooklyn on Utica Avenue . . .
You got to change your subway train at every stop or two . . .
And every time you come wearing a different pair of shoes.

We loaded in a taxi to haul us crost the town
And it registered a nickel everytime the wheel went 'round
He charged us 'leven dollars and eighty seven cent
And down in Texas that's enough to pay six months of rent

Now friend if you are from the South or either way out west
And got a wife and children that you love your very best
If you come to New York City, I wish you very well,
You'd better bring a wagon load of greenback dollar bills.

By W. (Woody) Guthrie
New York City
Dec. 2, 1940

The following, more or less a parody of the Biblical "Beati-tudes," was attached to the original manuscript of Woody's song "Jesus Christ (They Laid Jesus Christ in His Grave)," itself a parody (or at least a rewrite) of the folk ballad "Jesse James."

1. Brethren preach Jesus Christ and him crucified,
2. And King Tutankahmen and him mummy-fied,
3. And the electric chair and it electrified,
4. Yea, and preach the legs of beautiful girls, their sweet sunkist faces and rounded breasts which as ye remember that Hollywood glorified
5. And go forth bolder to serve and to work and let your going be your boldness and your learning be your work and your preaching of humanity unified and made into one big happy family and it stupified,
6. For truth, Brethren, Truth, that is your mission and your coming and going,
7. And unless ye seek and thirst after Truth even as a jackass brays to breed its mate, even as the doe and the deer seek the wilderness, even as the Oakies sought to find work picking fruit in the green trees of California and across the hot sands of the Arizona desert,
8. I say, beloved, if it be not Truth that ye seek in your traveling and preach, what use is it to travel, or to preach?
9. Preach the Forest of Arizona and it petrified, and curse Wall Street for it is putrified and rank and filthy and will one day be made clean by Love,
10. And that Love is so strong and powerful that it shall look like Hate,
11. But ye shall know it by this sign, and when Love shall appear as Hate—you shall know Love, for it shall contain no greed.
12. You are a worker and work is a way of loving,
13. Even so, work is also a struggle, and work is to wrestle— and work is good and so is the fight when it contains no silly greed.

Woody G., 1940

"Slipknot" has appeared in Guthrie songbooks before, but never with the dedication that closes the manuscript. Since Woody had, only a few months before, been known to tell racist jokes on the air in California, this song and note provide a useful measure of how far he'd come.

SLIPKNOT

Did you ever see a hangman tie a slipknot?
Did you ever see a hangman tie a slipknot?
Yes, I seen it a many a time, and he winds, and he winds
And after thirteen times, he ties a slipknot.

Tell me, will that slipknot slip? No! It will not!
Tell me, will that slipknot slip? No! It will not!
It will slip down round your neck, but it won't slip back again
That slipknot. That slipknot. O' That slipknot!

Did you ever lose a brother in that slipknot?
Did you ever lose a brother in that slipknot?
Yes. My brother was a slave . . . he tried to escape . . .
And they drug him to his grave with a slipknot.

Slipknot

woody guthrie

Did you ever lose your father in that slipknot?
Did you ever lose your father in that slipknot?
(Yes.) They hung from him a pole, and they shot him full of
    holes
And they left him hang to rot in that slipknot.

Who makes the laws for that slipknot?
Who makes the laws for that slipknot?
Who says who will go to the calaboose—
And get the hangman's noose, get that slipknot?

I don't know who makes the law of that slipknot.
I don't know who makes the law of that slipknot.
But the bones of many a men are a whistling in the wind.
Just because they tie their laws with a slipknot.

*Dedicated to the many negro mothers, fathers, and sons
alike, that was lynched and hanged under the bridge of the
Canadian River, seven miles south of Okemah, Okla., and to
the day when such will be no more.

Woody G.
2-29-40 N.Y.

————————

*By the time Woody arrived in New York, he was a full-time
proselytizer for Popular Front concepts. In that spirit, he not
only wrote songs, but appended to some of them instructions
on how potential listeners could craft their own. "The Govt
Road" is a particularly good example of how Woody worked—
including the flaws in his approach, since he was still address-
ing himself to fellow Okies even though he'd relocated to the
East Coast, where there were few, if any, Dust Bowl refugees
besides himself.*

THE GOVT ROAD

Hanover House
43rd Street & 6th Ave.
New York Town
Feb. 1940

Howdy friend,

This is the first copy of this song ever wrote. It shows you
how to write em up without the music. Songs come to me

best when walking down the road, and I've got fifteen or twenty road songs, I mean trying to catch a good easy one that everybody can sing the first time you hear it, and fit everybody in the country. The song New York has liked best so far that I made up is called "Why Do You Stand There in the Rain?" That is one about the American Youth Congress a going to Washington to stand in the rain and listen to the president. But this one I think is as good because it brings out the idea of plowing down the roots and rocks to build a big smooth road so everybody can travel easier on it, and it would be a government road.

Us Oakies are out of jobs, out of money, out of drinking whiskey, out of everything, except hope—and we're a walking down that old 66 carrying our work shoes, because our feet are blistered from walking. And since so many folks get killed ever day on our narrow minded highways, why dont they pitch in and make them wider? That would at least give us a job. So to the day that we grab our shovels and tractors and build that road, I would like to dedicate this little song. The Government Road. Thank you for the help you gave in buying this first original copy. It was a big help.

Woody Guthrie
2–'40

I'm a walkin' down that buffalo trail;
   Gonna build a government road;
Twenty one years I been in jail;
   Gonna build a government road.

   Build a government road, love
   Build a government road—
   Plowin' down the buffalo trail;
   Gonna build a government road.

Buffalo trail is sticks and stone;
   Build a government road,
It'll be paved when I get done;
   Build a government road.

Gonna grab my shovel in my hand,
   Build a government road,
Gonna hire every man I can,
   Build a government road.

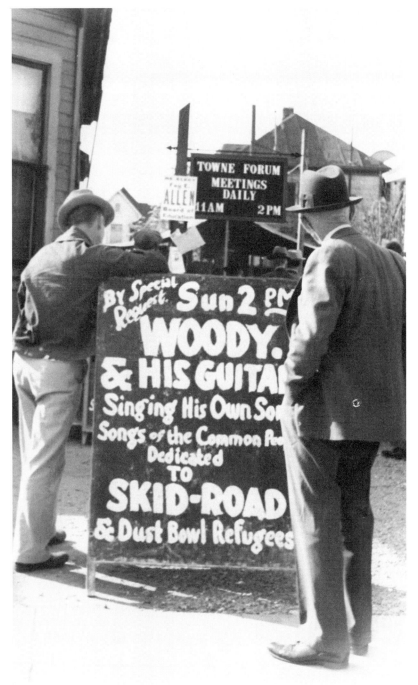

Sign board for Skid Row Show, 1941. (Courtesy of Seema Weatherwax)

"Skid Row [in Los Angeles] on Main Street around 3rd to 5th Streets was where he liked to go and drink beer, talk and sing to the men hanging around in the many bars in that area. On a number of occasions, Jack [Weatherwax] and another friend, 'Greenie,' went with him. The three made a good team: Woody with his guitar, 'Greenie,' who was a musician-composer, played the piano and knew all the working class songs, and Jack, who had a good voice and joined in the singing.

"During this period, there were meetings held on a daily basis at the Towne Forum in Los Angeles, where many of the down and out people gathered. Jack sometimes lectured there on current events and conditions that affected the lives of the people. Woody was asked to entertain there and it was one of the things that gave him the greatest satisfaction because he could really relate and communicate with the people who frequented the Forum." —Seema Weatherwax, 1988

Tractors, plows, and engines, too;
  Build a government road,
All be a workin' when I get through;
  Build a government road.

What you gonna do when the rent comes due?
  Build a government road.
Then we'll build a railroad too;
  Build a government road.

Whose a gonna travel down this a way?
  Build a government road,
Why, brothers and sisters every day!
  Build a government road.

What we gonna do when we get to the end?
  Build a government road,
Then brother, start right over again;
  Build a government road.

                    Almost 8 o'clock Feb. 24th 1940
                    New York, 43rd & 6th Ave. Hanover House
                    New York as a hole is okay.
                      Woody G.

On May 3, 1940, Woody received his Dust Bowl Ballads *for RCA Victor Records at their Camden, New Jersey, studio. Alan Lomax had persuaded RCA to give Woody the opportunity to make twelve records, exploring the possibility of marketing Guthrie as the label's answer to Columbia's Burl Ives. The label also encouraged Woody to write at least one song about* The Grapes of Wrath, *then kicking up a cultural storm as both a novel and a movie.*

The Dust Bowl Ballads *include some of Woody's most enduring music: "So Long It's Been Good to Know You," "Do Re Mi," "I Ain't Got No Home," "Vigilante Man," and, of course, "Tom Joad," a ballad based on* The Grapes of Wrath's *central character, which essentially restates the novel's plot. He also wrote the following essay as a booklet included with the release of the two-volume album.*

WOODY, 'THE DUSTIEST OF THE DUST BOWLERS' (THE TALE OF HIS TRAVELS) (MAKING OF HIS SONGS)

This bunch of songs aint about me, and I aint a going to write about me, 'cause every time I start to do that, I find that I run out of material.

They are 'Oakie' songs, 'Dust Bowl' songs, 'Migratious' songs, about my folks and my relatives, about a jillion of 'em, that got hit by the drouth, the dust, the wind, the banker and the landlord and the police, all at the same time . . . and it was these things all added up that caused us to pack our wife and kids into our little rattletrap jallopies, and light out down the Highway—in every direction, mostly west to California.

I got a letter from a lady down in Oklahoma that comes as a result of a Poor Farmer Broadcast over CBS, that said, "Only the quitters took to freight trains and broken down jallopies, in search of a LIVING WITHOUT LABOR."

I didn't think there was a human in the world that actually believed that about us Oakies. But it looks like there is one. Somewhere in this world there seems to be one. And, you know, if it's all right with everybody, I'd like to dedicate this album of Victor Records, and every other breath of air that I ever draw in this old world to that person, just that One.

There was a feller that knew us Oakies, and he knew what it was like in Oklahoma, and he knew about the dust and the debts that covered us up, and he knew why we blowed out to California, because early in the deal, he throwed a pack on his back and traipsed around amongst us, and lived with us, and talked to us, and et with us, and slept with us, and he felt in his heart and knew in his head that us Oakies was a lookin' for "A Living WITH Labor"—that man was John Steinbeck.

We followed the 66 Highway, the Will Rogers Road, from Oklahoma to the Pacific Ocean, about 1500 miles, and we wasn't all so lucky as to have a broke-down car to knock along in. Lots of us had to walk. Wife and Children had to walk. It's a mighty long stretch from Phoenix, Arizona, to Barstow, California, or Blythe, and if you slow down and look right real close, you can see a lot of sights. Sometimes, specially in summer time, the desert is awful hot, and the tar pavement is hotter, and you can see whole families caught and stranded out there under the signboards and cactuses . . . depending on the desert rabbits for something to eat . . . and the sun to guide 'em west to that "Living with Labor."

As just a little personal experience, I've made this stretch of desert lots of times. Once I remember I was a wearing a pair of shoes a lady had give me, and they was alright for ordinary walking, but on the desert they wore big blisters on my feet, so many that I had to take off the shoes and carry 'em in my hands, and go barefooted down that highway, and the tar was too hot to walk on, and so was the sand, and I made about 30 miles this a way, and was sitting on the side of the road on a gallon bucket, when two boys picked me up in an old roadster and hauled me to Barstow, California.

My relatives had wrote letters back from California a telling how pretty the country was and about the big rains and the big ocean and the high mountains, and the valleys with green trees that was loaded down with most every kind of groceries, and they said the whole landscape out there just spelt the word 'Work'—and back in Oklahoma it just spelt the word 'Sleep'—or the words 'Work Together,' yep, that's what it spelt.

Only trouble was that I got lost in California, as I lost the address of the railroad bridge my relatives was stranded under.

However, while going through the process of a lookin' for 'em, I looked into the lost and hungry faces of several hundred thousand Oakies, Arkies, Texies, Mexies, Chinees, Japees, Dixies, and even a lot of New Yorkies . . . and I got so interested in the art and science of Migratin' that I majored in it—in a school so big you can't even get out of it.

Get this down, once and for all, them folks are just a lookin' for one thing, and that one thing is what all of the books and bibles call Freedom . . . well, that includes 3 square meals a day and a good job at 'honest' pay. I say for all of them, "We crost this country once, and we'd cross it ten more times, if it would take us to Honest Work at Honest Pay."

"We're hard hit, we're hard hitters, but it's a dern cinch, we aint quitters.

Back south and back east it was the drouth. Down in Oklahoma it was the drouth that first hit us. Then come the Big Oil Booms here and yonder, and the first bunch to leave the farm and take off down the big middle of the road was 'boom-chasers.' They needed men and they paid big wages for Oil Field Work, $15, 18, 25, a day for Drillers, Tooldressers, Roughnecks, Roustabouts, Pipe-liners, Rig-builders, Tong Buckers, Ditch Diggers and Carpenters, Team-skinners, Cement Men, Truck Drivers, and so forth, and they wrote to the folks back stranded on the farm and said, "Come on, folks, the Boom's on, you can find more money along the streets in a Boom Town than you could make in fifty years on a dried-up farm with a mortgage on it!"

Whole families lit out. The little old farm went to rot, and weeds jumped up around the house, and the shingles blew off, and the windows got broke out, and the porch fell sideways to the ground, and the house slipped sideways to the ground like a young calf that had been hit with a sledge and stuck with a knife.

Them was the Boomchasers.

But you couldn't as a rule, afford to build a permanent house in a Boom Town. Reason why's because a Boom jumps up like a patch of toadstools and goes away the same way . . . and all that's left of the oil field is just a forest of rigs and cables that just set there and pump the oil out of the ground, and it dont take many folks to handle that, so—the money's gone and the chase is on, to another Boom Town, maybe 300 or 400 miles away somewhere, maybe even away out on the west Texas plains . . . around the northern panhandle of Texas . . . Skellytown, Panhandle, Pampa, Borger, Amarillo, Dalhart, Dumas, 'way up on the wild and windy plains, 3600 feet high, flat as a floor, bald as an eight ball, with nothin' in the world to stop that North Wind but a barb wire fence about a hundred mile north, and all of them barbs is turned the same way . . . where the oil flows, the wheat grows, the dust blows, and the farmer owes.

That's west Texas. Lived right in there north of Amarillo, around Pampa, Gray County, for about 6 years. Got married there. Bought us a little shack for $25, me and Mary, and we been married 6 years now, and got 3 of the nicest, youngest children you ever saw, Teeny, Sue, and Bill. Bill he aint old enough to vote, but the other two scribble letters to me while I'm away—and they know about as good as anybody how the 1940 elections are a going, and about the wars in Europe, they got that figgered out, too, 'cause they dont give a hoot about 'em, and dont want to waste no time on 'em, and wont take no sides with 'em, and wont spend a penny on 'em. (The picture on the front of this album is the town where they live right now, Pampa, Gray Co., Texas.)

Dust-storms is not exactly a new thing—but up till five or six years ago they was mighty few and far between. This business of such awful and terrible dust storms, so black you cant see your hand before your eyes, or a light in your room, or a dollar in your pocket, or a meal on your table—that's what's new, that's what the old timers cant figger out. That's what their kids grown and married cant see through. That's what the little fellers cant see through, nor the teachers, preachers, screechers, nor the police, bankers, nor politicians . . . and you might be able to stand the dust, if it was dust alone, 'cause

CHRIST FOR PRESIDENT

Let's have Christ our president.
Let us him for our king.
Cast your vote for the Carpen-
ter
That you call the Nazarene.
The only way you can ever
beat
These crooked polician men
Is to run the money changers
out of the temple
And to put the Carpenter in.

O it's Jesus Christ our presi-
dent,
God above our king—
With a job and a pension for
young and old,
We will make hallelujah ring!

Every year we waste enough
To feed the ones who starve;
We build our civilization up
And we shoot it down with
wars—
But with the Carpenter on the
seat
Away up in the capital town
The U.S.A. would be on the
way
Pros-perity bound!

you're made out of dust, and can take a lot of it for a little while, or a little of it for a long time, but when things just sort of fly loose and all happen at once, like an old clock, why—everything goes haywire, and everything seems funny, and your land turns into a sand dune, and your barn is half covered up, and you see tractors covered under, and farm machinery, and chicken houses dusted under, why, you scratch your head, and you pull your hair, and you walk the floor, and you think, and think, and think, but you just cant see your way out . . . you owe the bank money, you cant pay it, you cant get credit, you cant get fuel, coal, groceries nor a complete new set up of new stuff—so you hear of another place, say California, and you see herds and herds of people a pickin' up and leavin' out—and you just sorta say "Well, I aint got nothin' to lose, so here goes."

That's a migration. Even if you can't explain to the police all about it, that's what's in your head, you're a leaving a string of stuff behind you, and you could explain it, but it would take as long to do that as it took to live through it, and the police aint hired to write history books about you. They're hired to see that nothin' dont hurt you—even a deputy.

I guess you wonder how Oklahoma is right now in this day and time. Well, I heard a expert say the other day that Oklahoma is 'first in everything worst.' 1940 expects the shortest wheat crop in 40 years, account of the dust, and dry weather, and besides, they'd have to lay on 15,000 more deputies to corral the farmers—off of the 66 Highway.

I like to wore that 66 out myself, and when you bum around for a year or two and look at all of the folks that's down and out, busted, disgusted (but can still be trusted), you wish somehow or other, that they could get back to their old stompin' grounds, and pitch in and build this part of the country back up again . . . but you know they cant do it unless some things are changed.

They need a piece of land. You need a good house on it, with a coat or two of good paint, and three or four cows, and some chickens, and lots of stuff like that, farm tools, and stuff to eat, and some spendin' money in your pocket for a little good time once in a while, and a long time to pay your place out, about 40 years . . . and you need U.S. Government Camps for the Workin' Folks, with nice clean place to live and cook and do your washin' and ironin' and cookin', and good beds to rest on, and so nobody couldn't herd you around like whiteface cattle, and deputies beat you up, and run you out of town, and stuff like that.

You could pay a dime a day for your place to live, and you could do work around the Camp to pay your bill, and you could have a nice buildin' with a good dance floor in it, and you could have church there, too, and go to Sunday School, and Church, and have all kinds of meetings and talk about crops and weather and wages, and no cops would make you scatter out.

You could meet there and have Singings and Pie Suppers, and Raffles, and Banquets, and Eats and Dks., (abbreviated), and have your own Peace Officers to keep down fist fights, and your own women to keep care of the kids, and they could have games and baths and good toilets and clean showers and—the governor of the state could find out where the jobs was, and keep you hired out all of the time, building Oklahoma, and the whole Dust Bowl over again.

These here songs aint mine. The Government says so, and so does Victor Records, but really they aint, and I hope that when they are played on your loud speakers in these U.S. Camps, and over Radios, that you say, well, you made 'em up yourself, 'cause I'm just an old awkward Oklahoma boy, use to shine the governor's shoes and shine his spittoons, and aint too good to do it again, if I get a good chance, and the pay is 'right.'

This bunch of songs are really just one song, cause I used the same notes. Just fixed 'em a little different, that's all. Same old notes as ever.

I wrote a letter to Leon C. (Red) Phillips, present Governor of Oklahoma, and told him to make that 66 Highway twice as wide a comin' back from California as it is a goin', and I don't know if he done it or not, as that was several days ago. However I'm gonna tramp back to Oklahoma this summer and kill a couple or three months there, and will look over the 66 and see what he's done. In case he aint done it, I'll make up a song about it. In case he has, I'll make him as famous as Jesse James.

Well, folks, a word more, and I sign off. This is all taking place in New York City, and all of their street cars run under the ground up here, they aint got room for any more on the streets, and I'm writing a letter to the Mayor this morning about the cars, they're so thick they can't get the 1941 models on the streets, and I'm gonna suggest that they paint 'em a thinner coat, and that way they could squeeze 2 Lincoln Zephyrs and a kiddy car on every street.

Sing as loud and as long as you like, but dont mention my name. Take it easy, but take it.

True as The Average, New York State
Woody Guthrie New York Street
New York Town New York Everything
 N.Y., N.Y., N.Y., N.Y.,

No matter where he lived, Woody remained an amazingly prolific letter writer, keeping in contact with all his musical associates as he or they rambled. While Woody was in New York, Alan Lomax relocated to Washington, where he worked with the recording division of the Library of Congress, in which capacity he eventually took Woody into the studio. (The recordings that

(Courtesy of Seema Weatherwax)

resulted, which constitute an oral history of the Dust Bowl and a highly politicized version of the Okie attitude, are now available as a boxed set from Rounder Records.)

By 1941, Woody himself had returned to the West Coast, where he wrote a series of lengthy, amusing letters to his associates who'd stayed in New York to perform as the Almanac Singers. Lee is Lee Hays, who was a central figure not only in the Almanacs but later in the Weavers. Mill is Millard Lampell, who went on to become a radio, television, and movie scriptwriter. Pete is Pete Seeger, America's most famous folk singer, then known also as Pete Bowers.

31 E. 21 Street on the
Top Floor of New York

Dear Alan

Just thought I'd write you a few more lines tonight on as many different subjects as I can get down in one line. Mainly about a few thoughts that I been thinking about making up songs and stuff like that. A little dog just got run over down below in the streets, a taxi hit him. I could make up a song about how it sounded to hear the little dog yelping to the little boy a watching out of the third floor window across the street. I had a big dog once and all of the kids played with him and liked him and he would go and get their base ball when they knocked it too far or he would run in their football games and stand around with his eyes shot over and his ear stuck about half way up and his tongue running in and out of his mouth, his head cocked over sideways like and watching the kids shoot marbles. But an old neighbor lady with something haywire in her head went and poisoned the dog and it killed him and the kids all had a big funeral for old poochy they called him and they dug him a nice grave and painted his name on a flat rock and it was a plumb heartbreaking affair. You could write a song about that and it would contain enough of all of the high and low feelings to put it over if the blame was properly placed on the old lady that poisoned the pooch. I think one mistake some folks make in trying to write songs that will interest folks is to try to cover too much territory or to make it too much of a sermon. A folk song ought to be pretty well satisfied just to tell the facts and let it go at that.

You hadn't ought to try to be too funny because if you just tell folks the truth they'll laugh at every other word. The best of all funny stories have got a mighty sincere backbone. Those are the old deathbed and graveyard and parted lover songs that I sing more than any others when I need to cheer myself up. And there is something very funny about almost everything that happens if you do a good job of a telling just exactly what took place like in the song Why Do You Stand There in the Rain? or about Pretty Boy Floyd or the little BollWeevil. People that laugh at songs laugh because it made them think of something and they want you to leave a good bit up to their guesswork and imagination and it takes on a friendly and warm atmosphere like you was thanking them for being good listeners and giving them credit for being able to guess the biggest part of the meaning. Lots of songs I make up when I'm laughing and celebrating make folks cry and songs I make up when I'm feeling down and out makes people laugh. These two upside down feelings has got to be in any song to make it take a hold and last.

Usually I set down and knock off a song in about 30 minutes or a hour but in most of them I've been going around knowing and whistling it and a trying to get it all straight in my head what I want to say and why I want to say it and usually when I decide just exactly who the song is a going to help out if its the right bunch I can really blat or scribble her down in a hurry. The reason why you want to write songs is what keeps you going. If you get enough reason to write I say that you can knock off two or 3 pretty fair songs a week and a pretty damn good one over the week end. I know just honky tonk geetar thumpers that can whack out a song a day and a good one out of every 30. The main thing is to set your head on some subject you want to keep on and haul off and start and you can write 25 or 30 or 500 songs on the same subject if your subject is a helping people. I took as my subject songs that would make people want to help people, and I am now on my 202th—two oh tooth. I've wrote up songs and tore them up. I bet I tore up more than a orchestra feller could shake a stick at. And lots of folks are making up songs all of the time and they dont know it. I hear so many people coming around me and going on about where you get your words and your tunes. Well I get my words and tunes off of the hungry folks and they get the credit for all I pause to scribble down. I feel a little bit guilty for not taking more time out to jot down more. As you know I aint able to read no music notes. I just get the tune to grinding through my head and jot the music down on any old guitar. You know

That reminds me of the girl that shot her boy friend and buried him under the house. She sang a little song that went, 'Now I'm Walking the Floor Over You.'

pretty near everybody is a making up all kinds of tunes all along but they just dont know about it. You see a lady doing your housework and youll be a walking around a humming or whistling and half of the time youll mix up about three or four songs that are such a good mixture that you got a brand new song—but the reason you dont know it is because your mind is thinking about all kinds of stuff like dishes and dust pans and kids and husbands and ice men and the traveling salesman or debts you would like to be able to pay if you could only raise the money—and so the time fades away and thats the last of it. Everybody makes up music and some folks try to harness it and put it to work just like steam that you cant hold in your hand or vitamens you hear the doctor charge you three dollars to describe or electricity that makes big engines run and great big wheels go around. If it would of been left up to me I'd of been too busy trapseing around over the country and making a guitar sound like a freight train to of stopped long enough to catch electricity and make it help you but of course Mr Edison had some men working for him and tonight I'm a writing this by a light, a floor lamp with three shifts forwards and a radio with 3 backwards and I've got the light and the other folks can hear the music. Music is some kind of electricity that makes a radio part of a man and his dirt is in his head and he just buys according to how hes a feeling.

The best stuff you can sing about is what you saw and if you look hard enough you can see plenty to sing about.

As you may of already known me & Cisco sung one week up here on 4th Street in a joint called Jimmy Dwyers Sawdust Trail. I didnt see much dust but saw lots of trailing. The big reporters from the newspapers came down and they listened to the songs about the people in the dust bowl and about the ones that are chasing up and down that big 66 highway with empty bowls and the ones that went to California trying to swap a cracked crock bowl for a sugar bowl and the police and big farmers got the whole works—and the papers here, the Sun and others give a pretty good write up or two about the dust bowl and especially P.M. & the Sun sent 5th 1940 copy—and lots of people wrote in hollering that the reporter fell for a lot of 5th column stuff. They called me a communist and a wild man and everything you could think of but I dont care what they call me. I aint a member of any earthly organization my trouble is I really ought to go down in the morning and just join everything. I registered in California as a democrat and changed it in one day to a progressive just because I was passing the ladys house. I done that on a dare more or less from a girl I was out walking. So I wrote back to the columnist and thanked him and I dont care what number he is. Numbers is like a slot machine the guy that advertise them wins. He published a double column then about the letters he got kicking on me and he said he liked the songs no matter if I was sprinkled or babtised by drowning or soused down in a river of dust—and he liked me no matter if I believed what was right. Good columnist. I answered his second column by a letter and I thanked him for doing some hungry people a good hand. Other fellers ought to write some columns to help the folks that need help. Im as good of a preacher on hungry bellies as I am to sing on a full stomach ache.

Ive always knowed this was what I wanted to talk and sing about and I'm used to running into folks that complain but I dont ever intend to sell out or quit or talk or sing any different because when I do that drugstore lemonade stuff I just open up my mouth and nothing comes out.

And now I've got this CBS radio job and a salary that beats owning six farms in Oklahoma and I dont know just what or where or when somebody will raise up and try to put their foot in my good jungle stew because it is mighty apt to happen and it means so much not only to me but to my friends and relatives that I'll be able to help and my wife and three kids are feeling pretty good for the first time in a long time and a long time down in the dust bowl where they've been cooped up is just naturally a mighty long time. If I thought for two minutes that anything I do or say would hurt America and the people in it I would keep my face shut and catch the first freight out of the country. The library of Congress is good. It has helped me a lot by recording what I had to say and to copy all of my songs and file them away so the senators caint find them. Course they're always there in case they ever got a few snorts under their vest and want to sing. I think real folk stuff scares most of the guys in Washington. A folk song is whats wrong and how to fix it or it could be whose hungry and where their mouth is or whose out of work and where the job is or whose broke and where the money is or whose carrying a gun and where the peace is—thats folk lore and folks made it up because they seen that the politicians couldn't find nothing to fix or nobody to feed or give a job of work. When we get to a feeling sorta folksey and make up some folk lore we're a doing all we can to make it easy on you. I can sing all day and all night sixty days and sixty nights but of course I aint got enough wind to be in office.

I walked ten years from town to town on big hot blistered feet singing and trying to learn how to sing my folk songs.

And now you tell me I didn't do no work to win my little place. You say it was all handed me on a silver stick.

All I know how to do Alan is to just keep a plowing right
on down the avenue watching what I can see and listening to
what I can hear and trying to learn about everybody I meet
everyday and try to make one part of the community feel like
they know the other part and one end of it help the other
end—cause if a horse fly is dealing a horse trouble on the left
nose hole, its the tail that swishes and drives the fly off and
it sings a little fiddle bow song as it swishes. Horses tails
make awful good fiddle bows.

Take It Easy but take it
Woody Guthrie
Sept. 19th 1940
New York Town

1965 Preston Ave.,
Los Angeles, Calif.,
March 1941

Dear Mill, Howdy Boy,

How's the writers cramps? Making lots of money? It
looks like the more money you make the worse it cramps
your writing. Same way with singing or anything else. But
the way you old boys are set up there in your old loft I
imagine there ain't no way in the world you could let money
cramp you. The more dough you go to making the more you
get to run around with the white collars. I hope you dont
ever let their ideas soak in on you. It was such a good stew
that you old boys made and the best time was had right there
too. Your songs and the stuff you wrote were worth a lot to
either side and will attract attention for you from both sides.
The other side sucks you dry and dont give you nothing. Our
side gives you the real stuff you need and whole train loads
of good fresh material, but not much money. We aint on the
money side and dont fight with money, but we use the Truth
and its like a spring of cold water. Hows the Ciscoes and have
you seen them lately? I wrote to them and their address has
been changed. You big horse you must of been awful busy a
getting rich. You aint wrote me a drop. Old Pete's still a
throwing his head way back like a coyote and a frailing that
old banjo. Petes really been around. He's the Uncle Dave
Macon of the labor movement. Mary's a warshing the kids
faces and a yelling like she was a branding calves on a frosty
morning. How's the loft? Lofty enough to suit you? Dont let
old Pete & Lee go high brow on you. Just plenty of plain
common old stew and hot coffee. Wine once in while if you

Take it easy but
take it.

—GEN. DE GAULLE GUTHRIE

like it. Stay sober and fight fair, dont get drunk unless you're by yourself or with somebody. If that loft is big enough you might fatten a head of cattle up there. Jack of diamonds is a hard card to play. New York City is a hard place to be. Folks is few and far between that knows the right slant on singing the right kind of songs. Pete for New England. Lee for Arkansaw. You for the midwest. Im shore as hell anxious to get a look at your APM records & book. Stick together you guys. I got a traffic ticket to go see about this morning. Hay Judge, Whats a gonna be my fine? He says Po' Boy its yo' hard luck, not mine.

Course you take old Lee he's lived down there on skeeter stew so long that he dont know what to do with a gal on concrete. I seen him one night down there close to Philly ducking out of the spot light down under the trees with a Bee Line mama and her honey dripping like dew and of course it made you like him better.

Sometimes I set around and picture you old boys up there a hoeing your row and I never seen 3 fellers I'd of took any more stock in. Always busy. You come and went and come and went and after you come a time or two you went.

Old Mill had him a nice girl and she was smart and lots of days he'd want to show her a good time but he was broke and that would make it hard.

Sue's our middle class daughter. She's been out in the back yard with Mama chopping weeds. Mary tells the kids the weeds are pretty flowers to get them to help carry them off. Sue just now wheeled in at the door with a big bundle of loose weeds and says, Daddy I got a purty big bouquet, looky, looky! And I told her yes but shut the door. And she said, No, dont you know what for I left that door open? And I said, No, why? And she told me, Well, they's a whole bunch of stuff grows outside where mama is, I wanted to bring you some, but you got to leave the door open so's you can get back outside to where some more is growing.

Thats just about like a feller gets in the big town.

So maybe you say Theres a fight to be fit right here in the big Town. And youre right. There is. But a feller hadn't ought to ever close that door between him and his old friends thats out in the weed patch a pulling up by the roots.

Lee Howdy. Would shore like to get with you old boys and steal some watermelons and splash some branch water.

Stay up till morning and sing to beat hell.

Everybody write.
Woody Guthrie

Some feller from the Dept. of Interior is here in town. He just called and said he'd heard my records and wants to come out to the house and talk about a documentary film to be shot up along the Columbia River. Hope he gives me a job. Will let you know.

———— ▬ ————

6111 S.E. 92 Ave
Portland, Oregon
7-8-41

Dear Pete, Mill & Lee
My Beloved Talcum Powder Singers
Or Seed Catalog Singers,

No letter received from you and no real reason for writing except to say that I did not get no album of your records which I understood that you sent to me. However if you didn't send none they aint no hard feelings, because I dont remember of sending but a scant few of my own to anybody and never did own a album of them for over a few minutes at a time.

Boys, what I think needs to be done to old time folk songs is not to give over an inch to jazz or swing as far as the melody goes, but what we've got to do is to bring American Folk Songs up to date. This dont mean to complicate our music a tall, but simply to industrialize, and mechanize the words. Why should we waste our time trying to wind the calendar back? Our old standby songs were no doubt super stream lined when they first got out, and possibly that is the reason why they spread like a prairie fire. Within my visit to New York I did not have the pleasure of coming across but a mighty few songs of the wheels, whistles, steam, boilers, shafts, cranks, operators, tuggers, pulleys, engines, and all of the well known gadgets that make up a modern factory. Except for just a few work songs of this kind that I heard through Alan Lomax, I am sorry to say the others were almost equal to zero. Alan knew the good of these work songs ten times better than me, and I know that all of you had the jump on me concerning work songs, but this is to simply remind you that the idea is on me like a wild cat with 3 sets of razors in each foot.

I have visited the Oakie camps a time or two since I been out here and they put me on their programs and the crowds were almost too big for you to believe. 600 here, 500 yonder. 300 next place. And they just dam near tore down a perfectly good govt auditorium when I sung about Pretty Boy or Tom Joad. And I made it my business to go into lots of the tents and shacks this trip that I didnt make on other trips, and hear them all sing, the little sisters, brothers, yodelers, ma and pa in the old yaller light of a coal oil lamp, sittin in a rocker, or on the side of an old screaking bed, eyes about half shut, bottom lip pooched out fill of snoose, and they sang religious, hopeful songs and sentimental worried songs but hours on hour could sing and sing and sing. And I made a little speech in each tent and I said, You folks are the best in the West. Why dont you take time out and write up some songs about who you are, where you come from, where all you been, what you was a lookin for, what happened to you on the way, the work you done and the work you do and the work and the things that you want to do. Your songs so far are not your songs, but songs that somebody else has put in your head, and for that matter, not your own life, not your own work, trouble, desires, or romances; why had you ought to sing like you're rich when you aint rich, or satisfied when you aint satisfied, or junk like you hear on these nickel machines and over the radio? Every one of them would lean and look towards me and keep so still and such a solemn look on their faces, there in those little old greasy dirty hovels that it would bring the rising sun to tears. In a few minutes some young and dreaming member of the family would break down and say, I been a thinkin about that ever since I commenced a singin. And then the whole bunch would enter into a deeper religious conversation and decide that was right. On more than one night, on more than one day, I've heard my Oakie friends ask me, Say Mister, you dont happen to be Mister Jesus do you? Come back?

Where the works of the Oakies is mainly in following the crops and praying for a little forty of their own, and adopting a mental attitude that it'd all come from a machine that you put a nickel in, the workers in other parts of the country have their mines, mills, croppin farms, factories, etc., from which their songs of their work must come and the answer to Tobacco Road and The Grapes of Wrath. It would be a sorry world if there wasnt no answer. But it is just so arranged that there is an answer, not only to the grinding voices of us Oakies, but to the questions of city workers as well. And it is our job if we claim the smallest distinction as American Folk Lorists, to see to it that the seeds are sown which will grow up into free speech, free singing, and the free pursuit of happiness that is the first and simplest birthright of a free people. For with their songs choked and their pamphlets condemned, their freedom will be throttled down to less than a walk, and freedom of going and coming, of meeting and discussing, of course, freedom will just be a rich man's word to print in his big papers and holler over his radio, it wont be real, it will only be a word. As now the case about 90% of the time.

I read your war songs and like them a lot. But you ought to throw in more wheels, triggers, springs, bearings, motors, engines, boilers, and factories—because these are the things that arm the workers and these are the source of the final victory of Public Ownership.

> True as the average.
> Woody Guthrie

Our job aint so much to go way back into history, that already been done, and we caint spare the time to do it all over again. Our job is the Here & Now. Today. This week. This month. This year. But we've got to try and include a Timeless Element in our songs. Something that will not tomorrow be gone with the wind. But something that tomorrow will be as true as it is today. The secret of a lasting song is not the record current event, but this timeless element which may be contained in their chorus or last line or elsewhere. (Bill is about to quit shitting in the britches.)

> Woody

———— ▬ ————

In happier times—or, simply, a country with a better school system—we wouldn't need to point out that this is a parody of "Frankie and Johnny," written to chastise British Prime Minister Neville Chamberlain for appeasing Adolf Hitler's imperial intentions by allowing him to snatch a big piece of Czechoslovakia at a famous conference in Munich.

ADOLPH & NEVILLINE

Hitler and Chamberlain was sweethearts
Lordy Lord, how they could love;
Swore to be true to the rich folks;
True as the stars above!
   Hitler was his man; he wouldn't do him wrong!

Chamberlain flew to Munich
And he didn't go for fun;
He went to give Mr. Adolph
Some bullets and some guns!
    Hitler was his man; he wouldn't do him wrong!

Now Hitler started eastward
But he didn't get so far;
He saw a light that blinded him
Was that big red Russian star!
    He was Chamberlain's man, he wouldn't do him wrong!

Hitler hollered to Mussolini,
Says, What am I gonna do?
Mussolini declared, That big red bear
Is too dam tough for you!
    You're Chamberlain's man, you wouldn't do him wrong!

So Hitler grabbed Czechoslovakia
And then he bought out France
'Cause against them Soviet workers
He didn't have a chance!
    He's Chamberlain's man, but he's a doin' him wrong!

Hitler stole England's customers,
And he stole her business, too;
Chamberlain tried his appeasement plan
Till he seen it wouldn't do!
    Hitler was his man, but he's a doin' him wrong!

Chamberlain went down to the hock shop
And he bought him a gattlin' gun;
Said, I caint beat that polar bear,
But I'll kill that Hitler Hun!
    He's my man but he's doin' me wrong!

Chamberlain came to Mr. Roosevelt
Said give me a bullet or two;
I'm a gonna run that Hitler down
And shoot him through and through.
    He's my man, but he done me wrong!

Hitler lied to his people
He promised them a socialist plan;
He called in all of the rich guys
And he gave them the whole shebang!
    He was their man but he done 'em wrong!

Drops of water
Turn a mill
One by one
One by One
Drops of water
Turn a mill
Singly none

—LEE HAYS

Take, drink, this is blood
—JESUS CHRIST

Land. Bread.
—V. LENIN

He sent his planes to London
To kill the workers there;
And now the planes of Chamberlain
They fill the London air!
   He was their man, but he done 'em wrong!

And now the rich folks tell us
To jump into this war—
For a bunch of thieves and liars
That ain't worth dyin' for!
   Since Hitler and Chamberlain has done 'em wrong!

Woody Guthrie
3-12-41

In 1941, Woody, Pete Seeger, and Alan Lomax set to work on a book that would compile all the most militant topical songs— industrial ballads, protest songs, blues—that had been created over the preceding decades: the boom years of the twenties, the Depression, and the New Deal, when migratory homeless workers joined the mass of the urban unemployed and auto workers and sharecroppers first tried to unionize. From the coal miners of Kentucky to the union organizers of the Rockies and the Northeast, wherever working people united, they sang. Hard Hitting Songs for Hard-Hit People *was to be the record of their music.*

Lomax did the bulk of the collecting, with Woody assisting (mostly by recollecting old songs but sometimes by making up a brand-new one). Seeger came into the project to do the actual musical transcriptions, working from Guthrie's memory, records, or the in-person renditions of other singers. John Steinbeck, as big a fan of Woody as Woody was of him, was enlisted to write an introduction.

But no publisher was interested, and then Pearl Harbor happened and World War II began and the manuscript was lost. Fragments survived and were published over the years, but it wasn't until 1964 that a full copy was restored and not until two years after that that it was published. By then the bloom was off the folk revival and very few people ever saw the book. Woody's introduction remains one of his fullest statements of the worth and purpose of the folk song movement.

INTRODUCTION

Howdy Friend:

Here's a book of songs that's going to last a mighty long time, because these are the kind of songs that folks make up when they're a-singing about their hard luck, and hard luck is one thing that you sing louder about than you do about boots and saddles, or moons on the river, or cigarettes a shining in the dark.

There's a heap of people in the country that's a having the hardest time of their life right this minute; and songs are just like having babies. You can take either, but you can't fake it, and if you try to fake it, you don't fool anybody except yourself.

For the last eight years I've been a rambling man, from Oklahoma to California and back three times by freight train, highway, and thumb, and I've been stranded, and disbanded, busted, disgusted with people of all sorts, sizes, shapes and calibres—folks that wandered around over the country looking for work, down and out, and hungry half of the time. I've slept on and with them, with their feet in my face and my feet in theirs—in bed rolls with Canadian Lumber jacks, in greasy rotten shacks and tents with the Okies and Arkies that are grazing today over the stage of California and Arizona like a herd of lost buffalo with the hot hoof and empty mouth disease.

Then to New York in the month of February, the thumb route, in the snow that blanketed from Big Springs, Texas, north to New York, and south again into even Florida . . . Walking down the big road, no job, no money, no home . . . no nothing. Nights I slept in jails and the cells were piled high with young boys, strong men, and old men; and they talked and they sung, and they told you the story of their life, how it used to be, how it got to be, how the home went to pieces, how the young wife died or left, how the mother died in the insane asylum, how Dad tried twice to kill himself, and lay flat on his back for 18 months—and then crops got to where they wouldn't bring nothing, work in the factories would kill a dog, work on the belt line killed your soul, work in the cement and limestone quarries withered your lungs, work in the cotton mills shot your feet and legs all to hell, work in the steel mills burned your system up like a gnat that lit in the melting pot, and—always, always had to fight and argue and cuss and swear, and shoot and slaughter and wade mud and sling blood—to try to get a nickel more out of the rich bosses. But out of all of this mixing bowl of hell and

high waters by George, the hard working folks have done
something that the bosses, his sons, his wives, his whores,
and his daughters have failed to do—the working folks have
walked bare handed against clubs, gas bombs, billys, black-
jacks, saps, knucks, machine guns, and log chains—and they
sang their way through the whole dirty mess. And that's why
I say the songs in the book will be sung coast to coast across

the country a hundred years after all nickel phonographs have turned back into dust.

I ain't a writer. I want that understood, I'm just a little one-cylinder guitar picker. But I don't get no kick out of these here songs that are imitation and made up by guys that's paid by the week to write 'em up—that reminds me of a crow a settin on a fence post a singing when some guy is a sawing his leg off at the same time. I like the song the old hen sings just before she flogs hell out of you for pestering her young chicks.

This book is a song book of that kind. It's a song book that come from the lungs of the workin' folks—and every little song was easy and simple, but mighty pretty, and it caught on like a whirlwind—it didn't need sheet music, it didn't need nickel phonographs, and it didn't take nothing but a little fanning from the bosses, the landlords, the deputies, and the cops, and the big shots, and the bankers, and the business men to flare up like an oil field on fire, and the big cloud of black smoke turn into a cyclone—and cut a swath straight to the door of the man that started the whole thing, the greedy rich people.

You'll find the songs the hungry farmers sing as they bend their backs and drag their sacks, and split their fingers to pieces grabbing your shirts and dresses out of the thorns on a cotton boll. You'll find the blues. The blues are my favorite, because the blues are the saddest and lonesomest, and say the right thing in a way that most preachers ought to pattern after. All honky tonk and dance hall blues had parents, and those parents was the blues that come from the workers in the factories, mills, mines, crops, orchards, and oil fields—but by the time a blues reaches a honky tonk music box, it is changed from chains to kisses, and from a cold prison cell to a warm bed with a hot mama, and from a sunstroke on a chain gang, to a chock house song, or a brand new baby and a bottle of gin.

You'll find a bunch of songs made up by folks back in the hills of old Kentucky. The hills was full of coal. The men was full of pep and wanted to work. But houses wasn't no good, and wages was next to nothing. Kids died like flies. The mothers couldn't pay the doctor, so the doctor didn't come. It was the midwives, the women like old Aunt Molly Jackson, that rolled up her sleeves, spit out the window, grabbed a wash pan in one hand and a armful of old pads and rags, and old newspapers, and dived under the covers and old rotten blankets—to come up with a brand new human being in one hand and a hungry mother in the other. Aunt Molly was just a coal miner's wife, and a coal miner's daughter, but she took the place of the doctor in 850 cases, because the coal miners didn't have the money.

You'll find the songs that were scribbled down on the margins of almanacs with a penny pencil, and sung to the rhythms of splinters and rocks that the Winchester rifles kicked up in your face as you sang them. I still wonder who was on the tail end of the rifles. Also in the Kentucky Coal Miner Songs, you'll sing the two wrote by Jim Garland, "Greenback Dollar" and "Harry Simms"—a couple of ring-tail tooters you're bound to like.

Sarah Ogan, she's the half sister of Aunt Molly, about half as old, and a mighty good worker and singer—she keeps up the spirit of the men that dig for a hamburger in a big black hole in the ground, and are promised pie in the sky when they die and get to heaven, provided they go deep enough in the hole, and stay down there long enough.

Then the next batch of wrong colored eggs to hatch—out pops the New Deal songs—the songs that the people sung when they heard the mighty good sounding promises of a re-shuffle, a honest deck, and a brand new deal from the big shots. A Straight flush, the Ace for One Big Union, the King for One Happy Family, the Queen for a happy mother with a full cupboard, the Jack for a hardworking young man with money enough in his pockets to show his gal a good time, and the Ten spot for the ten commandments that are over-looked too damn much by the big boys.

Next you'll run across some songs called "songs of the One Big Union"—which is the same Big Union that Abe Lincoln lived for and fought for and died for. Something has happened to that Big Union since Abe Lincoln was here. It has been raped. The Banking men has got their Big Union and the Land Lords has got their Big Union, and the Merchants has got their Kiwanis and Lions Club, and the Finance Men has got their Big Union, and the Associated Farmers has got their Big Union, but down south and out west, on the cotton farms, and working in the orchards and fruit crops it is a jail house offence for a few common everyday workers to form them a Union, and get together for higher wages and honest pay and fair treatment. It's damn funny how all of the big boys are in Big Unions, but they cuss and raise old billy hell when us poor damn working guys try to get together and make us a Working Man's Union. This Book is full of songs that the working folks made up about the beatings and the sluggings and the cheatings and the killings that they got when they said they was a going to form them a Working

Man's Union. It is a jail house crime for a poor damn working man to even hold a meeting with other working men. They call you a red or a radical or something and throw you and your family off of the farm and let you starve to death . . . These songs will echo that song of starvation till the world looks level—till the world is level—and there ain't no rich men, and there ain't no poor men, and every man on earth is at work and his family is living as human beings instead of like a nest of rats.

A last section of this book is called Mulligan Stew which are songs that you make up when you're a trying to speak something that's on your mind . . . telling your troubles to the blue sky, or a walkin' down the road with your 2 little kids by the hand, thinking of your wife that's just died with her third one—and you get to speaking your mind—maybe to yourself the first time, then when you get it a little better fixed in your head, and you squeeze out all of the words you don't need, and you boil it down to just a few that tell the whole story of your hard luck. Then when you talk it or sing it to somebody you meet in the hobo jungle or stranded high and dry in the skid row section of a big town, or just fresh kicked off a Georgia farm, and a going nowhere, just a walkin' along, and a draggin' your feet along in the deep sand, and— then you hear him sing you his song or tell you his tale, and you think, That's a mighty funny thing. His song is just like mine. And my tale is just like his. And everywhere you ramble, under California R.R. bridges, or the mosquito swamps of Louisiana, or the dustbowl deserts of the Texas plains—it's a different man, a different woman, a different kid a speaking his mind, but it's the same old tale, and the same old song. Maybe different words. Maybe different tunes. But it's hard times, and the same hard times. The same big song. This book is that song.

You'll find a section in this book about Prison & Outlaw songs. I know how it is in the states I've rambled through. In the prisons the boys sing about the long, lonesome days in the cold old cell and the dark nights in the old steeltank and a lot of the best songs you ever heard come from these boys and women that sweat all day in the pea patch, chain gang, a makin' big ones out of little ones, and new roads out of cow trails—new paved roads for a big black limousine to roll over with a lady in a fur coat and a screwball poodle dog a sniffing at her mouth. Prisoners ain't shooting the bull when they sing a mournful song, it's the real stuff. And they sing about the "man that took them by the arm," and about the "man with the law in his hand," and about the "man a settin' up in the jury box," and the "man on th' judges bench," and the "guard come a walkin' down that graveyard hall," and about the "man with th' jail house key,"—and the "guard a walkin' by my door"—and about the "sweethearts that walk past the window," and the old mother that wept and tore her hair, and the father that pleaded at the bar, and the little girl that sets in the moonlight alone, and waits for the sentence to roll by. These outlaws may be using the wrong system when they rob banks and hijack the rich traveler, and shoot their way out of a gamblin' game, and shoot down a man in a jewelry store, or blow down the pawn shop owner, but I think I know what's on these old boys minds. Something like this: "Two little children a layin in the bed, both of them so hungry that they cain't lift up their head . . ."

I know how it was with me, there's been a many a time that I set around with my head hanging down, broke, clothes no good, old slouchy shoes, and no place to go to have a good time, and no money to spend on the women, and a sleeping in cattle cars like a whiteface steer, and a starving for days at a time up and down the railroad tracks and then a seeing other people all fixed up with a good high rolling car, and good suits of clothes, and high priced whiskey, and more pretty gals than one. Even had money to blow on damn fool rings and necklaces and bracelets around their necks and arms—and I would just set there by the side of the road and think . . . Just one of them diamonds would buy a little farm with a nice little house and a water well and a gourd dipper, and forty acres of good bottom land to raise a crop on, and a good rich garden spot up next to the house, and a couple of jersey cows with nice big tits, and some chickens to wake me up of a morning, and . . . the whole picture of the little house and piece of land would go through my head every time I seen a drunk man with three drunk women a driving a big Lincoln Zephyr down the road—with money to burn, and they didn't even know where the money was coming from . . . yes, siree, it's a mighty tempting thing, mighty tempting.

Now, I might be a little haywired, but I ain't no big hand to like a song because it's pretty, or because it's fancy, or done up with a big smile and a pink ribbon, I'm a man to like songs that ain't sung too good. Big hand to sing songs that ain't really much account. I mean, you know, talking about good music, and fancy runs, and expert music. I like songs, by george, that's sung by folks that ain't musicians, and ain't able to read music, don't know the one note from another'n, and—say something that amounts to something. That a way you can say what you got to say just singing it and if you use the same dern tune, or change it around twice, and turn it upside down, why that still don't amount to a dern, you have spoke what you had to speak, and if folks don't like the music, well, you can still pass better than some political speakers.

But it just so happens that these songs here, they're pretty, they're easy, they got something to say, and they say it in a way you can understand, and if you go off somewhere and change 'em around a little bit, well, that don't hurt nothin'. Maybe you got a new song. You have, if you said what you really had to say—about how the old world looks to you, or how it ought to be fixed.

Hells bells, I'm a going to fool around here and make a song writer out of you.—No, I couldn't do that—wouldn't do it if I could. I ruther have you just like you are. You are a songbird right this minute. Today you're a better songbird than you was yesterday, 'cause you know a little bit more, you seen a little bit more, and all you got to do is just park yourself under a shade tree, or maybe at a desk, if you still got a desk, and haul off and write down some way you think this old world could be fixed so's it would be twice as level and half as steep, and take the knocks out of it, and grind the valves, and tighten the rods, and take up the bearings, and put a boot in the casing, and make the whole trip a little bit smoother, and a little bit more like a trip instead of a trap.

It wouldn't have to be fancy words. It wouldn't have to be a fancy tune. The fancier it is the worse it is. The plainer it is the easier it is, and the easier it is, the better it is—and the words don't even have to be spelt right.

You can write it down with the stub of a burnt match, or with an old chewed up penny pencil, on the back of a sack, or on the edge of a almanac, or you could pitch in and write your walls full of your own songs. They don't even have to rhyme to suit me. If they don't rhyme a tall, well, then it's prose, and all of the college boys will study on it for a couple of hundred years, and because they cain't make heads nor tails of it, they'll swear you're a natural born song writer, maybe call you a natural born genius.

This book is songs like that. If you're too highbrow for that, you can take your pants and go home right now, but please leave the book—some people might want to look through it.

If you're so rich that you look down on these kind of songs, that's a damn good sign you're a standing on your head, and I would suggest that you leave your pocketbook and wife and ice box and dog and catch out east on a west bound freight, and rattle around over this United States for a year or so, and meet and see and get to knowing the people, and if you will drop me a postal card, and enclose a 3 cent Uncle Sam Postage Stamp—strawberry or grape, either one, both flavors are good—why, I'll send you back a full and complete list of the addresses of the railroad bridges that 500,000 of my relatives are stranded under right this minute. (From east coast to west coast, and I ain't a coastin', I mean, I ain't a boasting.) It's the—it's you wax dummies in the glass cases I'm a roasting. If you are one, you know it already, I don't have to sing it to you, and I don't have to preach it to you, your own song is in your own heart, and the reason you're so damn mixed up and sad, and high tempered and high strung, it's because that song is always a ringing in your own ears—and it's your own song, you made it up, you added a verse here, and a verse yonder, and a word now, and a word then—till—you don't need a book atellin' about songs, yours is already ringing and singing in your ears.

The only trouble is with you, you hold it back, you hide it, you keep it down, you kick it down, you sing over it, and under it, and you get lost in so called arts and sciences and all sorts of high fangled stuff like "intellect" and "inspiration" and "religion" and "business" and "reputation" and "pride" and "me"—and you say, talk, live, breathe, and exercise everything in the world, except that real old song that's in your heart.

Thank heaven, one day we'll all find out that all of our songs was just little notes in a great big fog, and the poor will vanish like a drunkard's dream—and we'll all be one big happy family, waking up with the chickens, chickens we don't owe nothing on, and a skipping through the morning dew, just as far as you want to skip.

I've got off the subject 719 times in less than 15 pages. I told you I ain't no good as a writer, but—well, looks like you're already this far along, and I feel so sorry for you a having to try to wade through my writing like a barefooted kid though a sand-burr patch—I think I'll just thank you for your visit, borrow fifty cents if you got it to spare, and try to throw some sort of trash or weeds or rags or something on this infernal typewriter—and may be it'll sort of quit.

True as the average,
WOODROW WILSON GUTHRIE, or just plain old Woody

The folk song movement exhibited a resistance to new musical technology that came close to caricaturing Luddism. But the English Luddites of the late eighteenth century, who smashed the new "labor-saving" mass production weaving machinery, had their reasons: They hoped to preserve their jobs. Woody's note here, from a 1941 journal, suggests that the origins of that animosity (which caused so much turmoil when inappropriately applied to Bob Dylan at the Newport Folk Festival a quarter century later) emerged from the same spirit as the originals.

"Nickel phonographs," if you haven't guessed, are juke-boxes.

Nickel phonographs has really throwed lots of musicians out on their ass and I don't mean perhaps. Almost every little old saloon use to have 3 or 4 or 30 musicians and nowadays you put a damn nickel in a bastardly slot and a whore house light turns on and you got your music—but have you got as much real old red blooded fun? I doubt it. I like real people better. Put them back to work. The world would be a lot happier.

Paul Robeson—All-American football star, attorney, celebrated Shakespearean actor, accomplished art singer—was by far the biggest star that the Popular Front produced and certainly the most prominent black American radical of the first half of the twentieth century. But however congenial their politics, he and Woody barely knew one another, and it's unlikely this letter was ever sent.

To:

PAUL ROBESON
from yore olde buddy
Woody Guthrie

I was writing my funny little colum for the
Peoples Daily World (every day)
When somebody handed me a free ticket to go out to the
  Pasadena Ritzy Ditzy Auditorium there and listen to you
  (and your piano player) sing & play;
I saw then that them big highup rich folks couldn't make a

small dent in all of the good things you believed in in the broad and general ways of racial and social equality;

And so, I stood there in our long line of handshakers with a pritty eyed negro girl who was also from the Peoples Daily World, and I told her then that I was trying my very best to think up some kind of a good joke to pull off on you;

And so, there I stood in my first handshakey line shaking worse than a blue goose with the greeny ganders, and, even though I was a mediumly well known balladsong maker and singer and a professional jokester in my own right, I thought to my very soul that I was stuck this time, I was getting ootched and boosted on up one step closer to your shaking hand and your big friendly smile, and I had not figured

What in the name of the very devil I could say to you that would be funny and at the same time a tribute and a compliment, and also something just a little bit risky; so I go my first idea for my joke as I heard several hundreds of other linestanders there telling you:

Marvelous. Excellente. Magnificent. Fine. Wondrous. Wonderful. Good work. Elevating. Elating. Exalting. And several thousands of these kinds of words with a, You Are Very, hitched onto the front of them.

I listened to this long line both that had gone before me and also to the ones waiting their chance to congratulate you in back of me;

I shook your hand just the same way as I shook Joe Louis's hand, because I knew the two of you to be champions at your trade(s), and, I always did argue and defend the simple truth that when you find anybody that's a genius or a champion at any one single thing, like Pete Seeger on his five string banjo, or like Leadbelly on his Twelve String Blues Guitar, these champions are not just only a champion at some one single kind of a trick or a trade or an art or a science or a profession; but they are champs at a good many other things, too;

I stood there in your Pasadena lineup wondering what I could say that would not make you too sadly sore at me; and I couldn't think of one earthly word when my time did come and when you'd already lifted me up several inches from the floor just being friendly to me;

I said something like: It's really that piano player of yours that makes your voicebox sound as good as it does.

You doubled up your left hand into a fist and tried to wipe a coming laff off of your mouth and shook me up and down at the same time without really knowing how high your laffs were lifting me up;

I heard you break and say: I don't know where you come from, friend, but you sound like a kindred spirit, a fellow soule of some kind; listen to this, George . . .

And your piano man sat on his bench and told you, "Yes, I heard him. I heard 'im before you did. Or 'longa 'bout th' same time. Must be a musician? Huhh?

And I said: Yepp. Guitar. Folk ballads. Songs an' stuff. Peoples World.

I heard the legs of the piano stool scoot across that waxy stage and heard your piano man tell me again: We're havin' a bit of a house . . . a get together . . . sort of a woodsheddin' . . . over at . . .

And you broke in to tell this world: Yess. You are the first to be known to buy a ticket and to stand in my line to tell me backstage that my voice depends mostly on this, ahhh, my pianoman here . . . which sure is true this night . . . throat . . . knowww . . . ?

I just said: (Ohhh something like) I didn't think tonight that you sound'd like y' used y'r throat . . .

And you told me back, things getting a good bit bouncey: Pasadena Playhouse. I didn't wanta, wish to use up my gifts and talent too muchly here, as, ahh, since we're gon'ta have this woodsheddy singin' affair later on where y' really need about seventeen throats;

And your piano pounder told us all, Yeahhh man. Three ta eat with, two more ta draink with, and then about sixteen more t' do my drinkin' with. I'm way behind.

And the girl I was with said: I'm awayyy up front.

And some of your (our other friends there) said: OKay. Sounds good t' me an' I'm hard ta please.

And other opinions, other phrasing, other soundings and other breathings of the same breath of the same hope that all of us would meet at this friendly singing house a few short running hours after this.

At which all of us did.

To which all of our soules repaired.

Under which richlooking roof our physical bodies ganged in.

And in betwixt which rocky stuccoed plasted walls our spirits did unite and our minds untied their bashful knots and our dreams undone their hairdo, and our hands did some warmer shaking, I firmly believe than any we'd been able or had the time to do back yonder backstage of that pitchdark Pasadena Playhouse; and the best of our playings didn't barely begin till all of us had got out and away from that hired fake foney flashybulb called a Playhouse;

I well remember and recall how I met Blacky Myers around those cockytaile glasses there, and I remember how Blacky said to me in that highly organized friendly way of his: Woody, if the labor movement ever does need a real good Jesse James man, I think you will make a good one.

I told Blacky I sure did hope so, sure did hope, I mean, that I could make the labor movement a good Jesse James; because, at that time, I guess I was hoping lots of fairly bright thirty year old hopes, in spite of several of my own bodily raisings and mental habits which got in the way of lots of my hopes at that time.

I was going through that same season a lot of us go through in order to find and to try on and to stick with a way of thinking and working and being useful and living and loving that I liked; I mean to say, I was parting in those days from my first wife, Mary, who's head got stuck so full of catholic religious notions that she hated all of my new books and new friends and my newfound thoughts with a poison in her belly that killed everything I tried to learn and to work at faster even than I could tell her about them.

The worst pity of our sad mismatch was that we had three small baby children, two girls and one little boy, to share the mental benefits of our mean despiteful and hateful kinds of arguments, up against which side neither talker, neither yeller, neither curser gained or lost an inch of useful grounds. She said she could see why I would fall for such a fibby line as that old trade union labor movement stuff, since I me, myself really did think that I was helping the workers of the country by going around and making up songs and playing and singing for them; but, that I had a ring of ratty friends around me, stealing not only my laboring movement stoney blind, but, stealing me just as blind from early to late, and the worst part of my sad situation was that, yes, I couldn't hear and see and know all of what she saw and heard and I wasn't in any position to judge what was being done to me in this bloody mess of robbing these very working folks we all so piously pretended to be 'helping.'

I was pretty well unjointed in lots of ways as far as being a worried man singing me a worried song; and I was living at that time through, as I've said heretofore, in some times that a good many mismatched and mismated pairings of this fleshstuff have to, or choose to, or by some way do so live through until such a time comes when neither one of us could take each others presence any more and we just closed up our ears and eyes and minds toward each other, till she moved back to Texas's Pannyhandle to be on the same vacant lot with her daddy and her mommy and her brothers there in Pampa;

I tried, I think, working along in my own ways, reading my own pages, studying my own papers, and eating up my own books, pamphlets, leaflets, records, and movies, and plays, and radio shows, and house parties, and, trying as best I could to cover these forty eight states putting down what ever scene or sight or happening or current event I came upon in my own words to fit my own balladsongs and to suit the sounds of the strings of my own guitar(s). I wrote my piece daily for the P.W., and sang sometimes for pay and sometimes for free around at any place where my labor movements friends offered me the possible chance; I was in such stews, juices, spirits, and humors, I guess, when I pulled my joke on you up there on that half crazy Pasadena Playhouse that went so bunko later on.

I sung you a song here under the dimlit lights of this real warmling cocktail party where you acted like you didn't know the song, and sort of hummed it along with me, and it gave you a good excuse, too, to let me take the light while you rested up a good lot on a big sofa . . . (it had to be a big one) . . . to fit such a big man living here on such a (could be) big free world . . . if every human alive and trying to live on it would live, work, pray, go, come, sing, smile, act, and hug all his peoples up as warm and as tight in his bearhuggy arms . . . as I felt this particular night that you did . . . just about every day and every hour of every night given unto you here to spend for the uplift good of every labour and every seed and seedling of man's kinds here all around us.

This ballad I sung was one I didn't write by my own hand, but I felt so sorry and felt so much sympathy for these Missouri farming boys that our system of lackamoney forced to get their good money (if there is any such a thing) at the wrong end of a gunbarrel . . . that I decided right then and there to keep on going with my job of turning out such kinds of balladsongs for folks a hundred generations from us to learn how things were with our bunch here:

Poor Jesse Had A Wife To Moan For His Life, Three Children Brave and Strong, (Strong & Brave); But, One Dirty Coward Called Little Robert Ford Has Dug Jesse James Down To His Grave.

4

SONGS TO GROW ON

1942

I struck out for old New York
Thought I'd find me a job of work
One leg up and the other leg down
I come in through a hole in the ground
Holland Tunnel. Three mile tube.
Skipping through the Hudson River dew

—"Talking Subway Blues"

During 1942, Woody finally settled down in New York more or less full-time. Although he was, as you'll see, unable to scare up any more recording work, the Almanacs were still singing together, and his mind remained very much on writing and singing, but the war was impinging on all such commitments. Meantime, Alan Lomax had arranged for the Library of Congress to procure and preserve a copy of Woody's extensive songbook.

On the home front, Woody was now living with Marjorie Greenblatt Mazia, whom he'd met when both of them were appearing in Sophie Maslow's dance piece, Folksay; they were married that year, and she became pregnant with their first child, Cathy Ann. While waiting for Cathy, Woody dubbed his anticipated offspring "Railroad Pete" and wrote the baby a whole diary full of letters so addressed (including one passage meditating on what happens if Pete's a girl). For another writer, "Railroad Pete" might have been a full-time job. Woody knocked it off amidst an assortment of other projects, literary as well as musical.

Dance magazine commissioned this diary of Woody's involvement with the Sophie Maslow dance company, as they prepared Maslow's piece Folksay, and it's memorable, among other things, for Guthrie's insight about the difference between recorded music, music made for dancing, and music that needs to pay attention to nothing more than the singer's own metrical whims.

SINGING, DANCING AND TEAM-WORK

I've had a funny problem here lately. Working with a group of dancers, the New Dance Group.

My special problem was to sing some old time songs count for count and beat for beat as they were on some records. The New Dance Group had been rehearsing their dances by the use of a phonograph and they'd created and built their dances in this way.

I couldn't possibly have been with the dancers on all of the days because my work of writing and making up songs and singing at different places kept me busy. My trouble wasn't that I didn't know the songs because I'd known all of them for years.

But it was here that I learned a funny thing. People that sing folk songs never sing them twice alike. If you're the same the weather's different and if the weather is the same and even you're the same, you breathe different, and if you breathe the same you rest or pause different. The problem I had was to memorize these folk songs according to exactly as they were on the records.

One of the records was my own. A commercial record called I Ride An Old Paint. Imagine how funny I felt trying to sing this song in exactly the same speed and rhythm as I did on the rainy afternoon that I recorded it in the studios of the General Record Company. I was on my way out of town with the group of singers who got to be so well known "The Almanac Singers." We were headed for Frisco and the whole West Coast—we had an old 1931 Buick rattletrap car—and we was all in a rush and a push and we needed some money to buy gas because our old car was mortally a gas eater. We had 3 thousand 500 miles to travel and at the last minute we got the job making the two albums of records for this particular company. We shut ourselves up in the studio and sung the songs over a few times and the man cut

them onto records. Then he played them back for us and we all stood and listened to the songs and then we run and jumped in our junk heap and took off and I never heard of the songs or the records again till several months later—after our Almanac tour—I was back in New York and the New Dance Group called at my living quarters because there was a big empty hall with a hardwood floor and we all got limbered up and tried the songs along with the dance they had worked out.

First they played the records on a phonograph and went through the dances. I watched their pretty bodies and wished I was a dancer. I swore to quit whiskey and tobacco and start out taking physical exercise. I next tried to sing the same songs but I sung them all wrong. I sung them according to my old philosophy of "inspiration" and "feeling" but I sung the wrong counts, paused wrong, got the speed wrong and the time wrong. I

Woody with Tony Kraber, during performance by Sophie Maslow's New Dance Group, New York City, 1940. (Courtesy of David Lintow)

figured a dancer with any sense at all could make a few quick changes and invent a few steps if he had to in order to keep in step with my singing.

The dancers tried to do exactly this and they bumped and tromped on one another and flailed their fists and heads together and poked each other in the ribs and faces and in the small of the back with their elbows.

I learned a good lesson here in team work, cooperation, and also in union organization. I saw why socialism is the only hope for any of us, because I was singing under the old rules of "every man for his self" and the dancers was working according to a plan and a hope. (I learned that a planned world is what you need.)

I was nervous and scared. The dancers looked so good and so hard working and so honest. The old hall was fogging full of dust from between the cracks and I got my mouth full of dust everytime I laid my head back and my mouth open to sing. My hair was catching dirt and trash out of the air. The dancers all tried it over and over. I watched them puff and sweat and slave and work. Dirt stuck to them and they looked like statues dancing.

I would do all right for a while and then I'd miss a beat or put in a note too many and everybody would run over everybody else.

Because of a shortage of life insurance policies and in order to save human lives for the war effort we called a halt and talked the whole thing over. I fell in love with two of the dancing girls just by the horse sense they used in explaining to me the business of organization. One girl told me the theatre was like a factory. The people are like the wheels. If they don't all turn the same way at the same time they'll tear each other up.

I learnt a whole lot that first afternoon with the New Dance Group.

Sophie Maslow and me got together and I watched her play the talking machine and do the dances she had made up to a couple of my dust bowl songs. One was Dusty Old Dust and the other was I Aint Got No Home In This World Anymore.

With the record playing Sophie done a good job of dancing. I can't tell you how pretty and how nice Sophie is. That first day I had my suspicions that she was an awful good person—you know—one of the kind that works hard and likes everybody she sees.

Sophie's body looked so healthy and so active it looked like it would do almost anything she told it to do. All she had to do was to notify it.

I watched her do her dances to my two Dust Bowl Ballads. I remember how I watched her feet. Dancers all have got a busted foot or ankle or back or shoulder or some certain mixture of it all. It's like a cowboy gets bow legs or like a cotton picker gets thorny hands. Yes—dancers have always got their troubles too. You can shake one's hand and always some other part of their body will fall off, a leg, an ear, their hair. I shook hands with one lady and her left hip dropped four inches. But I was all interested in Sophie's feet somehow that day.

I wondered how such a pretty woman could have such big feet. I don't know just how big they was but they seemed to spraddle out like and cover most of the floor. The floor was of white oak if it will help to clear your mind up any. I really don't think it will make much difference one way or the other because it is generally understood that most halls have got a floor. The only possible difference would be between some kind of a hard spruce or pine or oak. As I said this floor was white oak. It still is. And Sophie's feet are still as big—or well—at least I had good reasons for thinking her feet covered the whole floor because she danced and brushed and scraped around so much that she really did cover the whole place.

She wore a little skirt—a long dress to rehearse in. She had a red looking hat she used to slap herself with and in this way to suggest how dusty it was in her dust bowl dances. The hall was so dirty and so dusty she didn't have to pretend much. It was as dusty and dirty as the dust bowl ever was.

After she got done with her dances she tried to teach me how to sing these same two songs like they was on the phonograph record. You'd be surprised how hard it is to sing a song the same way twice. Especially when you can't read music notes. I never could. I always just run my bluff, and sung them how I felt them.

But I'd come to the end of my rope. My jig was up. I'd been fooling the audience too long already, and now I fell in love with this whole gang of New Dancers and told them I would sing these songs for them. And one more song which another Almanac singer by the name of Lee Hays had put on a record—The Dodger.

I had to imitate Lee's voice in every way—not really imitate him—for I naturally have got my own way of singing. I don't sing out of books and neither does Lee very often. He's a boy from Arkansaw that's had a lot of hard luck piled on him and has got one of the best folk singing voices in the country. What I heard in Lee's voice was his tough luck. I liked the song but I found out that I had to also memorize and sing his song exactly like it was on the record. Lee had the asthma or bronchial trouble of some kind and he was under the doctor's care I knew on the day that he made this record. So he sung when he felt like it and he breathed and he rested and he paused when he felt like it. The outcome was that the record was all out of balance—not when you just listened to it in person—but—well—not—either—when you made up a dance to it. Because dancers like to dance to songs that are out of rhythm. It gives more dancers work. In other words if a song is just the same number of pauses and holds and the same rhythm all the way through it don't give a dancer much of a chance to show how good a dancer he is. But if a song ain't regular—that is—if it's different all of the way through with a different number of beats between each verse—then you see—this gives a dancer a chance to come out and do something new and different every time and it surprises you because it aint the same every time—and you like it because it surprises you.

I was surprised when I seen the way the dancers danced this song The Dodger but I still desired and wanted to sing it for them. My only trouble was how to imitate Lee Hays' bronchial trouble and how to sing like I had his asthma and how to imagine all of this when I was physically in pretty good shape. How to rest and pause and how to take my breath as if I, too, had a case of bronchial trouble. No. I'm laughing at the very fact that I'd never had such a thing as this happen to me before. Oh I guess I've learned hundreds of songs off of records and then sung them in my own way but with the dancers I had to sing them so exact as to make it sound like the other singer felt on the day he made the record. To lots of trained musicians this wouldn't have been much of a trick but to a folk singer and an ear player like me—I'd always just sing like I felt—this was one of the hardest jobs I ever had to do.

The name of the dance is Sophie Maslow's Folksay which got such good reviews in some of the dance magazines and a couple of times in the New York Times. But these good reviews didn't grow like flowers. This young bunch of dancers worked their heads off practicing these dances that make up Folksay and then they worked their legs off and their arms off—worked like dogs to teach me how to sing these folk songs with them.

Marjorie dancing.

Although its byline ascribes this piece to the Almanac Singers, every word cries out that it was written by Woody, as does his signature at the end.

BIG GUNS (BY THE ALMANAC SINGERS)

There's several ways of saying what's on your mind. And in states and counties where it ain't any too healthy to talk too loud, speak your mind, or even to vote like you want to, folks have found other ways of getting the word around.

One of the mainest ways is by singing. Drop the word 'folk' and just call it real old honest to god American singing. No matter who makes it up, no matter who sings it and who dont, if it talks the lingo of the people, it's a cinch to catch on, and will be sung here and yonder for a long time after you've cashed in your chips.

The language of the working people is their working and fighting to fix up a better world to live in, what's good about it, bad about it, what's okay, and what's out of kilter and needs a fixing.

Good times, bad times, boom times, slack times, times of work, no work, worry, celebrating, raising cane, making love, getting married, having kids, or getting let down with the silver chain.

The world aint all good or all bad, things happen fast, and change around . . . wars break out and folks are first on one side, then on another, because they believe in something, because they hate something, and because they get together with other people that think like they do—and gradually, out of all of our isms, new isms, and new songs grow like weeds and flowers.

The slave war was fought and little pieces of it are still being fought. Jim Crow still makes the Negro people slaves to all kinds of things, mean and low treatment, hard work and starvation wages, and mistreated by all kinds of narrow minded bosses everywhere . . . so any talk about American songs, ballads or music has got to first shake hands with the Negroes, and find out why their music and singing is the best, longest lasting, and by far the plainest that has sprouted in our midst. It has scattered and sprouted time and again, here and yonder, everywhere, till it has cropped up in lots of styles and colors.

The same as the midwest had its Jesse James, the southwest its Billy the Kid, Oklahoma Pretty Boy Floyd, the deep south its Stack O'Lee, the Virginias had their desperate little man.

John Hardy was his name. In the day and time when one

state was a so-called free state, the next out and out slave state, and so on, John Hardy done some thumb busting on the West Virginia line—but here's the song:

John Hardy he was a des'prate little man
Carried a gun and a razor every day . . . ;
Well, he blowed down a man on the West Virginia line;
You ought to seen John Hardy a gettin' away,
Poor Boy,
You ought to seen John Hardy a gettin' away!

There was an old vacated coal mine tunnel, called it the Free Stone Tunnel, big hunks of soft, loose coal. Same way as you would say free stone peaches, or cherries, or anything else that turns loose easy. But to the Negro people, it meant a thousand times more than that.

Underground railroads were almost a religious thought to the Negroes, because it meant a train that would come and carry you away from here to a land where you could be free to do your work and live your life to the brim. Imagine how tales and songs got started about the Free Stone Tunnel: You got loose from your mean boss and made a run for a better place, a free state, and you went in a slave, and you come out in a free state. And that freedom is the same freedom that men and women are fighting to keep today—. The people have kept singing the life of little John because it means more than just another bad man gone wrong:

John Hardy he stood in his jail cell;
The tears rolling down from his eyes;
Said, I been the death of a many a deputy sheriff;
But my six shooter never told a lie, god knows,
My six shooter never told a lie.

What is an outlaw? A person that breaks the law? There's lots of laws, too many. The world is full of laws and the jails are full of people. And the people are full of songs. Every time a man gets disgusted with trying to live decent in the rich man's system, and jumps out with a couple of forty fives on his hips to try to shoot his way through—the outlaw is beat. Beat to start with. The whole world is against him. Reason why is because he's not organized. He's just by his self. Wants to holler, cuss, fight, work to change the world around a little bit better . . . but he's by his self. Bound to lose. Police will shoot him down like a mad dog on the county road. Why do people set down and write up great songs and ballads about their outlaws? (And never about governors, mayors, or police chiefs?)

Here's why. An outlaw does it wrong. Police do it right. And the Union does it right. The outlaw tries to whip the world down to his own size and then he finds out that the world is a whole lot bigger than him . . . so by yourself, even with a couple of Tommy guns, you're beat before the cards are dealt. But . . . an outlaw does one big thing. What? It's easy.

He tries.

Tries his best.

Dies for what he believes in. Goes down shooting.

Politicians dont try. They shoot the bull and the hot air, but they dont try their best to make the world better . . . and people just dont waste any pencil lead on their politicians, unless it's to write up a song showing how bad they was compared to the outlaw.

American songs have never glorified the outlaw . . . other than to just make him a common everyday man with a lot of guts and nerve. But a man needs more than that to be glorified. He needs a good level head on him, call it intellect, call it anything. He needs it. And most songs hold this against the outlaw.

Best way is to join the union and bring your complaints to the shop steward, or from the floor of the union meeting. This keeps your job, and you dont have to turn out to be a bad man to get some changes made.

Maybe it's like the song of the Kentucky mountains wrote by the two little daughters, 8 and 11, of a coal miner and union organizer, the night after the thugs and deputies of old sheriff J. H. Blair had raided the miner's house . . .

> Come all of you good workers
> Good news to you I'll tell . . .
> Of how the good old union
> Has come in here to dwell . . .
> > Which side are you on?
> > Which side are you on?

There aint but two sides, the working people's side and the big bosses side. The union side and the Hitler side. The first thing that Hitler cracked down on when he took the Nazi Chamber was the Trade Unions. And it will be the Trade Unions that will beat Hitler. The best job you can do for your country, next to being a good soldier for the working people,

The Almanac Singers (from left): Woody Guthrie, Millard Lampell, Bess Hawes, Pete Seeger, Arthur Stern, and Sis Cunningham.

FDR Bandwagon group shot. Standing: Ed Royce, producer; Fran Baker, office; Al Hall, bass; Jackie Gibson and Sam Moskowitz, publicity; Woody Guthrie. Seated on chairs: Mary Lou Williams, pianist/singer; Helen Tamiris, Dan Negrin, dancers; Rollin Smith, Bill Coleman, musicians, leaning over drummer Jack "The Bear" Parker. Seated on couch: Bett Rope, piano accompanist; Lou Kleinman, writer. Seated on floor: Bina Rosenbaum and Cisco Houston; Jack De Merchant; Laura Duncan, dancer.

is to be a good union member—and stick up for what you know is right.

Us Almanac Singers started out singing down across the country, in saloons, little churches, political meetings, and gatherings of all kinds. We sung for the Dairy Farmers up north and the anti-poll taxers down south, for the right of the poor white man and the colored people to have a free vote and say so in the way this country is run, for the Oakies to get together and have meetings and decide on how much to get for picking cotton. . . .

Gradually, little by little, we kept seeing that the only way to ever get a nickel out of a multi-millionaire on Wall Street was by our unions, and so we just naturally fell in with the union folks and have been working for them ever since. Our idea is to bring songs and fun and serious enter-tainment into the union hall so as to make it a better, livelier, peppier, and lot more sensible place to come to than a pool hall, gambling game, or horse racing board . . . or even a theater. The job is too big for just a few entertainers. It takes more of us. It takes me and you and him and her and them and those, and everybody and his dog.

There's some long hair experts that claim that we aint got no right to change old songs over to new words, or to make up new songs that yell out the working man's side of this deal. Our job is to show these professors that they are sadly mistook.

What about the hundreds and hundreds of songs that have been made up by the unions to holler back at the cops, vigilantes, deputies and hired thugs of the rich guys? There's train loads of songs to prove that the best songs are always waiting to be wrote down. A song dont have to be as old as the hills to be good, true, or honest. Songs that tell the true battle of our people to get better and better conditions everywhere, are as good hot or cold, new or old, just so's they're honest.

It don't matter who makes them up just so they're made. How big it goes over with the people is the only thing that matters.

The rich men first used songs as a weapon against the workers. To keep men doped and women floating around in the dim lights and low clouds—sentimental crap to make your heart nice and tender so's you wouldn't raise no fuss.

But the working people have always known that songs are a good way to say what you got to say about work, wages, school, cats, love, marriage, keeping house, or doctor bills. If

STAGE LIGHT

Don't swap this raw sun-shine for too much stage light. The fight is here lots more than on the stage.

the fight gets hot, the songs get hotter. If the going gets tough, the songs get tougher.

And a song will shoot straighter than a long bore 32-20, and do more damage than the biggest cannon. The crooked politicians know this. That's why they pay actors and actresses such ungodly wages to put out this crap and corruption that you see smeared across the movie screen, the radio, phonograph, newspapers, and magazines. Who makes the most, a worker in a cannon factory, or a movie worker? It would take ten dozen munitions workers ten years to make as much as Crosby rolls in in a little while. Reason, because music is a weapon, the same as a gun, and can be used by the slave just the same as by the big boss.

Why did Hitler take the radio stations first in every country that he invaded? To keep down floating news and political broadcasts? Yes. To keep down music and singing? More. A news report says something once or twice and that's that. But a song says it over and over and over again, and people flock around by the great herds—to listen.

Songs say in a quick spreading language what politicians grunt in a slow spreading glue. Politicians must have songs to put them in office or keep them there. Songs to keep the people hoodooed, fooled and buffaloed. That's another reason why 'successful' artists are 'successful.'

This is so in Europe, as well as right under your nose.

You dont have to make a trip to Europe to find a crook. You dont have to go to Europe to find plenty to do to beat Hitler. Unions here working with Unions there will dig his grave, but your job is close to you, closer than your hands and feet . . . stick up for what's right, freedom of speech, press, radio, meetings, collective bargaining, the right to get together for decent pay, hours, rent, prices.

It's a mighty big job.

The biggest thing that's happening right now in the United States is us.

> Hello folks
> Woody Guthrie

Alan Lomax arranged for Woody's old songbook to be procured and preserved by the Library of Congress, an ironic honor any nativist radical could appreciate, though few would have acknowledged in quite the way that Woody did in his open letter to potential users of the volume.

Woody and Ford flivver "on the road," ca. 1942.

Notice: Please put this in as the front page in my song book you got there, you know, Songs of Woody Guthrie . . .

New York Town
New York City
New York Street
New York Everything
N.Y. N.Y. N.Y. N.Y. N.Y. N.Y.

Dear Library of Congress

I just got the copy of my song book that you printed up. I got a carbon copy, and about a third carbon at that, but it is pretty fair, so I guess that's all right. I just sort of wanted to write and say that it is about the neatest thing that ever had my name on it. I want to sort of thank you and Alan Lomax for copying it. But you kept the original. I would like to kiss it good bye while I'm at it. Is it handy there for congressmen and senators to come in and sing? I hope they bring their fiddles and guitars around and hit off a few of the most radical tunes. They are awful easy to sing, and you can sing them drunk or sober, it dont matter, just a matter of personal choice. I tried them both ways. The senators, too. You can elect just about as good a one one way or the other. I'd like for them to specially learn to sing #56, Looking for That New Deal Now, which is a good one for the boys to recollect once in a while between poker games and #134, That Gal of Mine Made a Horse Collar Outta Me . . . only you leave out the gal and put in a representative. #158 is the Capital City Cyclone which shows where a big high wind got a loose and tore up jack, it cut down everything in the country, this song aint a prophecy, inasmuch as it is just something that goes on all of the time. They can sing this one sort of in unison; if they aint union men, they can get around in some alley and hum it to their self while nobody aint a looking. This is a sure nuff classy job of printing up this book, and it was done by the PWA, I dont guess the senators knew what was going on, or the president either, or they would of left off the copying of these books, and cut my original book down by about half. Thank goodness we got it through.

True as the average,
Woody

Looking at both his patriotic duty and the main chance, Woody tried to drum up some interest in new recordings by writing to R. P. Weatherald, the RCA Victor A & R man who'd recorded the Dust Bowl Ballads not so long before. Woody wrote an almost identical letter to Columbia Records, RCA's main rival, and received an almost identical response: No.

The Victor Recording Co.
Mr. R. P. Weatherald

Dear Mr. Weatherald:

In these days of a war to the death against fascism, when our whole nation is buckling down to the job of working and fighting the greatest war that ever come over the face of the whole world, I feel of the notion that war songs are work songs and hit a lot harder than empty slogans, zippy rhymes, etc., such as has mostly been the tone of the radio and phonograph up to this time.

I would like to make arrangements with you to take an audition of your own selection of the songs enclosed in this letter. I can't read music notes as you know, but I could play them over and show you how the tunes go.

I hear you are not able to put out as many records as before, due to shortage of materials or priorities, but if recording is cut down, I think it ought to be the cocktail numbers and not the songs about jackhammers and diesel engines and saws and axes and sledges that build our railroads. There aint no better way to get more work out of anybody than to tell them how proud you are of the work they already done, and the working folks that I've met didn't build America in a sissy tone of voice such as the nickel machines are full of.

I'm writing a novel under contract for the E. P. Dutton Publishing Co., Inc., N.Y. City, and it will be a lot about my traveling and singing. In a way, this should increase the sale of the dust bowl ballads, and a natural step now to take would be to release an album or two of songs titled 'War Songs Are Work Songs.' Could you hear an audition of these as soon as possible?

Woody Guthrie

"The Debt I Owe" was clearly meant to be the beginning of a longer piece of family history, probably mainly about Marjorie's family, the Greenblatts. Woody's marginal notes on the manuscript concern getting accurate ages for her parents and correct birth dates for their children, and their moves to Philadelphia and later Atlantic City. Apparently, though, this is as far as he got on the project. It's enough.

THE DEBT I OWE

Every day, and several times a day, a thought comes over me that I owe more debts than I can ever pay back.

I walked around the streets here of Coney Island and I look in at every window, windows of the stores, windows of houses, in the doorways and steps, and I feel this debt I owe. I walked home tonight from a movie that showed the people on the Waterloo Bridge in London during a couple of air raids, and all through the movie, this feeling ran through me. You see, I've seen that Waterloo Bridge in London, I've seen their Waterloo Railroad Station while the Buzz bombs, those Nazi Rocket bombs, were jarring the rocks, the concrete, the iron works, and tonight I feel my terrible debt plainer than I could see it ever before.

The feeling is a crazy mixed up whirl, a world of fallen wreckage, a garbage heap, a tangled, wild sort of a salvage yard, a vision called up by a loose blown paper, a curb stone of gum wrappers, struck matches, empty paper cups, the smell of trash cans, the looks on every face, the ways that people hump, stroll, saunter, and crawl along the sidewalks. It comes over me like a mist rising or a fog falling, like a danger bell ringing out here in the channel.

When it hits me I see not only my three Invasions and two torpedoes of my days in the merchant marines, not only my eight months I spent in the Army Air Corps, but I see my whole life stretched out in back of me. I owe everybody this same debt.

I wonder some times when my new found feeling comes how I can ever pay any such a debt, I mean, such a debt as you can't even see, only feel, only know, but can't speak about it. And when I feel this way, I feel the same way that Marjorie feels when she cries.

I got a few good hard whippings when I was a kid back in Oklahoma. The first few beatings made me cry, not about the hurt of the strap or the stick, but just to think that the whipper really believed in his whip. The next few frailings I cried lots louder, to get the whipper to take pity on me and stop. The last few, I didn't cry at all. I've never been able to really break down and cry anymore since then.

I've heard Marjorie cry plenty of times in our 5 years together. I tell her I wish to my soul that I could just break down and cry a few times a day. I've seen our daughter, 3½, Miss Cathy, cry like a baby, like a devil, like an angel, cry just like her mommy cries.

Nobody will ever know how much I would give just to have that first gift and clean talent it takes to turn on your tears and cry. No eyes shine quite as bright as your own while you are having a real good cry. It always looked like to me that you can see how honest a person is by watching them cry. But, if this is true, then I must not be a very honest man.

Oh, I guess I do cry. I guess I cry inside of my own self somewhere. I suppose I cry down here on paper. Ink and tears run just about the same rip tides.

A torpedo knocks a lot of things out of you, and if you live through the shake up, it knocks a lot of new things into you. It puts a lot of your thoughts straighter in your mind, and sets your hopes and your plans up clearer and plainer. If I had sunk down in the waters I know that I would have gone on down saying, "Take it easy, but take it" and, if I had plenty of water and time to make a longer speech I'd have said, as I've always said, "This world is your world and my world, take it easy, but take it."

This is not a tale, though, about cute sayings. This is not a tale about funny wise cracks. I can't make it a story about wise proverbs, nor sound advice. I can't even write down an outline of it, not give it a shape nor a plot.

I can't write it down like it was a love diary nor a daily cash book. I can't get it said if I put it inside a frame, because there's not a frame in the world big enough nor costly enough to hold it.

You'll just have to be my expert listener, my psychic doctor or just my good friend, and act like I am paying you Seven Dollars an hour just to listen to me spout off. And if I don't get it said to where it makes sense, and if you don't listen, well I'll get up and I'll walk down under the Coney Island boardwalk, on down to the ocean's damp sands, and start walking. I'll walk a thousand miles around the breaking waves, and I'll hum my story and my feeling to every empty life jacket that I see float in.

I'll start with Marjorie. I'll take you through her dance studios and stages. I'll take you out and lead you by the finger through our three Invasions, through our two torpe-

APPOINTMENTS ✦ MEMORANDA ✦ REMINDERS ✦ 1942

| OCTOBER 1942 | NOVEMBER 1942 | DECEMBER 1942 | NOVEMBER |

19

THURSDAY

8:00 WRITING:
8:30 *Tracks behind*
9:00 *a baby mind*

does, through air raids, V Bomb raids, through the magnetic
mines, through the wet poker decks, and on through the oil
strangled sailors, and on through our walks across north
Africa, the mountains of Sicily, the heather hills of Scotland,
the hard oak of Wales, the peat bogs of Ireland, the old rock
houses of Liverpool and those grey slate rooftops across
London, and then back home again on the hospital ship, and
always back between ships to Marjorie and to Cathy. I give
you my word, I won't harm you nor hurt you. I'll take you
through eight months of Army camps and bring you right
back to Cathy and Marjorie.

Marjorie is small in size. Her hair is thick, shiny, curly
and sparkles when she shampoos the big city soot out of it.
Since the day she was born twenty nine years ago she has
kept on dancing, except for a few weeks here and there of
busted ankles, blistered feet, bones and muscles out of joint,
and ligaments and gristles pulled out of socket. Even when
her body was too bruised and broken, her face, her eyes, her
mind has gone on dancing.

Her mother is Aliza Greenblatt, a fine Yiddish folk singer

and well known poetess. I doubt if Mrs. Greenblatt ever took three strong drinks of spirits in her life. She is more of a fine actress than anybody admits, and can take a whole afternoon to act out a whole tragic comedy, playing all of the characters, mama, papa, neighbor, sister, brother, aunt, uncle, grandpapa, grandmama, visitor, friend, rabbi and all, while her blackmarket chicken burns to ashes in her new modern oven. Aliza Greenblatt has been moulded by sculptors, painted by artists, sung by poets and toasted by drinkers, recorded by recorders, and published in song books. She has that moving and living fire in her face and in her eyes that same sort of an honest strength about her that you could see in the movement and hear in the words of Franklin Delano Roosevelt. She was born in a little town somewhere in Roumania, was raised there, married there, and came to the U.S. along at this same time.

Izadore Greenblatt met Aliza at the gang plank, took her to their first home in Coney Island where he turned the pages of radical and anarchistic books, as well as big thick ones about Capital and Labor, Socialism, Trade Unionism, and Communism, as well as through the several kinds of religious books, pamphlets, newspapers, and text books of the history, growth, evolution, birth and life of the whole race of humans. He walked the streets by day as a street peddler, sold ties, handkerchiefs, and novelties of every useful sort. By night he was mostly at home again with his new found wife and the words printed down on his pages in Hebrew, Jewish, Yiddish, and English. His walking by day with his pack of wares kept his feet strong, his belly hard, his shoulders straight, his arms strong, his appetite good, and his body full of life, spring, bounce. He craved to learn more and more and then to learn some more. His books were his wine, his drink was hot tea and lemon juice. By hard work and honest sweat, Isadore Greenblatt worked his way from a small street peddler, to a busy dry goods salesman covering several large cities. He kept his good health and worked his way on and on, up and up, till he came to be the owner of a fair sized clothing factory. He tried to be as honest as the day is long, and his less honest friends and relatives cashed in on the fat and licked up all of the gravy. They had good union spirit and free working conditions in Izzy's factory and he liked for his workers to have a good union. It made them work and feel better. But closer friends and finer relatives stole him broke and borrowed him flat. He lost his factory and all of the work hands cried to see him go. He tried to go to make his friends and relatives pay him back, but treated them so

Lenin: "Where three balalaika players meet, the fourth one ought to be a communist."

Me: "Where three communists meet, the fourth one ought to be a guitar player."
—FROM 1942 DATE BOOK, JULY 19

nice that they put off their payments. Isadore took up his grips and suit cases full of dry goods samples and went back to the trains and the big towns to get him and his family a fresh start. Money came and money went in some awful funny ways to Isadore and Aliza Greenblatt. Every single night, and at odd hours out of each new day, Isadore turned through the thick books that told all about good folks, bad folks, politics, economics, business, money, religion, and salesmanship.

10-25-46

Woody presents "How to Write a Folk Song (And How Not to) in Two Simple (If Not Easy) Lessons"

> 148 West 14th Street
> New York City, N.Y.
> July 9, 1942

Dear Mrs. Greenblatt:

Your poem is enclosed. Marjorie just copied it for you, and then she caught a train to Philadelphia. And so she will be back Monday, and spend some time with you next week.

Your poem is the kind of an honest poem that makes me want to say something about it. It is not all of the time that I feel like talking about songs or poems, because, after all, the most important thing for anybody to do is to just keep on and on, writing, writing, writing. This will, in time, either correct the style and the message in the poetry, or wear the poet completely out, and cause him or her to put the pen and paper away and forget all about writing poems.

Your work attracted my attention from the start, when I felt and saw the deep personal, human, homey content of your writings. This is more true when you work in your Jewish language than when you try to get the same message across in any other. I know enough of the Mexican language to carry on a conversation with a peon, but I certainly don't try writing any songs or poems in the Mexican tongue. I worked along the Mexican Border for several years, but I doubt if I could get hold of their hundreds and thousands of little twists and turns, phrases and sayings, proverbs and folk say, well enough to turn out a song or a poem in their lingo.

All art and all industry and all work and all play, in these days, should point to the defeat of fascists the world over. Naturally this includes poetry and singing.

The main job is to describe the enemy. What is fascism? What is freedom, liberty, democracy? The true. The brave. The free. All of these are empty words unless they are taken apart and defined in terms of the war against fascism and nazism and any other kind of slavery. Words change their meanings when a new situation comes along. All the words are good for then is to expose, tear apart, throw light, on the enemy; because no army, without the very highest morale it can muster, has any real business walking out in front of Hitler's war; and the very best fighting morale, pep, enthusiasm and power that can be put into an army of freedom and democracy, is to tell in all of our works what Hitlerism is, how it came to be, who brought it about, where it first arose and in what forms it is to be found in Europe, in China, Asia, Russia, or right here in our own United States. And the same as Nazi Slavery must be shown up, for the hideous, bloody, murderous evil that it is; so must democracy, unity, freedom, equality, and the whole Allied philosophy, be spread, and instilled a thousand times into the mind of every thinking human being that lives in these days of the common people's war against fascist slavery.

Art is a weapon and as deadly as steel cannons or exploding bombs. Art should not be pacifist nor mystic, but should send fighting people to the field of battle filled with the clear knowledge of what the real enemy is, and what the people of the world are [fighting] toward. Art that simply causes soldiers to trot blindly out onto a battlefield without the least historic understanding, in terms of the past, the present, and the future of the whole human race, is far from being useful art; it is actually national morale for the fascist enemy. Three enlightened soldiers with the right understanding of these things, are worth more than three hundred who are only fighting because it is better than loafing, or because somebody told them to go and fight.

I am going to rewrite your poem, I Gave My Son To My Country, in the light of what I've been talking about. You can see the whole meaning of what I am getting at, and I feel sure that it will enter into all of the future writing that you will do.

I gave my son to my country	(This is a very good line)
My oldest I gave to my land	(This line is very good)
A soldier so brave	
My country to save	(Save? From what?)
He will fight for what's right	
To the end	(I suppose Hitler tells his boys this. But, give actual, concrete proof, that your son's side is the right side.)
Cheer up! American mothers!	(Very good line)
Heads up! How proud we shall be!	(Very good line)
Our Johnnies are young!	
Our Johnnies are strong!	(The young will save the world)
All nations our Johnnies will free!	(Free from what? Where is the actual proof? The Nazis also believe they are freeing the world. Nazism is doomed to lose. How do we know?)
I shall give my third to my country!	
I shall give my babe to my land!	(Two very good lines. But for such a great gift of patriotism, the next lines should tell the best reason on earth why you are giving, and why they are fighting and why we will win.)
Should the enemy dare	
I am ready to share	(The Axis Powers are famous for daring. For striking deadly, murderously, quickly and without warning. Millions of homes wrecked. Families killed and driven around over the face of the earth like cattle! Pearl Harbor. Over 300 American ships torpedoed! Europe and Asia blasted asunder! Are we still waiting for some undescribed enemy to dare?)
	I am ready to share what?

So you see it is the job of poets to untangle all of the knots, wipe away all of the clouds and fog that have been hiding all of these inner meanings. What is the enemy fighting for? Surely he believes in his fight! It is the job of all artists, painters, dancers, writers, singers, sculptors, musicians, critics, actors, everybody everywhere, to join hands with the war workers and work harder to root out, expose, and kill out the fascist enemy everywhere, at home and abroad. Words must be turned against the Nazis like red hot machine gun bullets and 500 pound bombs, mowing their poor, misled soldiers to the ground like brutes and monsters, blowing their factories and munitions dumps into ten million pieces. Unless words do this job, they are useless, and the Nazis smile and keep crashing ahead. Words that expose Hitler's Axis for what it is, are words of truth, words that are deadlier to our enemy than all of the pretty, empty rhyming in the world.

---

300 NAZIS

Ludmilla Pavlachenko is quite
   well known to fame
She's from Russia's deep forests
   and sniping is her game
I'll love you, I'll love you
   For all time to come
More than three hundred Nazis
   Have fell by your gun

Chorus:
Fell by your gun, love
Fell by your gun
More than 300 Nazis
Have fell by your gun

Over mountains and canyons
   quiet as a deer
Down in the forest
   knowing no fear
Raise up your sights and down
   comes a Hun
Yes Three Hundred Nazis
   Have fell by your gun

Let's see now—for a song like this it shouldn't be too long. The main thing here seems to be to get folks to sing the chorus, "Fell by your gun, More than 300 Nazis have fell by your gun!" So the song, the whole song, may have to be sung over a time or two to get people to join in on it. So it should stay as short as possible.

There are two kinds of ballads, both good, both useful. One is the longer kind where you tell the story as the main thing and other people learn it and sing it because they want to tell the same story. This is the long ballad usually where even the time is not very important, but monotonous and repetitious, but lulls your mind along like suggestions from a hypnotist, and you see the story plainer than you hear the tune.

The second kind of ballad is shorter, usually a livelier tune. And it is shorter, usually full of repetition, so it will be

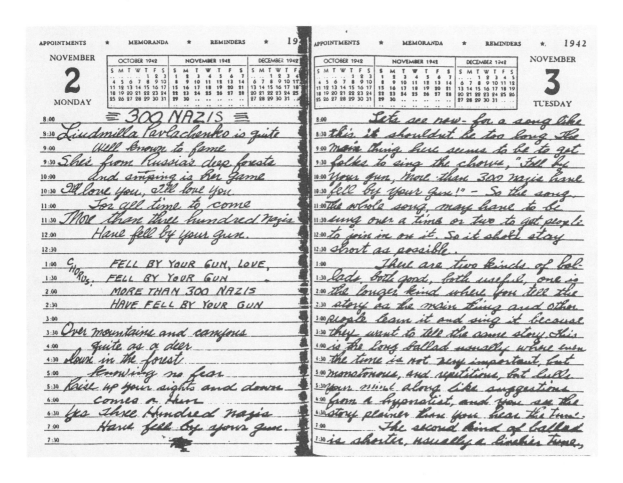

awful easy to learn, and as a rule, has some kind of an easy chorus, such as "Jesse James had a wife that was proud of her life, 3 children strong and brave—" and although there is quite a story told which causes everybody in the crowd to think about the same thing at the same time; still the ballad singer's main thought in using these chorus songs is to break down social icicles and get a crowd of people to let their hair down and have fun.

And so it goes. Songs are a high art because singing lifts your mind free of your usual run of thinking and often shows you a world of new thoughts and stories and ideas and principles and ideals are seen plainer while singing or while listening to singing. This is why singing is part of all of us— it is nothing in the world but pure hypnotism and is used to either put you to sleep or wake you up. Singing brings your mind out onto an impersonal plane. It puts action and the ways to action clearly before you and educates you about things that have happened in other parts of the world and calls your attention to things happening to other people now. It makes you feel glad and mad and sad and bad and uplifted and fine and dandy, and compares your troubles and hopes and daily work to the worries and hopes and work of everybody else.

And so the world rolls on singing.

Woody wrote so many loving and often hilarious letters to his unborn child that they should have a book of their own someday. As these excerpts show, he turned himself loose in those pages in the hopes of creating a most philosophical child.

LETTERS TO RAILROAD PETE

I think this is a good place to bring in some things about your mama. Although you'll know her in lots of ways better than I will, I'll know her in some ways better than you will and it will be just about an even break.

Do you know what a hoper is? Well, that's what your mama is, a hoper. She has more hopes per square inch than almost anybody else. Hopes about this, and hopes about that, hopes about you, about me, about all of the relatives, hopes about lots of people, all people, I ought to say. She's what's called a planner. I guess she makes more plans in a day than fascism could tear down in a century. I really believe this was what made me like her. Sometimes, you know, when I found myself running short of plans, well, I'd just go and borrow some of hers, like a neighbor borrowing flour. Every detail of her life is not only a plan, but it is a dream, and the whole plan of a better world is one that she dreams about always. And she dreams it so plain and so strong that everybody who gets close to her notices it, and picks it up like a radio taking music out of the air.

Her particular dream is to see her plans of dancing reach the most people in the best way—and of course this is to improve people's work by brightening their bodies and lighting their minds—and shows the real joy and fun of being a human being in the first place; and do you know that this is a thing which so many people lose sight of too early in life? The work is the dance and the joy is the doing it. The job is the fun of being here.

She don't even know I'm writing this for you. No. She's in for a big surprise. But that is something else between us. We surprise each other new every day and worse than a couple of six year olds.

Maybe this is because we come from such opposite ends of life. I have let myself wonder at times if this wouldn't cause a distance to grow between us, but it works like a magnet every day and what one end says, the other end knows and that is the way culture is spread around.

These are pretty hard days with your mama, because her dreams are so bright and things are so unsettled. But there will come a time when she will do her chosen work again and then we've all got to do our part, not only to make her feel better, but to see to it that we put as much power into our own dreaming as she does.

Our own separate plans can still look on the outside as a whole lot different from hers, but there will be a big deep undercurrent where all will roll along just like one.

Knowing her as I do, friend, I can tell you that you'll never be allowed to live any of this planless, unorganized, meandering existence. Even if you are a professional rambler in heart and mind, she will see to it that your walking and breathing, eating, celebrating and sleeping, fits in with the higher aims of the people's struggles to live better lives.

Even now we talk about you as a rambler and—as a boy. Why, I don't know.

Of course, as I scribble this, I almost hold my breath— what if you are not a rambler—and not a boy?

Yes, that, those two things, are what make me hold my

breath. And, once in while, when she talks about you, she says, what if her boy turns out to be a girl?

I'm all wet—shirt, shoes, socks and pants. I went down this morning to Charles Street to rehearse some songs with a seaman called Cisco. On my way back about noon, the rain soaked me from stem to stern and I'm going to peel off my wet duds and crawl into bed for awhile. But while the clothes are drying and I'm in bed I know what I'll be thinking about.

Wondering how in the devil you are. How you're coming along. And hoping you're all okay.

You know, already your mama tells me by the hour, all of the great things you are going to do when you get your two feet set down solid on this old earth.

Says you're going to be the World Champion Spitter.

Now ain't that a hell of a thing to look forward to?

The World's Champ Spitter.

That's some title, especially the way she described it.

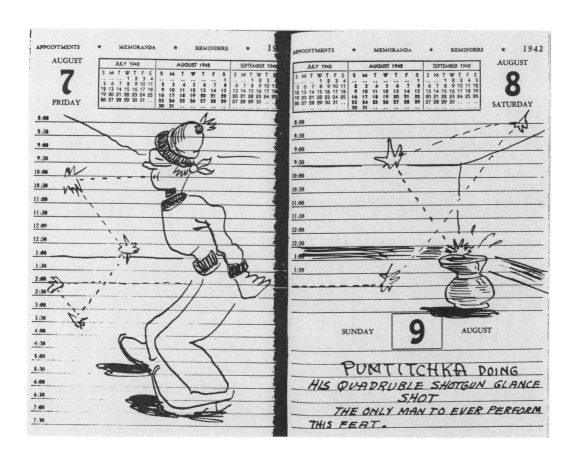

PUMTITCHKA DOING HIS QUADRUBLE SHOTGUN GLANCE SHOT THE ONLY MAN TO EVER PERFORM THIS FEAT.

Not just a useless, wishy washy, kind of spitting, either, but an organized, socially significant kind.

Where you walk into a town, look it over, shake hands with all of the workers; then spit, and the whole town organizes into one big CIO—and every person gets 100% back of the issues at stake—like a Western front. Or like beating Hitler in '42—or like winning the world for the working people. I see Joe Louis does a lot of this for people, but your mama says that her champion spitter is going to go to every town in the world and shake hands and spit and organize the whole shebang, just like that.

So you see how I am looking forward to getting to knowing you?

Already, everybody is working for you, asking questions about you, and doing everything they can to make you a good, big healthy guy, so, maybe, they can see some of this organizational spitting; but you're just a little squirt now, about the size of the 40 cent fish; and only your mama knows that already, you are practicing spitting 48 hours a day, and—really—this 9 months start you're getting on the rest of the world's great spitters is what gives you the upper edge on all of them, and, when you meet enemies who are also good spitters and have often used the art of spitting to draw big crowds and mislead whole sections of the people—when you meet them as I have met musicians—

Like down south where the good art of good music and good singing is used like a weapon by the politicians to mix up, keep down, divide, keep poor, confuse, keep ignorant, the people—

You're going to run onto them in the science of spitting—these people that only master an art to shoot workers with—

And when you meet their spitting experts, they will be as good and as expert, as sly and as wicked as they can be, because you see, they have practiced and rehearsed, practiced and rehearsed, all of their life since the day of their birth—

But already they are beat.

Because, you will be the first Spitter to jump in the fight,

Who has been practicing not only since the day of his birth, but nine months before.

Of course, if you are a girl, why, this spitting business can all be changed over to any kind of work you choose, because nobody really knows how and why we ever come to get off on either the subject of boys or spitting either one. And if you're a girl, my God, look what your mama done! Look how hard she works to see her plans come through. And the new people are the planning people. As far as that goes, girl or boy, you will be loved an equal amount. And if you are twins or quintuplets or something like that, then there will just be that many more to lick fascism. A girl can do just as much in any field as a boy, to beat fascism—although I'm hoping this is one monster that your eyes won't have to see—; yet you may—because the world is full of hesitators and long waiters.

Boy or girl, you will just have to see how awful hard it is to talk to you in a book before you're born.

You will know of course that there is no real partiality on the part of your parents.

Your mama and papa kept trying to talk about you in advance of your arrival and one would say 'she' and the other would answer back 'he'—and they nearly got into an argument because neither of them ever knew what you'd be. So both of them then decided to call you 'it' and, naturally, 'it' is already such an overused word—sounds all right when you're talking about the weather, saying it blew or it rained, but not about a baby. People say, How far is 'it' to the next town, but never say what this 'it' is. They call animals 'it,' and so we didn't want to call you 'it.' So we agreed to call you Railroad Pete—boy or girl—Railroad Pete would be your name until you came in the mail. All of this business of picking a name can come then.

And so, Pete, you see why we call you Pete.

There is wind in your lungs that is wild in your blood, and there's eyes in your mind to go see with.

Wherever you go and whatever you see, just remember, you're going to see a lot of the same kind of country and some awful large weather—and it will be, maybe, the same kind of weather that I saw hanging over that same stretch of country.

And you know this is what really makes friends out of people, this going and this looking and this seeing the same things—

But I guess I'm old fashioned already if I think this, because when you go and when you see, the old country and the old weather that I saw will all be changed—it'll be new—new life out there building up—and new wind shaking new seeds out of old limbs—

So go the new road and see the new things—feel the new way and breathe the new air—

That's best.

—From 1942 datebook, January 19–31
(but written in August)

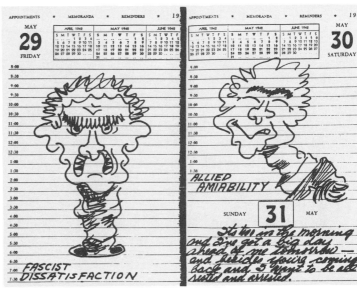

Rubber Face John (from "Railroad Pete").

I can't seem to go to sleep tonight—just thinking about the world in general.

So I'd like to write in this book when I feel like this.

The world is so full of all kinds of good things—except of course the fascists—and on this particular night, some of the god-damdest biting mosquitoes that the human body has ever been punctured with.

Newspapers call them Jersey Swamp Mosquitoes—and they are supposed to be hatching out of the waters of the Jersey Swamps, just across the Hudson here, at a rate of 250 little baby mosquitoes to the teaspoonful of water.

It's pretty late—I suppose 2 or 3 a.m., and Sis and Gordon are supposed to be asleep; but every few minutes I hear them rave and cuss out in the dark, moan in bed, and then jump out naked into the middle of the floor and pull the light cord, grab up the Flit gun—and send up whole clouds of the most noisey anti-aircraft fire that you ever heard.

Mosquitoes hit the floor like horses falling.

Almanacs hit worse than that.

Now maybe you will hear all or most of the good mosquito stories there are in the world by the time you are a few years old. I hope to mankind that the human race finds some way to at least make extinct the bite of the mosquito before you have to face them—but if we don't—if we who go before you fail to overcome them, then there will still be mosquitoes and mosquito jokes—so here is the best one I ever heard.

You can tell it if you ever run for office:

A mosquito was flying along with a dray horse he'd just stolen out of a livery barn. He was thinking "How good this horse is going to taste!" Just then another mosquito flew along in the air beside him and hollered, "Where are ya takin' th' horse?"

"Over here on top of this hill to eat 'im!" the first mosquito said back, and he kept on flying.

"Why dontcha take 'im back down along the river to eat 'im?" the other one said.

" 'Cause!" the first one said, "if I was to—I'm afraid one of them *big* mosquitoes would take 'im away from me."

—From 1942 datebook, February 2–4, 1942
but written in late August

Your mama and me are just holding our breath now and waiting to see what's going to happen to our book, "The Boomchasers" which is now named "Bound for Glory."

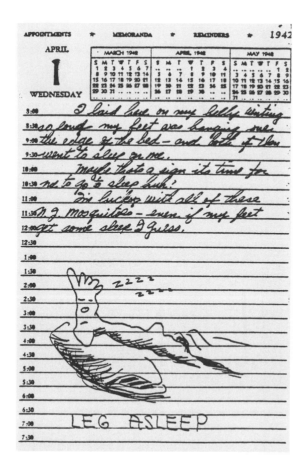

Leg Asleep (from "Railroad Pete").

How long did we work on it together? It must have been several months. I don't know where the time went. It was all so foggy before the book got under way, because my business was so scattered out and so badly disorganized before the book became the main job.

I will always believe that this book was a symbol of my whole life—the mess and the mixup of the past—the terrible and the good and the funny times; and that it was the job of getting the book wrote and rewrote—organized and reorganized that caused me to go to casting my eyes about for a secretary—and that was where your mama came in. She jumped in and took about three or four flying leaps, and sailed handfuls of loose papers all over Fourteenth Street—and when the air got clear again, I was surprised to see all the notes, and papers, and papers stacked in their proper order, clipped together in the right fashion, all tagged and labelled and naturalized—all meaning something—all pointing to each other, all united and all union, and all aimed at telling a tale that was born and raised directly under the shadow of the whip of fascism. And you see why you've got to pull in your belt and expect all of the loose ends of your life to be equally as well arranged and as well directed as was all of my old loose, babbling papers before she sailed into them.

I got a letter from her today which said, "Get up right this very minute and go and scrub your teeth, shave, take a shower, do a lot of work, and don't waste your money." You will receive without a doubt many such letters. And that is one of the main things that she is doing to socialize her household and teach people the real use of a higher standard of living. She's a materialist double plus a maternal dialectician. I am stormy like the weather and I do a lot of useless tossing and whirling and pitching but she is as well organized as the sky and everything goes to its place. I've mentioned to you so many times how well organized her mind is—and she don't know it—that is, not in a sentimental way, but she was what I was looking for—a long time before I found her. As long as there are enough minds as well planned to the least detail, fascism doesn't have a chance to sneak into the home of the human race—not even a corner or a crack or a crevice where a fascist bug, or a fascist germ can hide and breed and cause people to waste their time.

—From 1942 date book, February 27–March 3,
but apparently written late August

Maybe I could talk to you about fascism.

It is a big word and it hides in some pretty little places.

It is nothing in the world but greed for profit and greed for the power to hurt and make slaves out of the people.

Fascism is a bully too dumb and too thick skulled to think out a mental reason or explanation or a hope or a plan for us, so it says the world belongs to the bullies and the gangsters who grab clubs and guns the quickest and rob and kill us first—before we can get ready mentally and bodily to fight back. But fascism can no more control the world than a bunch of pool hall gamblers and thugs can control America. Because all of the laws of man working in nature and history and evolution say for all human beings to come always closer and closer together—to know and understand all races, creeds, and colors better; and fascism says for us to split ourselves up into the thousand cliques and klans and beat our own chains of slavery onto our ankles by wasting our strength fighting our friend and neighbor—and allowing the fascists to nip us off one by one, little by little, group by group.

How come me launching off into a talk about fascism to you—only 4½ months on the way—not even here yet? Because in the whole big world, (out here where your mama and me are, and where you're gonna be one of these days)—fascism and freedom are the only two sides battling—every other early argument, and talk, shades into the fight somewhere—and—well, I'm not worried about where you'll be standing—but—how could I ever get this book wrote full unless some of it was cussing out fascism?

—From 1942 datebook, March 4–5

There's a feeling in music and it carries you back down the road you have traveled and makes you travel it again—

Or it takes you back down the road somebody else has come and you can look out across the world from the hill they are standing on.

Sometimes when I hear music I think back over my days—and a feeling that is fifty-fifty joy and pain swells like clouds taking all kinds of shapes in my mind.

Or—music gives you a lift when you are recalling or thinking about a friend—and music helps you to go in your own reveries into the mind of the friend—because music makes you tender and sensitive—and this is why the feel to me is half of sadness and half of joy. If it is joy it is of such a treasured sort and such fine make that the thought of its passing is near to pain—and if it is pain, it is seen so plain and known so true that you can see how pain has paid you a profit in its own strange way—and the joy of the sadness is like a raindrop falling in the sun—some say rain is dreary but it's not—and some say clear skies are gay, but not always—it's all a mood—millions of words swirling and whirling like grains of dust in a storm—but when the worst of the dust storms blew—the people pressed in closer got to be better friends. And this is what music helps to do—live again the days you made good friends and dream again the tears you shed for joy and for sorrow in the nights of your meeting and parting.

Music is on the radio—organ reveries and the music itself need not be either depressing or uplifting—I notice that as I listen, I think of my mistakes, ill words, wasted time, and feel like a water eel buried in 20 feet of Mississippi mud—and the next note I think of who I love and who I hate and the success I've had at both and of my tomorrow's chances and feel like a singing god riding on a cloud, snapping my fingers and ruling a universe.

Music is a tone of voice—a tone of nature, a sound life uses to keep the living alive and call us back many times a day from the brinks of torture and the holes of superstition. Music is in all of the sounds of nature and there never was a sound that was not music—the splash of an alligator, the rain dripping on dry leaves, the whistle of a train, a long and lonesome train whistling down, a truck horn blowing at a street corner speaker— kids squawling along the streets—the silent wail of wind and sky caressing the breasts of the desert. Life is this sound and since creation has been a song and there is no real trick of creating words to set to music once you realize that the word is the music and the people are the song. How sorrowful sounds the jarring of cannons to an army losing a war—and how gay and cheery those same guns to the ears of a people winning a place in the warm sun of freedom! How sad the funeral song and dirge, unless, happy and upright, it is the last long ride of the enslaver? The world is filled with people who are no longer needed—and who try to make slaves of all of us—and they have their music and we have ours—theirs, the wasted songs of a superstitious nightmare—and without their musical and ideological miscarriages to compare our song of freedom to, we'd not have any opposite to compare music with—and like a drifting wind, hitting against no obstacle, we'd never know its speed, its power, and the whole movement of nature.

Music is the language of the mind that travels—that carries the pass key to the laws of time and space where distance is at least understood and visioning works with marvelous clearness. Now, in the days to come, Pete, you are going to see many newer and newer things—things that I never knew very well nor deep, but of which I did give considerable thought to. Things, some will say, of the outer or the material world, and other things of the inner or mental world. Yes, your new day is going to turn up a whole field of new ideas—new inventions—new ideas about old ideas—which I am sure will surpass any that I in my time have been able to think or vision or help to bring to light. That's why I guess, I like music so, because, when I listen to it and think of a fallen leaf, all of the fallen leaves—and all of the fallen people and bugs come to me plainer—or when trying to imagine or see pictures in life—music the mirror and the voice of life make it all plainer and the laughs and the yells and the jokes and the wails of the people in the undercurrent come so plain—

Music is the winds that sigh in the leaves on the tree of life and I find it pretty hard from day to day to keep from getting out on a limb. But in my day there was lots and lots of folks out on limbs—I'm just hoping that in your day there won't be so many.

—From 1942 datebook, March 16

Gene Austin just sung a song on the radio—I guess you remember Gene—he was sorta the Bing Crosby of his day—I remember once when I was living with a drunkard barber and his crying wife—yes—it was in the year of 1927. My home town had been dead for a couple of years, since 1925 (the grand year of the dance known as the Charleston)—and even at this time, Petum, I was a worried old man, looking at life through too dark glasses, and all too sensitive, too dreary and too sentimental about life. Yes, I remember this year very well, and that I drank hard liquor already—and already played the fox chase, the train blues, the Lost John, Lost Indian, and done jig dances on the sidewalk and took up collection. The most I ever made in one night was seven dollars.

Yes—no—I don't agree with the sentimental bellowing of Bing Crosby—but the old songs bring up lots of memories.

Your ma wrote me a letter today that was awful funny—and now because I want to have a copy of it, and know you'll want one too, I'm copying it here—that is—parts of it.

Now there are two parts—one pretty sad and the other pretty glad. So I'll take the sad part first and end up with the glad part. That will be like the sun coming out from behind a cloud.

It says:

"I keep wondering how long I'll be able to make these N.Y. trips. I don't know what I can do for Martha. And while I know you'll help me find something, I still want to be around the studio—or just forget about New York!!"

And that was the part that is just a shade rough—not too rough but pretty dam rough.

—From 1942 datebook, April 27

I used to say I wasn't sentimental and said it for quite a long time—and then I wasnt emotional and said that for quite a spell—and next I said I wasnt ever lonesome and lied for a good long time—and then it seemed like when I met you I found out I was one of the world's worst at all of these.

Grownups are more babies than the kids are.

—From 1942 datebook, June 19

Of course, Pete, you understand that under the circumstances, you being 3 months B.B., I'm forced into writing in this double talk way.

You and your mama are both wearing the maternity girdle and I'm trying to just write to the folks wearing it.

I aint so hot on this mushy stuff either, but you know how women are.

—From 1942 datebook, June 20

MARCH 20 FRIDAY

8:00 come, Pete, you are going to see many
8:30 newer and newer things — things that I
9:00 never knew very well nor idea, but of
9:30 which I did give considerable thought
10:00 to. Things, some will say, of the outer
10:30 or the material world, and other things of
11:00 the inner or mental world. Yes your new
11:30 day is going to turn up a whole field
12:00 of new ideas — new inventions — new ideas
12:30 about old ideas — which I am sure will
1:00 surpass any that I in my time have
1:30 been able to think or reason or help to
2:00 bring to light. That's why, I guess,
2:30 I like music so, because, when I
3:00 listen to it and think of a fallen leaf,
3:30 all of the fallen leaves — and all of
4:00 the fallen people and boys come to me
4:30 plainer — or when trying to imagine or
5:00 see pictures in life — music the mirror
5:30 and the voice of life makes it all plainer
6:00 and the laughs and the yells and the joke
6:30 and the wails of the people in the undercurrent
7:00 come so plain —. music is the winds
7:30 that sigh in the leaves on the tree of life and

MARCH 21 SATURDAY

Just thought I better knock off a couple of fascists.

SUNDAY 22 MARCH

I find it pretty hard from day to day to keep from getting out on a limb. But in my day there was lots and lots of folks out on limbs — I'm just hoping that in your day there won't be so many. But with all of this writing, Pete, it's

From "The Railroaders' Cannon Ball Gazette," an occasional mimeographed newsletter Woody spewed out for friends that summer. Obviously, he was now beginning to get the hang of his adopted city's cultural rituals.

SWIMMING POOLS IN NEW YORK
IN BAD SHAPE

N.Y., July 21, (Open Letter). I dropped in on a family of my friends who are doing their part to win this war. The husband is a seaman who has sailed on several tankers and troopships through all sorts of waters. I found his wife returning from her daily job at a small eating joint. I found everybody in their shirt tails lolling and mopping sweat, suffering from the Greenwich Village heat. We walked a few blocks to spend the rest of the day with a shipbuilder and his wife in their top floor apartment, hoping to find something that had some similarity to a breath of fresh air. On reaching their place, we found his wife and himself panting through their rooms like shaggy coyotes in the high rabied stage. It was like dog days in a slaughter house slum. I was so slick and wet with sweat that I found it hard to keep my clothes from sliding off.

So we decided to walk down and take a good cool, healthful, invigorating swim in a New York City public pool.

It was my first.

Three in our crowd took along their own trunks and bathing suits. The others, being too far away from our living quarters, decided to rent suits upon arriving at the pool.

A block or two away from the water, I heard the loud cheering and laughing, spitting and booing that I took for a heavyweight union fist fight in Madison Square Garden. But my friends told me the yelling was coming from the people swimming in the pool. I said I could imagine just how big the pool was, about the size of Lake Ontario.

They pointed over a fence and told me the crowd doing all of the yelling was inside that fence. I not only have heard, but am a personal friend of every frog along the Gulf of Mexico. I've watered the bull elephants and put new straw in the beds of the animals at feeding time on the Al G. Barnes and Ringling Brothers circus. Also watched and heard the 6,000,000 vampire bats fly out of a little hole every night just at sundown at Carlsbad cavern. Heard Paul Robeson get a 15 minute cheer and applause at Madison Square Garden. But never have I heard any such volume of noise and racket as my friends pointed and said

647 Hudson St. . . .
     Last night I went to the Village Vanguard to hear Leadbelly sing—I took with me a party of several friends.
     For about an hour before his time to perform—Leadbelly sat at our table with us.
     I told him I was writing him into a script for a new show and would like to have his phone number.
     And he says to me:
If you've got anything
For Leadbelly to do
Call Gramercy
Number 7-4192
Cryin' Ho!
Baby, shout you want to go
     To the Village Vangarden
Just to see the show!
                    8-17-42

was being made by the people swimming there inside that little fence.

We come to a door that said it was the entrance for men. So we men walked in and tried to buy a ticket off of a man. He said we had to buy our ticket around at the east door of the building. I walked in on a rubber mat that should be somewhere on the eastern front and handed a lady a $5 through a little hole in a cage. She said she had no change, and sent us across the street to a saloon where a drunken janitor was pouring a bottle of creosote disinfectant around inside of a phone booth. We got our change and went back to the pool and bought our tickets.

The ladies went one direction and we went another.

I don't know what all happened to the ladies, but guess it was something like the men [had] to go through.

We slushed along on a wide floor that no buffalo in Texas even on the hottest gnat and beel fly day, would have wallowed in. A tribe of naked boy scouts skidded past us running and cracked blisters on each others rumps with wet towels. Several hundred papas talking all kinds of lingos peeled and tore clothing over the heads of little kids that looked so much alike naked that no 2 pappas could possibly have managed to get back home with the same kids he started out with.

We come to a big room full of green lockers which I put my clothes in. My comrades also slipped around over the tile floor, soaking their clothes and falling flat on their faces in an effort to undress. Our clothing was so wet and soggy by the time that we managed to get them off over feet, that no floorscrubber in any slum tenement house could have used them for a mop. I flushed my shirt and trousers down a drain and they landed, purely by a streak of luck in locker #213. Some of my friends were trying to pull each other up off of the slimey floor, but there was no real foothold anywhere on the tile floor and they always jerked each other down until 12 or 15 rank strangers got involved and piled up along with us.

I could tell these were working class people. They organized. They worked. They tried several systems. Finally they worked out a sort of a walking grapevine hold where everybody choked everybody else, and managed to stand there naked waiting for somebody to come and rent us some trunks and give us some keys or tickets or at least a pari mutual chance to get part of our clothes back. The only way we could manage to stay on our feet was to skate around and around the lockers holding around each others bellies.

Finally an Irishman almost as old as the lockers walked in and we grabbed brass checks out of his right hand as we skated

OCTOBER 19 MONDAY

SEPTEMBER 1942 · OCTOBER 1942 · NOVEMBER 1942

Drops of water
Turn a mill
One by one
        One by one

Drops of water
Turn a mill
        Singly none.

=LEE HAYS=

OCTOBER 20 TUESDAY

SEPTEMBER 1942 · OCTOBER 1942 · NOVEMBER 1942

Take, drink, this is
blood
        Jesus Christ

Land. Bread.
        V. Lenin

Take it easy but
take it.

        Gen. de Gaulle Guthrie

I read the bible from
generous to Revolution
        =Leadbelly=

OCTOBER 21 WEDNESDAY

SEPTEMBER 1942 · OCTOBER 1942 · NOVEMBER 1942

Aunt Molly
JACKSON
        I wish I was
        twenty five years
        younger∘∘∘∘∘∘∘
        But hell
        Folks like me
        Aint never goin'
To die
        noway.

        I dont believe in
hiding books I believe in.
        How's anybody gonna
know I believe in 'em?

OCTOBER 22 THURSDAY

SEPTEMBER 1942 · OCTOBER 1942 · NOVEMBER 1942

"I was singin' down
on Fannin Street in Shreveport
Louisiana when them big
silver dollars was in
rotation."
        Leadbelly

Well I was a pretty
bad man
        But
        never did
        Hurt nobody
        That didnt hurt me
                first

the next few times around. Then we handed him dimes and he stuck out his hand holding our trunks.

Now I never have entertained the idea that there was any real material for a great American novel in just a pair of trunks, but my next 4 books, in order to contain the right revolutionary slants and aspects, must push past the secondary problem of a mere 5 or 7 million migratory workers and get to the real contradiction, the real friction, the real cause of all that is socially wrong, swimming pools, swimming pool floors, swimming pool lockers, swimming pool janitors and foremen, and ten times more, swimming pool trunks.

The trunks in the first place were not worth 10 cents, the rental price. Originally spun out of some kind of a yarny sack cloth, they were older than the Irish caretaker and did not come within 15 sizes of fitting a single soul that rented them. This had been a rich part of town right after the first World War and the millionaires had got fat and stretched the trunks to just about the size of a window curtain.

He brought me and my seaman friend a piece of string off of a undershirt in the ladies department and we tied ourselves into the netting. We skated off to take a shower and our trunks fell off 3 times. We got pushed out into a runway like Chicago cattle and got 5 dippings for our feet, vaccinated twice, once in each arm and once on the cheek of the rump, and shot down a coal chute and rolled out onto a sidewalk beside the pool full of water that looked like green paint.

We both dove in on our heads and there was so many people so close together that we just wedged there and couldn't come up. I opened my eyes under the water and recognized the faces of most of my friends down in under there blowing bubbles. We made signs at each other goodbye and good luck.

This is all I remember about the New York swimming pools.

Woodrow Wilson By God Guthrie

—From "The Railroaders' Cannon Ball Gazette,"
Vol. II No. 6½, 1942

5

BOUND FOR GLORY
1943–1945

We are seamen three
Cisco, Jimmy and Me
Shipped out to beat the fascists
Across the land and sea

—"Seamen Three"

By 1943, the Depression had ended decisively but the price was World War II. Bound for Glory, which Dutton published in early 1943 (soon after Cathy Ann was born), appeared not only as Woody's biography but as the voice of the whole Okie generation. It was a critical and, to some extent, commercial success. Woody was as respectable as he was ever going to get—he even found himself writing for the New York Times.

But the war ruled everyone's lives. In his mid-thirties and the father of four children, Woody was an unlikely candidate for the draft. He worked on rallying support for the war against fascism on the home front. But toward the end of 1943, it became obvious that the military was going to need·even men in his situation. Rather than risk being drafted into the Army, whose disciplines were unlikely to match well with his personal eccentricities, Woody and his friends Jimmy Longhi and Cisco Houston signed up with the Merchant Marine. After spending Christmas at home, they boarded ship, where they served in the crewmen's mess.

Woody's ships were sunk three times during the war, and although Cisco later testified that Woody was about the worst seaman ever to lose sight of land, he bravely stuck with it, doing his best in real life to beat up on fascism the way he did in his songs. He was intensely proud of his membership in the National Maritime Union, one of the most radical in the country and an organization for which the Almanacs had often sung at benefits. But no matter what else was going on, Woody never stopped creating: Along with his regular journal entries, he contributed to the Communist Party's Daily Worker and Sunday Worker, the NMU's Pilot, and other publications during the war.

His tour in the Merchant Marine was relatively short—he was blacklisted by Naval Intelligence for his Communist associations. Ironically, that meant he'd be drafted to serve in the Army for the duration of the war. He was inducted on May 8, 1945—VE Day, when the Nazis finally surrendered and free people all over the world danced in the streets. He served out the remainder of the war at Fort Dix, New Jersey; Sheppard Field, an air force base in north Texas; Scott Field, in southern Illinois; and finally, at the air base near Las Vegas, Nevada.

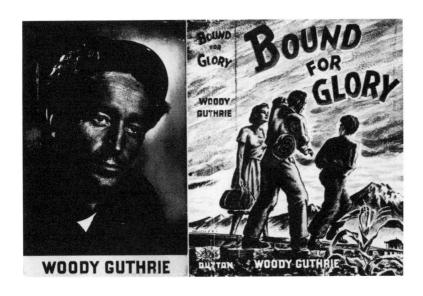

The dust jacket for the original Dutton hardback edition of *Bound for Glory*.

AMERICA SINGING

Author of 'Bound for Glory' Recalls What The Plain People Sing

By Woody Guthrie

Bumming my way around over forty-five of these here forty-eight States I heard plenty of folks singing.

Singing and working and fighting are so close together you can't hardly tell where one quits and the other one begins. Where you find one you'll find the other two, because folks that sing are always our best workers and hardest hitters.

Music has got to say what we're all trying to say.

People everywhere across the country all working on the same big job. You hear them talk in the wheat fields of North Dakota, and it's just about the same words as you'll hear down in the celery patches or along the docks in lower California, and they say, "We got to all get together, and stick together, and work and fight together."

People's songs say this same thing. The migratory workers are trying to turn every grain of good dirt into a green leaf. They have contests to see who can turn out the most of the best quickest. They sing a song called: "Truck Patch Trooper" and another one, "I'm a Pea Pickin' Poppa." Down South you'll hear their work songs made up to fit the work itself. "Me an' my wife can pick a bale of cotton, me an' my wife can pick a bale a day!"

CLASSICS AND FOLKSONGS

I ain't out to say that real honest classical music is better or worse than what you'd call folk music. Both are twin brothers and sisters. Both can learn plenty from the other. As far as "modern" music goes, or folksongs either, there's plenty of it that's good and plenty that's worse than useless.

If you've got war workers playing hooky from the job, I ain't a bit surprised. If you want to smell the rat in his neon-lit hole, take a sniff at this floating, drifting, aimless, pointless, mentally, morally and sexually confusing dope that is drummed into a hundred million ears day and night, day and night, on your pretty nickel phonograph.

I got picked up by a man in Washington not so long ago and he asked me: "What's that there label say there on yer music box?"

"This machine kills Fascists," I told him.

"How'dya figger that?" he asked me.

And I says: "Well, you see this guitar makes me feel like beatin' th' Fascists, an' then that makes me sing how much I hate 'em."

I don't believe in hiding books I believe in. How's anybody gonna know I believe in 'em?

"Yeh?"

"Then, well, I sing fer a bunch of folks, folks workin', fer soldiers, sailors, seamen, that sort of makes all of us whip it up a little—then we all get ta feelin' a little more like beatin' 'em, an' 'course if a Fascist then just sort of happens to git in our way, he just naturally comes out loser, that's all."

And the man stopped and let me out. He drove through a gate into a big orchard, yelling back, "Kinda like my plow, by God!"

To me these war days, any fool, any sort of a gadget, trigger, spring or what, any kind of a horn is a war horn, any kind of a wheel is a war wheel, any kind of a smoke is war smoke and any kind of talk is war talk, any kind of singing is war singing, any music had ought to be war music.

Woody in Army uniform.

MUSIC WE NEED

People need work music. People need music to march by and to fight with, and if you composers don't dish it out right on the split second, you'll find folks passing you up and making up their own and playing and singing it.

An apple is just like a song, no matter if a ditch digger, a jeep-jumper or a college professor or a rich dame eats it—it's for you or for your war. The best love and kissing songs in the whole world had ought to be on the jukeboxes right this minute. But where are they? Maybe the jukebox don't know there's a war going on.

Well, the people know.

The people always know.

And rather than me to keep on scribbling here, it would be a whole lot better if we both always keep our eye peeled and our ear cocked to what all of us are trying to say— because all any kind of music is good for anyway is to make you and me know each other a little better. That's the most modern thing in the world.

—The New York Times
April 4, 1943

WORK IS ME

I have always sort of felt
That this land belonged to me
And my work belongs to my land
Because my work is me
And it's all I've got to put into my business
Take my work away from me and I wouldn't amount to much

But I never could really put my work into anything
If I didn't have that old feeling that
It belonged to me

I've been working now for a long time
Trying to think about this
And trying
To someway say it

I heard a man talking last night and he said
I could actually make more money when the depression was on
And a lady laughed at him and said
Oh you couldn't either
How could you
And the man told her
Yes
I could
I made more money during the depression. I made more
    because I could steal more. Nowdays this dam war makes
    it awful hard to steal and besides, I don't know, I just don't
    enjoy stealing like I once did. This dam war is a hell of a
    thing.
And she told him
This war has just opened your eyes up to how many people you
    hurt by stealing
And a scared look was on his face and he looked all around up
    and down the street and then he said
That's it.
That's what I mean.
When I look around all over the town
And see
All of these pictures
Pictures of
Hungry kids looking at you
And see
These pictures of hungry soldiers needing a doughnut or a cup
    of coffee
And the faces
The all sunk in faces
Of the folks
In all of them there bombed towns and Hitler countries
I don't know
I just feel like I don't want to steal no more
Till after
This dam war's over

I stood there in the dark for a little while and I kept still with
    my ear bent
Listening
And I heard the lady say
You look like a pretty good guy to me
How would it happen that you would want to steal
And I heard him wait a bit and say
Dam'd if I know
Nowdays

But I used to like it. I just naturally
Got a kick out of stealing
Hell
Everybody
Was stealing
Them days
So
Why hadn't I—I mean—why shouldn't I
I was just By God stealing
Because everybody else was
I stole stuff
Because the rest of them was stealing it off of me
One way
Or the other
Everybody was a thief
Thiefs
The whole damn mess of them

And she pulled a red fire on the end of her cigarette and her
    face lit up in the old dark night
And the light struck over onto his face under his hat
And both of them looked
Just about like
Me
Or you
Or both of us
And she said
It's been very few green dollars that I've lifted off from men
And the times I had the chance was more than once
Why
How many is the wallet that they dropped on my floor
And
Money fell loose all over my place
And you nor nobody else
Could hardly of kept from
Stealing it
I hooked onto a little years ago when I didn't know no better
But I learned better
You know how I learned
Well
Tell you
I found out, we'll say,
That if you was—well—if I was to meet you right here on the
    street
And give you back your wallet
With all of your papers and cards

Some days I'm wild
Some nights I'm tame
But no two minutes
Am I the same

And pictures and stuff in it
And your money too
Twenty or thirty bucks
In it
Not even touched
Not even bothered
Well
You'd like me for that wouldn't you?

And he said
Sure
Sure I would

And she kept on
And said
Why would you like me?
It would be because you thought more of your pictures and
    cards and
Things
Than you did of the money
Wouldn't it?

And he shook his head yes and told her
A fellow don't just forget something like that with a snap of his
    finger

And she said
And you might steer me onto a whole lot more than what
    money was in your
Wallet
Huh
Say in the next six months
Or
A year's time?

And
The man said
Yes
Hell yes

Why sure
You're thick headed
She said
And green as they make em but you still got a little speck of
    brains or something like brains
Rattling around inside of your head

How dumb are you sister
How thick is your block
He asked her
There ain't a dry bitch in this town no more ignorant than you
     are
How the hell come you to say how dumb I am?

You're dumb because you're here with me
She said
That's how I know you're dumb
I know I'm no good and you ain't neither or you wouldn't
Be here with me

And he said
No
There's something about you
I always did like
No matter how dumb you are, no matter if you ain't worth
     much
Maybe
You're still worth a little
You ain't burnt your lamp out yet.

Yeah.
But you ain't no account as a man
Or you wouldn't
Be here
Wasting your time no way like this
And it ain't just tonight
Hell
It's all the time
You poof your time away on me and I don't like it
You hadn't ought to be missing out on your sleep
You gotta hellof a hard days work ahead of you tomorrow
And every other day
So
What in the hell do you want to suck around after me for?

You teach me a lot of stuff
He told her
You always do
You ain't nothing fancy
Or nothing on a stick
But
I don't know—I always feel like you know a dang sight more
Than you act like

And she said
Well
So does everybody
You're still a dam fool
For being with a dam fool.

Just because somebody is a dam fool
He said
And somebody else is with them
It don't
Always mean
That both of them are dam fools.

'Most generally
She said.

Not always
He told her.
Then he went on to say
I learnt a dickens of a lot just by being around you
I always feel like you teach me something
Something most women
Can't

What
Makes you ever feel such a way as that? She asked him.
You don't mean that baloney.
I ain't worth the price of the beer we soaked in tonight
And whose work
Whose hard earned money was it we blowed?
Yours
Your own.
Gone. Wasted.
Drunk down. Pissed out. Then drunk down. Pissed out. Cold
     going in. Hot coming out.
You're a liar
You're a liar to me
You're a liar to the whole world
You're a liar to
Your own self.
What under the sun could you ever learn off of an old satchel
     like
Me?
You know good and well you don't really give a particular good
     god dam
About me.

So he said
No
No I don't
Not this long time stuff
But
I mean
Not in a way like two sweeties about to get married
No little cottage with a rose bush and a gate
No
I don't really mean to say
This
Is how I feel about you
But you see I'm not even ready to think about that stuff
Right now
Anyhow
So I like to spend my time in a lot of crazy ways
Just to learn
About the world
People
Who they are
Where they are
What they are and what they think
And how come them to be
Who they are where they are doing what they are—

And while he was talking she walked up the street and he
    walked along behind her a few steps

UNION AIR IN UNION SQUARE

I walked out in New York town to the place called Union
    Square
Where trees are thick and people bark and the pigeons fill the
    air
Where pure manure and bird drops are flying from the sky
You'll get it in your ears and brain as well as in your eye

Old Paunchy shoots the Trotsky line and waves his hands and
    struts
Reef Wilson sweats for the socialists and the pigeons think he's
    nuts
Herb Solomon howls to get the dough to rebuild Jerusalem
And above it all there waves the flag of your good old Uncle
    Sam

I walked around and I heard the sound of voices of all sorts
The Slav, the Dutch, the heavy Swede, the Negro, longs and
    shorts
The broad flat A's from the Western plains, the thick ones and
    the thin,
The same old flag flew over them all—all free, but different
    men

Three Negro girls walked through and read the words carved
    here in stone
Words that told of the rocky road that our forefathers come—
The sparrow chirped and the jaybird squawked and the sweat-
    gnat plied his trade
I guess the sweat in Union Square is surely Union made.

A bigger fly just now buzzed by and he flew to earth to land
And he sat there and laughed at me as he licked and washed
    his hand
He knows dam well this country's free for him to bite my skin
(And I know, too, its free for me to take a crack at him).

One guy says "Why I'm free to sleep where it says Keep Off the
    Grass!"
And a cop says, "Sure! An' me, I'm free to kick your lousy ass!"
The sun shoots down on many a head, some bushy and some
    bald
But away up high the stars and stripes waves on above us all.

I put my feet upon the seat of the bench and the cop came
    'round
And he swung his club and say "Hey, spud! Ya better take 'em
    down!"
So you see you're free in our country to do as you dam please
And other folks are just as free to put you in your place.

A bald headed man with glasses on is humped up over a book
He feels like he has got the right to look where he wants to look
The book he reads is filled with mystic symbols of masonry.
The fellow next to him reads "How to Plant and Grow a Tree."

The copper badge of the N.M.U. on a fellow's coat lapel
Tells me that he is from the sea where the fascists raise their
    hell
Oh yes—you're free in the U.S.A. to be a fascist, too—
And of course the rest of us are free to dig your grave for you.

The cold shoulder dag-gery knife of commercialism kills lots of ability on every street every hour of every day.

All of us are just about as able as the next one.

Our least able persons make our laws of life and death. I saw this when I got one short good look at Sir Taft and Sire Hartley one day in a Coney Island news reel.

Left side of booth: Brownie McGhee and Woody Guthrie. Right side of booth (outside in): Bob Harris, Stinson Records; Sonny Terry; "Zacky"; Jackie Gibson.

Group shot at CBS Radio, ca. 1940. Identifiable are Cisco Houston (fifth from left), Woody (seventh), Lee Hays (eighth), Sonny Terry (ninth), Burl Ives (eleventh).

This union air in Union Square is breathed by many a lung
Some good, some bad, some sick, some well, some right ones
    and some wrong
We haven't got a Super Race nor a God sent maniac
To make super dupers out of us nor chain nor hold us back

What have we got? There's two little girls that climb a statue
    'round
And they laugh and pat the marble breasts and jump down to
    the ground
And one says "Hey! I'll be a statue! Looky! Hey! Watch me!"
And the second girl pooched her lips and said "I'd rather be a
    tree!"

"I'll stand here with my clothes off and be a statue real!"
And she scampered through the park with the other one
    barking at her heel:
"You ain't s'pose to take yer dress off just 'cause that statue
    did!"
"Girls dont have much fun as statues!" was the only thing
    heard said.

—Undated; found on separate pages;
    probably ca. 1943/44

I stopped in several stores to try to buy you a Christmas present but saw nothing in our price range that was personal enough to suit me.

I looked all around with Cisco and Bina trying to help them spot some kind of an apartment. Cisco sails out to sea tomorrow and Bina will go back to her job in the war plants. I think she works in two or three at the same time. Well they headed up toward the nineties to try to find some younger roaches for the price, the Greenwich Village bugs, you know, are very old and their whiskers are as long as a cat's. I was too tired to go up to the nineties so I told my friends I would go to a movie for a couple of hours, then meet you at the studio at 5:30. I exhausted myself plying through shops and stores and all I came out with was one pair of gloves for your present. I purchased also this empty book in the five and ten and now I'm parked out here in the fog in Union Square.

Its December here in Union Square. Foggy old December. I suppose it's foggy all around the world in December. But although the tops of the buildings are in the fog around me, I dont want this letter to sound grey.

Woody and Cisco Houston pose at 1944 FDR Bandwagon appearance.

Woody and Cisco perform at 1944 FDR Bandwagon event.

I want it to sound as funny as Charlie Chaplin and as gay as the kids on the streets.

Jimmy, Bina, Cisco, Gabby, and all paid us their visit last nite and I felt awful glad because it was their [first] visit since we moved into our house in Coney Island.

I never will forget how Cathy woke up in the middle of the night and how you went into her room, turned on the little dim light, and invited all the guests to come in and amuse your daughter—I mean—inspect your daughter.

The room was lit with such a faint blue light that we reflected about like a crowd of snowmen. We kissed, we smacked our lips, threw kisses, made googling eyes and goo goo sounds, and we waved and tittered at Cathy to try to attract her attention.

She looked up at us with such a clear and sober face that her eyes seemed to shoot entirely through us. She held her eyes wide open and gave each one of us such a looking over that all of us fell under the power of her stare, instead of bowling her over with our bags of tricks, it was she that bowled us over.

Jimmy, Gabby, Bina and Cisco was amazed puzzled. They had expected to impress Cathy with their sly and colorful antics and their tricks of imagination and influence. I was so tickled that I kept quiet.

And you kept quiet, I think, to hear them oh and ah and brag on the little monkey. You made a few little noises to let Cathy know that you was bolstering her there in the dim lights and it was fine to see how quickly she found your voice and knew you, how she felt assured and nodded half asleep and smiled. Yes she has come to know your voice in the sun, the fog, the rain, snow, darkness, and I think that, well, so have I. I'm pretty sure that both of us hear it, feel it, and know it wherever we are.

Cathy was no more than half awake for the first several minutes. She doubled up her fists and rubbed her eyes, then she blinked, smiled, and looked us over again.

Bina stood bent over the rail of the crib. She wore a large white flower in her hair which was to Cathy the brightest thing in the room. Cisco leaned over with his arms around Bina and Cathy won him over with only a puff and a grin.

She looked at Gabby somewhat longer, Gabby's dress-blouse was a deep red, she wore a pair of black slacks, I think that with her dark hair and skin, she was very hard to see. And Jimmy leaned over, hugging Gabby from behind, his eyes, like ours, were glued on Cathy. Cathy gurgled and spoke a few words in her private special language, winked once or twice, caught hold of a button on her pajamas, and also worked the magic of her personality on Gabby, moreso, Jimmy.

Now we didn't turn on the bright light for fear of it being too strong for Cathy's eyes. I switched it on for a short moment as you lifted her out of her bed in your arms, but you said "Turn the light down again, it's too strong for her!" So down went the lights again. But everybody in the room strained to get a look at her during the five or ten seconds while the light was bright. About all they said was,

"Mmmm! Ohh! What a darling baby!"

"Look what a kid!"

"Hey! Look! Oh! Oh! I want one just like her! Quick! Quick!"

"Isn't she simply adorable?"

"Wonderful!"

"Who does she look most like?"

"I thought I wanted a little boy! Now I want a little girl!"

Now the feelings of pride that arise from public praise are varied and are many and yet in all realms of work, I supposed the pride feels just about the same. But, mama, tell me, whoever did, whoever could, how could anybody in the world ever feel any prouder of a work of creation

Than we felt last night?

Foolish to ask you, did you feel proud? It would be an insult to ask you this silly question. I know you felt proud. I think I know, partly at least, how proud, because I was judging your heartbeats according to my own and my own were as fast and as wild as my body could stand. I put my arm around you after you had put her back down into her bed, for the purpose of testing your temperature, your pulse, pressure, and the speed and power of your heart.

I know you couldn't have been an ounce or an inch more prouder, because, frankly, you would have not been able to live through it.

You have had many other visitors, the Greenblatts, Mazias, others, me, Mrs. Bergher, Ruth's friends, Mrs. Goff, and all, even Sophie rode all the way out from New York to spend a couple of hours with us. She is such a good person, and such a long time friend of yours, that you naturally felt an added pound or two of thrill pressure, or rather, the pressure of plain old pride.

Who has ever seen, who even ever hopes to see a machine made by the hands of men which grows each day into a living soul, or looks at you and knows you, answers your motions and responds to your call, which is warm as you are warm, living as you are living, growing and learning, hurting, and hoping the same as you. People will mould fine metals into uncanny machinery to do their work, but man will never invent a machine that knows him or hopes with and like him.

The only thing that people have that bugs, fish, animals, and machines do not is hope.

Possibly you and all who read this will remark how childish are my words and my thoughts because all of us have thought all of these old things a thousand days and a thousand nights. Yet I must write things down as though I were the first man on earth to think them. Otherwise I would get lost in a maze and couldn't write a word.

—From 1944 datebook, pages dated January 3–12 (probably late 1943)

PORT HOLE
RECOLLECTIONS

this good climate into her lungs.

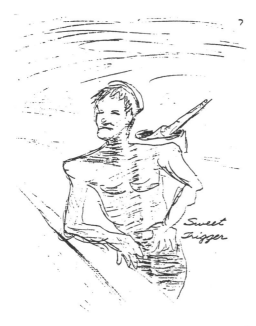

Sweet Trigger

June 18, 1944
At sea

Please print

Hello Pilot and Readers: (How are you? We are fine.) (How are all the folks?)

I cant think of a worse problem aboard our ship than the one of the gunners mess. I cant tell you exactly how many gunners there are, but they number more than forty. They are young and full of wild energy. They are loud, quick, good, and have a great appetite. Their first talk is of women, and their second is for something to eat.

One messman is required to serve these men. That is me. So again I have succeeded in getting the short end of the stick. I say this because on my last trip I worked on the William Floyd a Liberty job, and also fed this same number of gunners. Before our last trip was over I had transferred to washing dishes and two messmen took my place. The steward even helped these two men serve and carry their stores. This made three men who did the job that I had done alone. I was put to washing dishes because I couldn't hold down a three man job. The gunners, most of them, signed a petition telling that this was true. A lieutenant took my petition and failed to return it saying that it was not right for the members of the armed guard to *take* such a part in N.M.U. affairs. Of course the lieutenant is wrong. The naval armed guard ought to write letters, petitions, resolutions, to help us N.M.U. men to give better service. This, as I say, was on the William Floyd.

The second point is the same old problem. Two messmen are needed to serve our gun crew.

We have less than half as many officers in the officer's mess. They enjoy the use of three food servers, one pantry man, and two messmen. They don't have to take over three steps to pick up their orders. I have to walk over fifty feet down from the messroom to the galley to pick up each order. I have to carry these plates back down the alleyway on my own and yell at the top of my lungs to get people out of my path. I have to walk to the pantry for my coffee. I have to go down below to get my bread and to slice it myself on a machine. This takes up a lot of time. I pick up my butter, and condiments in the pantry now.

We usually run short of plates during each meal and I'm rushed to grab them off my table almost before my men are done.

I can strain and get through the job on time but I cannot do the work as it should be done. I can't keep tables clean, wash extra silverware, and sweep and mop up my deck as it should be. The boys get sore and think that I'm in favor of filth and all this mess. The truth is that I am just forced to work through each meal as best I can. They get nervous and impatient and yell orders all at once. I get all mixed up. I make many extra trips back to the galley for second helpings, a spoon potatoes, some more of this or that. The boys don't eat as well as they should. I want to see them eat well and in a clean hall. The food is good. Our cooks know their stuff. The whole trouble is that no one messman can serve these boys and do it right.

It is a problem of morale to make men feel better. It is for sanitation to keep down diseases. It is for health and energy and for all human decency that we call for and demand that these American Navy Fighters get the food and the service that any body deserves.

Imagine. If forty two men were to walk into a cafe to eat, how many people would be there to serve them. Why, there would be three or four, or in a rich joint, nine or ten!

Down below in the medical ward, two men serve 18 or 20 officers! In the crew mess hall, four messmen serve about 80 men. Why should one lonesome messman try to serve forty some young, loud, reckless gunners? Why? Why is it?

There is no earthy excuse. It is downright silly and an insult to human intelligence. It creates nervous friction, arguments, and quarrels of silly and useless sorts. It is sabotaging the morale of the gunners as well as the merchant crew. Whoever in the USA is in charge of this sad but serious set up should do as most all of our ships have already done, put an extra messman in the gunners mess.

I am sure that we can get letters signed by the members of our gun crews demanding that an extra messman be given.

Yours truly
Woody Guthrie
Book No. 86716

———— ▬ ————

Although some of Woody's quintessential American rube routine was a put-on, in many ways he remained very much just what he seemed: a heartland innocent. Consequently, landing in Sicily and England during World War II qualified as truly exotic experiences. His notes on the U.K. are merely amusing, but his descriptions of Sicily after its liberation reflect how disquieting he found not just war but poverty, wherever he encountered it.

SICILY WILL RISE FROM ITS RUINS

By Woody Guthrie

Well, my first trip to Sicily on a Liberty Ship taught me a lot of things, yet I'm sorry that we had to get hit by that torpedo. Trade such a nice big ship for such a stinking little torpedo, well, it may look like we came out loser, but I just want to assure you that the hot-stuff which we hauled into the war zone will cost the Nazis and the fascists far more than a Liberty Ship costs us.

We unloaded our cargo of invasion supplies at the city of Palermo. This is a place of about four hundred thousand. After severe bombings by the British and Americans to drive the Nazi-fascists out, the city was a dusty pile of wreckage and destruction. My buddies and I took long walks all over Palermo, even strolled out across the mountains to the small peasant villages. We hitchiked on donkey carts, horses and buggies, and army trucks, and rode with thousands of homeless people, both old and young.

OVER THE WAVES AND GONE AGAIN

Our cargo it was TNT
Our ship she was the William Bee
Over the waves and gone again
Over the waves and gone.

Tell you what a bos'n he will do
Break your neck and your backbone too
Over the waves and gone again
Over the waves and gone.

We had a poker game on our ship
Lost my pay the first dam trip
Over the waves and gone again
Over the waves and gone.

When we crossed the whole dam sea
Landed over in Sicily
Over the waves and gone again
Over the waves and gone.

As from Sicily we did go
We got hit by a torpedo
Over the waves and gone again
Over the waves and gone.

We did not see in Palermo any buildings that had been missed by bombs. Every wall was either cracked, scarred, chipped or else completely smashed. Homes gaped open like blasted corpses, whole blocks of living quarters were ripped away, old broken windows stared across the town, and appeared like shell-shocked eyes. Palermo, once a fine, healthful ocean-resort, excellent beaches, mountain trails, and a tropical climate very similar to California's, was now no more than a smashed toy town, and the people like homeless ants. A thing of this kind has always been hard for me to describe.

Underfed, stunted boys and girls ran up to us in wild herds, their clothing aged, ragged and filthy. Torn britches struck the boys above the knees, an old sour shirt, or no shirt at all, and their ribs plain to see under their dark, sunburnt skins. Skinny little faces with sunken jaws looked hungrily at us and asked, "Halo, Jo, cigaret?"

The people of Sicily and the people of Italy understand that fascism cannot be dynamited from a nation with ice cream cones. No, it takes the bomb. It takes the three inch, the five inch, the twelve and sixteen inch shell. The shell explodes and the shell does not know the difference between the hideout of your enemy or the parlor of your friend. The wreckage must be, now, because we waited so long, it must be. Oh, had we only joined our hands and destroyed Hitlerism on the young battlefields of Spain, France, Poland, then the wreckage would have been ten times less. But we waited until the fascist germ wiggled its way into every street, alley, neighborhood. The cancer of slavery actually found its way into every home. Now, it is good to see that the people of Italy and of Sicily understand the terrible blasting that is necessary to dislodge and destroy the fascist disease. The people know.

The streets are dusty, rocky canyons, piled with scrap-iron and cement dust, and the dust seems to hang in the air like a vaporous mist, and we hadn't stepped more than a block or so before the dust, too, was all over us, in our clothing, hair and eyes. All of the men, women, children, were powdered and their shirts, dresses, their skins were like the earth itself. No water with which to wash. Here and there in our walk we saw rusty, broken water pipes, no larger than your finger, from which trickled a few drops of water. People carried it long distances in tubs, buckets, vases, even small wine bottles.

SEAMEN THREE

We were seamen three,
Cisco, Jimmy and me;
Shipped out to beat the fascists
Across the land and sea.

We were seamen three,
Cisco, Jimmy and me;
We outsung all o' you Nazis
Across our lands and seas.

We were seamen three,
Cisco, Jimmy and me;
We talked up for the NMU
Across our lands and sea

We were seamen three,
Cisco, Jimmy and me;
Outsung all of you finks and ginks
Across our lands and seas.

We were seamen three,
Cisco, Jimmy and me;
Worked to haul that TNT
Across our lands and seas.

We were seamen three,
Cisco, Jimmy and me;
If you ever saw one you'd see all three
Across our lands and seas.

A New World in the Making

This is a picture of one bombed city. I think I saw more than just one bombed city here. I saw all cities that are bombed and shelled. I think I glimpsed Warsaw, London, Madrid, Stalingrad, Kiev, and all of the others. I saw what a sad and terrible thing it is; yet, on the other hand, I saw that it is not going to keep the people from finding their independence and their freedom to build a new world where all are needed, and every work-hand is wanted, where nobody can tell you that you are to remain idle, unemployed, a prisoner of the world around you.

The kids were our best guides. They followed us in bunches and big droves. They joked as they pointed out the sights of their city to us. They playfully bowed and motioned their hands in artistic poses, with smiles on their faces, showing us first up the left alley, then up the right alley, or a particularly crowded street where the people pushed and shoved to buy a drink of wine, a bite of fish, leathery meat, squids, nuts, seeds or a small loaf of bread for 42 cents. The sun was hot against the buildings, the dust caused it to feel hotter, and the mobs of people sweated, marched, carried their bundles, baskets, babies and clothing, their crucifix-crosses, their belongings from one part of town to another. Barkers, peddlers, hawkers, yelled so loud that the weak walls shook and quivered, with potato cakes, knishes, molasses candy and vino. Every person seemed to offer us a bottle of vino. It was the only earthly way to make a penny or two with which to stay alive.

The children appeared to be homeless, as they followed us for miles about the town. We saw soldiers carrying wine bottles, and postal cards and other trinkets wearily over the streets. We saw servicemen in all branches get their wages exchanged for local currency, and stand in a narrow alley tossing the bills out over a howling mob of people.

I decided to do the same, so I stood in a wider street and said, "I will give money to babies only!"

In less than ten seconds there was such a crowd pushing around me that I could hardly breathe. I tried to be careful and put a small bill only into the baby-hands appearing before my eyes. I knew the bills were of very small denominations, one-lire (one cent), and two-lire, three, five or ten, none larger, so I shouted jokes and told several of the older girls that they were not babies and there was no use to pretend. They joked and laughed far louder and longer than I did, and ran into their homes nearby (the bombed ruins),

We were seamen three,
Cisco, Jimmy and me;
Torpedoed twice and robbed with dice
Across our lands and seas.

We were seamen three,
Cisco, Jimmy and me;
Not many pretty lasses did we miss
Across our lands and seas.

We were seamen three,
Cisco, Jimmy and me;
Ocean's still a-ringin' with songs we sung
Across our lands and seas.

We were seamen three,
Cisco, Jimmy and me;
We fight and sing for the Willy McGhees
Across our lands and seas.

We were seamen three,
Cisco, Jimmy and me;
Keep a-fightin' and a-singin' till the world gets free
Across our lands and seas.

We were seamen three,
Cisco, Jimmy and me;
Gonna keep workin' and a-fightin' for peace
Across my lands and seas.

and rushed back out with little baby brothers and sisters of all sizes. The merchant seamen, soldiers, have made many friends in such ways with the Sicilian people. It was in this way that the people met with us, and started talking about themselves. These street scenes of glee and fun, they said, most certainly did not ever occur while the Nazis held their city.

Nazis Acted Like Wolf Packs

They described the self-proud, arrogant, bullying way in which the Hitlerite soldiers swaggered through the sidewalks brandishing their swords, knives, bayonets, and firing guns, demanding wine, taxis, carriages, shoe-shines, haircuts, food and women. The girls and women went on a strike, refused to flirt, to date, or even to be seen with the Nazis or Fascists.

Several children escorted us down a blasted street and pointed out a three or four story building which was ripped open from its belly like a gutted Chicago beef steer. "It was a place where the officers took their girls."

"But now we are rid of them all. We are rid of the fascists, the nazi. The British came. The Americano came. But when will the Americano stop bringing bombs and bring food?"

"When will you bring us the tools and the things we will need to fix our city up nice again?"

And we told them.

"Well, just as quick as we drive the Germans, the Fascists to hell where they came from, when they are destroyed, then we will sail the Liberty Ships to bring you the food, the things that you need to fix your country back up new again."

The workers of Sicily will discover their own form of government and reconstruction, and in them I have complete faith. There is no looking backward, no traveling back into the past for them, their future holds their fate, and in spite of the horrible destruction, they will raise up a newer and a better nation. The leaders are there. They have grown up from among the people of the land.

I took several trips on foot through the peasant villages, the mountains, valleys, foothills, and farms, the orchards, pastures, creeks and rivers around Palermo. I haven't got the space to tell you all that I saw, because that would take a pretty thick book.

Torpedoed Off Bizerte

Back to our ship, we left Palermo, and sailed with a detachment of soldiers in the direction of Bizerte, North

Well I was a pretty bad man
But
Never did
Hurt nobody
That didn't hurt me first

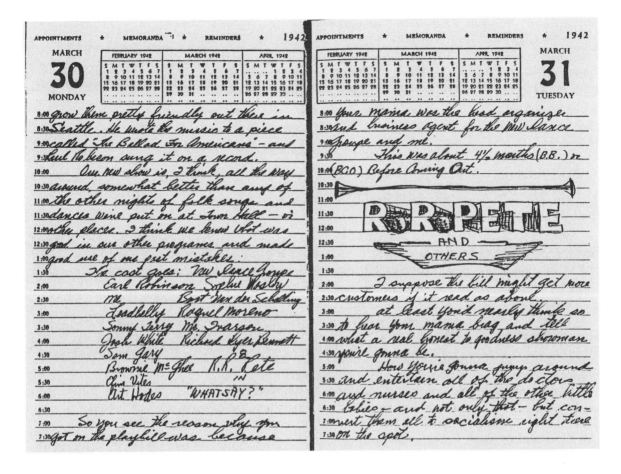

Africa. Six hours out of Palermo, our ship was torpedoed. On a cool, clear, moonlight night, just seventeen miles from Bizerte. We were hit in the front section, in our fuel tanks, and several soldiers were strangled on oil, some blown into the air, suffering sprains, bruises, fractures and shock. We were lucky to lose only one man.

We steered our crippled ship into the harbor, into Lake Bizerte, and when she sunk, she settled onto the shallow sands, and thus we saved her. The torpedo, in a way, caused all of the men of our crew to become more closely united, better union brothers. We were sent back aboard another Liberty Ship a few days later, and arrived here okay.

Well, now, I'm about to sail again. Don't know where. Don't know just when, but I'm pretty positive that I know a little more clearly now. I think I know why.

Stuck in the postwar Army with almost nothing to do—less after the Japanese surrendered in August 1945—Woody wrote continually: about the Army's daily drudgery and about the beauty of music (from which he wasn't quite cut off, since he kept a guitar in his bunk), long letters to Marjorie and to business associates like Folkways' Moe Asch, some of the most contemplative (not to say depressed) journal entries he ever compiled.

Saturday, January 6, 1945

The pages that we left blank in this book are an insult to the human race.

Sunday, January 7, 1945

I tell you right now just like I told you before. I don't want to live one single day here under your shelter if it is me that causes you all of your miseries.

Monday, January 8, 1945

In this book about these thoughts of my life I have always marked the weather squares to suit my own self and if you can't make any sense out of them the ways I've marked them, all I can ask you to do is to lay my weathery leathery book over to one side and forget that you ever met up with me. [*He'd checked off both "clear" and "rain today."*]

—From 1945 calendar book

FIDDLE A LITTLE

I've seen debates and fights lots of times between the true finger (or drop finger) fiddler and the slide finger (or hunting finger fiddler).

The true drop finger holds his fiddle up under his chin nice and tight and drops the end of his fingers down on the very note he wants and does not hunt around nor feel his way from note to note. He plays quick, clear, crispy and the notes are all clear and sound separate, and very good for rhythm and time. The clearer each note is the better he likes it. He feels that any three year old baby can pick up a fiddle and hunt, slide, skid from one string to the next and that all slide finger men are babies.

The slide finger man makes his fiddle sing, walk, talk, and weep and mourn. He puts all of his troubles into his fingers and makes each note speak. At cross sounds, discords, wild and nervous songs and chants he is at his best. Worried not like a fiddle unless it sounds like his own voice, like the voice he feels and hears in the air around him.* He plays on every inch of each string. Each string is worn down thin and lots of strings break on him. His fingers are stained with silver or cut deep with gut from pushing and sliding. He thinks a drop finger fiddler misses all of the space in between each note, wastes strings, sounds like a lawn-mower or a sewing machine. A two year old kid could grab up a fiddle and a mail order book and hold it under his chin, drop each finger like a piston rod, but the music would empty every house in a slide finger county.

This letter to Marjorie was found in a looseleaf notebook but not torn out, so maybe it was never sent.

A LITTLE GITBOX

Oct. 3, 1945

The sun is gone and another day done. This is the muddy time of the year in the rivers. Suntan uniform is out of style by law and I must wear my tie with my wool one.

You didn't write. If you did it didn't come through. I am back in my war room after another day. My second day as the one and official sign writer of Squadron L. I missed your daily letter but you always have good cause. Four other men are here at tables. I sniff at my nose and then somebody else tries to outsniff me. Colds.

OLD BANJER

DRY RATTLER

BUG JUICE RUN KNEE DEEP

*The copy is garbled here.

"Four Musicial Instruments"

I had a bad case of aches and pains last night. A headache nightmare with all the details. I have had nights as bad, but never a worse one that I can recall. All day today I felt too sick to paint, but I kept going, thought it would pass off.

I painted 28 PT Field signs, like grass signs, only there was numbers of yards from one to 50 on each board up to 1400 yds. Had to have them out by one p.m., for a big P.T. field meet, but they must have postponed it, they never came after the signs.

Painted some news items on a big bulletin board and used words that would make closer (instead of colder) unity with Russia and Britain. I have to reword the items to fit my board.

It was lots of fun. I couldn't tell you what all my sign brushes in my hands made me think of. It is a fine thing the way old memories come back when your hands touch old objects or tools.

The thousands of days, the hundreds of towns, the miles of paint spread, chalk and pencil lines drawn on windows, on boards, walls, buildings, fences, on rooves. On trucks. In sun so hot it knocked me over, wind so hard it pushed me down, cold so cold it made me shake and caused my brush to fall out of my hand. Four or five years in Pampa with Mary and the kids in our shack, then four or five more years of it on the roads, out to California where I used my brushes to make the bread to go with the beans. There is not a main street, and few side streets in Los Angeles and the whole state of California that I did not drive, walk, look down for jobs.

I painted for service stations and got gas, candy, beer, wine, oil, tires, tubes, patching and a little jingling money. No better way to see the roads could be invented. I painted fence signs for farmers, desk signs for clerks, name plates for officers, silver dust signs on windows of any sort of store. I learned what eats at the paint along the salt sea and alikily desert, up the wet mountain and under heavy shade trees. I had to work a thousand tricks to get the job and a thousand more to make it stick.

The average person you see doesn't have the least idea of how welcome the painted word is out along the open trails where no sign man ever comes. I worked big towns too. Houston on to Denver and Phoenix on to Portland. I always decided on some famous spot and painted and sung my way there. Lake Tahoe, Death Valley, Tia Juana, Columbia, Dodge City, Frisco, Hollywood, all over. I got to where, I barred none when it came to speed or size or even my line of sale.

You hit the town from the outside edge and hustle all the neighborhood stores, drugs, dry goods, hardware, theaters, saloons, the churches, the libraries, pool hall, road stands, the open air markets, and the office buildings to do names on plaques and tobacco stairways.

You do special price tags and banners for drug stores and markets. You do Holiday Post Cards on big plate glass windows. A Turkey. Santa Clause. A firecracker. Ice cream dishes all fancied up. You make icicle letters and sweaty ones, wood ones, hot and dry sand and leather ones. You hit every man with a new style alphabet to suit his name, birthday, personality, business and location.

There are traveling salesmen, artists, musicians, showfolks, crop chasers, gang workers, road, dam, bridge, railway, and house builders. There are lots more. And there was me there in the run with my guitar in one hand and my brushes in the other.

Lots of brushes I lost, some fell out a car or truck window, out a box car door, over a cliff, into a river, down an elevator shaft or somebody's cistern. But I went on and found a man that needed some words painted and borrowed enough to buy one brush with. I worked all day with one, then borrowed enough to buy a second one with.

When I first got to New York and looked it over, with all this nice salty air to chew paint off, I figured that I was looking at a sign painter's paradise. Coney Island is even better because the paint has got to be changed once or twice a year on account of the sea shore so close there. But there are so many complications about being a sign painter in a big town, for me, that I just never got around to doing it.

Buy a permit or two. Join the Union. Buy your stock. And rent your place. I always put in so much of my time on the guitar that I never had time left to look at my paint brush. But I still like a good paint brush as you will find out. I would like to be a good sign painter.

It's all in your brushes. You can pick up a good brush and cut a good chain letter out and you warn people, you tell people, you help to tell them where to go to get it, how to round a curve, how to stay healthy and living. It is a long time ago that we first started to squeeze berries and paint letters on rocks and leaves and the feeling of being in on the deal is bigger than you think.

If we do plan to travel some you will have the pleasure of seeing how much more regular you eat when you are prepared to serve in more than just one capacity. No matter how good you are in your one work there will be many folks

THIS MORNING I
AM BORN AGAIN
(revised version)

This morning I was born again
And the light shined on my
    land
I no longer look for heaven
In your deathly distant land.
I do not want your pearly
    gate
Don't want your street of gold
This morning I was born again
And light shines in my soul.

This morning I was born again
I was born again complete
I stood up above my troubles
And I stand on my two feet
My hand it feels unlimited
My body feels like the sky
I feel at home in the universe
Where yonder's planets fly.

This morning I was born again
My ball and chain is gone
This great eternal moment
Is my great eternal dawn
Every drop of blood within me
This breath of life I breathe
Is united with these mountains
And the mountains with the
    seas.

I feel this sun against me
It's rays crawl through my skin
I breathe the life of Jesus
And old John Henry in
I see just one big family
In this whole big human race
When the sun looks down to-
    morrow
I will be in a union place
NEW WORDS JANUARY 17, 1945
3520 MERMAID, BKYLN. N.Y.

that do not feel like laying down gas and food money for your chosen and beloved talent. They may be so commercial as to demand that your talent help them to produce and sell their stuff, and this is as true of entertaining as it is of painting.

I do wish that we could work up some songs to your dances. They would really hit in lots of good money places, roadhouses, nite clubs, street meets, stages, schools, churches, possibly in some big stores. You would go wild with joy when you made the first few miles of such a journey as this. We could book in enough union halls to fill in the gaps and the satisfaction you feel from seeing so much country and people is one of the best things that is found in this life.

Lots of your dances could be just made up on the spot. Others would work out as we went along. We could have one or two as well rehearsed as "Old Paint" or "Sweet Betsy" or "Old Smokey." With a work song or so we could have a whole evening's show for country schools, theaters, or anywhere. There are all sorts of fairs, rodeos, picnics, conventions, carnivals, festivals, dance seasons, and routes are easy to pick out of Show Biz Mags.

What am I trying to do? Sell you on something? No. More than that. I think what I crave most of all is just one good chance to show you my side of the world. Where I feel my best and know every minute how to get on to the next. Most, though, it seems like to me that there is something of a family sort sadly lacking between us. In the whirl of your work and mine and the bigger whirl of the town, I get lost in a current and float all around. I see you, your time to run. You see me and it's my time to run. We see Cathy and it's her time to run.

This can be stood up under for a good long spell, but it is wrong to let it be the whole story. We need to take some season out of every year to do some different sort of work.

I will state I've sung with two or three girls under these same situations and none of them had a better voice nor as good an ear and finger as you've got for music. You can chord well enough right now to play your first job on the mandolin and before you were out two weeks you would be an expert with a slick finger.

(I didn't eat any today. I always feel better when I get sick if I don't eat. I drink lots of water, milk and coffee and give my innards a chance to clean their walls out. I have not been on Sick Call for once even since six months in the Army. This is because of your good teachings. And because of Cathy's nice pictures and letters. Cathy, your letter and your picture that you drew for your daddy made him feel awful good. Write some more.)

Tell your Mommy to write her daddy a good nice sweet pretty big little fat skinny letter about TRAVELING. Being socked on my rear here for so many months in this wire fence makes my old vine climber brain look up and over every wall and around the next bend in every road.

I want you to look out our Busway window mamas- trudes* when you go over our big bridge and see our prettiest place in all of New York. I still think of how we use to sleep along and hug till we come to our one little spot and then one of us or both would punch the other one and say the speech. This is our speech. We own this speech. We own that Busway, bridge, and that prettiest spot, too.

I am trying to make this letter a long and drippy one because I want to keep you thinking about us all I can. If I can. And I believe I can. I mean all of the stuff that we have took in as a part of the "Us" Company. The Rancho, 5th Ave. Bus, 14th Street, and so on. We didn't take no more than our fair share. We left plenty for everybody else.

I'm going to get some coffee.

The PX is full of guys with the Xmas feeling buying all kinds of things to send or carry home. Prices here are cheaper than on the outside. And Payday was only Three Days ago. The PX is getting in more stuff since Peace come.

I bought Two Cups of Coffee. I told the girl with a cigaret in my mouth, "Put lots of cream in them." She put all of the cream in one cup. So now here I sit with one very white and one very dark cup on MY table.

I can't hardly wait for morning to come so I can paint my news bulletin and my signs. I'm working on a desk name plaque for Lieutenant B. J. Moseley. I made him a door sign today and spelled his name wrong. He's been in the Army so many years that I couldn't refuse him when he asked me to, "Make me a name plate like I seen them other lieutenants with."

A young G.I. just bought a sheet out of this notebook. He asked how much and I said Twenty Five Dollars Chinese money. He tossed me five pennies. I told him, "Take it back. It's not Chinese." He drew a naked girl and named her "Stinky" and said, "That'll show you what I'm thinking about."

This is his pen. It's an Eversharp just about like mine.

*The copy is unclear here.

Portrait taken for *Bound for Glory* dust jacket.

Only a more limber point. Maybe I can get him to give me the picture of "Stinky."

Which makes me think, I got to buy a new bottle of ink and a bottle of glue. For my clippings book.

We ought to write Helen Robinson and Earl a nice letter on account of the loss of their new baby by miscarriage. I know how hard a thing this is. It seems like so many of our friends all around us have lost. We are mighty lucky that it hasn't happened to us.

So it is Wednesday and what do we mean by Wednesday? It's just another word that means that seven more of our days have gone. Good days, too. Good whether we tried or believed to make them good or bad. Good even if they are full of our worst and best feelings. I believe that these fears we feel every day are good exercise. I love you more away from you because I can feel afraid, worry, wonder, and imagine you. I can see you walk and ride and dance as I read your letters or as I wander around the field here. I know that I must love you because I think so much about you. Us.

The men all feel the same. I'm back at the War Room. They look at the walls, maps, pictures, emblems, papers and books, they scratch and scrounge and look and try to set down on paper how they feel. They have my feelings and I have the same as they do. This is one of the most valuable lessons I've learned here in camp, that is, that no matter how foggy and droopy my head feels, I can just study the faces here all around me in these chairs and see that every motherly son is feeling the very same itches and stitches that I feel.

You can see this all around you. I know you can because we talked it over several times before, once by the ocean, once on dry land and once on a fast train from somewhere.

The posters on the walls say for us to "Enlist in the Regular Army" for "Travel. Education. Career." "See the Job Through." "Guard Your Victory." But I can't see that I am any too well suited to Army life any more than my time already put in. I get too dadgum cold these nights.

There's a little New York dancing gal that I want to snuggle up with and shackle onto. I'm more of a shackler than a fighter. Or even a traveller. I would quit anything to build my days up around yours. I don't know of any preconceived habit nor notion that I would not give up just to be with her. I always did know that I could feel this way about her when I found her. And this old brown grass weather

makes her look just about as pretty as the mist falling along over a hand rail.

Nobody ever saw her like I did. She never saw her own self like I saw her. She has only got one that saw her better than I did and that was a little kinky headed Stackabones.

Your Papa
Woody

Your mama wrote me and said:
It's the rest of us that have hurt you
But that's wrong
The rest of you are good
You've found something
Something I missed
You found a gladness being here
And how to stand up proud to laugh with everybody else
You found your work
And your notch
And where you belong
In a chain of others that can't be broken and a stone foundation
  that can't be shook down

So far, I haven't found that
I found a drifting wind and a blowing rain
And a coward and a stranger to people's pain
And people never will show you their laugh
Till you find it out through their pain
Maybe I'm learning
That secret of all secrets, (and it ain't even no secret).

———————

3505 AAFBU
Scotts Field, Ill.
July 8, 1945

Dear Moe:

Out of the bare Texas plains and into the Mississippi Flood basin is what they done to me. This is a stretch of our country that I have always wanted to see at real close range.

It is raining right now all over the farmlands around and I have never seen prettier nor hardier land and houses mixed in with so much poverty and filth. I am here to learn how to be a teletype operator and am okayed for overseas. Course here will take about six weeks they say. I hope to hear from you birds. My new home here is a fifty foot tar paper shack with forty or fifty double story cots and two depot stoves. The boys all came up from Sheppard field to study Radio, or this or that.

I am gradually coming around to the most important part of this letter. Please send me fifteen bucks and put it on my account and if I have no account get out your bastardly pen and make me one. I ain't gamboling nor fornicating the canine. Just need a few things and charge it up to advertising your Asch Records amongst the Army, Navy, and Merchant Marine.

Woody

One reason why I have to write to you for money is that I sit around and write letters to people that ask how to get ahold of folk records. Or am telling a bunch of men where they can buy Asch Records. I told nine down at Sheppard Field and one here at Scott Field already.

This causes the chow bell to ring and also causes me not to make it and then causes me to have to eat my coffee in a canteen here for twenty cents. This happens three times a

Woody's reaction to his
December 22, 1945, discharge
from the United States Army.

Discharged
Honorable
From The
Good Army

Hooop
Hoooop
Hoooppeee

Uniform in Dark
Closet.

day which is sixty cents. This is eighteen dollars a month. I will only charge you fifteen dollars a month because Marjorie sends me three dollars a month which just makes eighteen.

I thought that I could tell you ten good reasons why I had to ask for money but I have only been able to list eight.

Ninth is that I get only nineteen bucks a month which we call Dirty Thirty. My stationary, sodie pop, stamps, and bus rides (all for purposes of collecting or creating Progressive Folk Songs), all of this hits me pretty hard.

Ten is that I had to buy some new clothes last month. I lost a jacket somewhere and had to buy a new one. Are you going to include "Ludlow Massacre" in the album?

If you want to do your share to end this war and record union history, send me one of those Parker Fifty ones. I can't see any ft. pens nowhere around here.

*for my Birthday is July 14th and I will be Fifty One.

Pvt. Woody Guthrie 42234634
Squadron "L" 3505 AQFBU
Scott Field, Illinois
July 10, 1945

6

PEOPLE'S SONGS
1946–1949

As I went walking, I saw a sign there,
And on the sign it said "No Trespassing."
But on the other side it didn't say nothing,
That side was made for you and me.

—"This Land Is Your Land"

The postwar years at first seemed a promising opportunity for the folk-singing left. Within a week after Woody's return, he, Pete Seeger, and more than a dozen other performers held a meeting at which they formed People's Songs, which succeeded the Almanac Singers as the center of the left-oriented folk song movement. People's Songs, which was a cooperative among singers and songwriters, not a musical group itself, soon began organizing regular hootennanies—folk sings featuring professional and amateur performers, traditional and contemporary topical material—and soon afterward, formed an auxiliary, People's Artists, to book folk singers, both radicals like Guthrie and Seeger, and others less so, like Josh White and Oscar Brand, at engagements ranging from political rallies to actual concerts. There were, as always, more of the former than the latter, *especially initially. Nineteen forty-six was a year of big strikes; one of the biggest, by the United Electrical Workers at Westinghouse Electric in Pittsburgh, featured a rally of several thousand for which Seeger, Guthrie, and Lee Hays—the core of the Almanacs—flew out.*

Woody was also overjoyed to be back in Coney Island with his beloved Marjorie and Cathy. Though his homesickness for the West still sometimes showed through, most of what he wrote about his domestic life in this period, especially the great children's songs collected on the two Folkways albums called Songs to Grow On, *marks it as his period of greatest happiness. Still, the bulk of the material he wrote in these years came straight out of his leisurely morning readings of the New York* Daily News, *the city's premiere tabloid. He accepted a commission of several hundred dollars from Moe Asch to write a cycle of songs about Sacco and Vanzetti, the anarchists railroaded to the electric chair in Massachusetts twenty years before, but most of his work was far less historical: "Deportees (Plane Wreck at Los Gatos)," his most beautiful postwar ballad, concerned a plane wreck that killed migrant farmworkers in California who were being forced back to Mexico because harvest was over. As long as people were struggling, it seemed there was an unending supply of topics to write about, and all but limitless energy and spirit to do it.*

But it couldn't last, or at least it didn't. Already in 1946, the political situation had begun to unravel as the World War II alliance between the U.S., the U.K., and the U.S.S.R. unraveled into the ceaseless hostilities of the Cold War. In America, one result was the greatest anti-communist hysteria seen since the end of World War I. As material prosperity and conservative pressure increased, unions—even Woody's beloved National Maritime Union—began purging communists from their ranks. The House UnAmerican Activities Committee, the Senate Internal Security Subcommittee, and a variety of nongovernmental purveyors of blacklists intensified an effort to run radicals—not just communists but anyone deemed socialist or anti-capitalist or, for that matter, "prematurely antifascist"— out of public life. It was a time of witch-hunt and hysteria and by September 1949, when Paul Robeson attempted to play an outdoor concert in Peekskill, New York, less than a hundred miles up the Hudson River from the CPUSA's strongholds in New York City, he was run out of town by jeering, rock-throwing crowds.

Woody's home life also deteriorated. For one thing, his rambling ways weren't conducive to a stable marriage. For another, the early symptoms of Huntington's chorea began to show up, in lack of coordination and sometimes obsessive behavior (particularly involving sex and erotica). But the crushing blow came on February 9, 1947, when his daughter Cathy Ann, who had just turned four three days earlier, was severely burned in a house fire. She died the next day.

Woody's life didn't completely disintegrate, of course. In fact, he and Marjorie had three more children: Arlo Davy, born in July 1947; Joady Ben, born in December 1948;

and Nora Lee, born in January 1950. He continued to sing and write. But the most creative years of his life were drawing to a close.

Coney Island where the Yiddish speak on the streets in a mountain voice and the ocean is their mountain.

The ocean has made and torn down whole strings of mountains.

I stand here for a minute free from desire and use my trick key to see Coney Island in the land of pure rythm. I feel an ancient and a modern feeling here along these Jewish streets of people wise and friendly.

Wake up and face this old new morning sun. There's a long old hard day's work that's got to be done. My troubles they would make a garbage truck full. And on top of this is a big long hill to pull.

I'm like Mr. Whitman with six mouths to feed. Along this curb I'll dry and blow my seed. I'll come back every season or two and see how high and wide the wind here has fanned my seed.

I walk into a candy store to drink my cup of coffee, and to buy my Daily Worker and the man is rushed and in a hurry. I ask him to sell me one loose cigaret and he tosses one down on my table. I give him a penny but he won't take no penny, so I won't take no cigaret.

Took Cathy to school a piggy back this morning. She talked to everybody in the store and along the walk. She knows every window and all that is in it. She said one fellow had funny eyes. She hugged and kissed Dorothy her pal and the kids all played a game with colored pegs.

Samples and examples of rising above little things and getting above worries both big and small. These are easy to see up and down the streets here in Coney Island. I would like to try to write a book where the setting was here and the heroes are all of these people I see here.

—From 1946 datebook, pages for January 3–10

You took mama or did mama take you or did you and mama take one another to school today and this was your very first real day of school. And it is a little rainy and a little cold but the sun just sets back and smiles and waits and says, "I'm bigger than the cold. I'm bigger than the rain. I'm bigger than the clouds. When they finally do get tired butting their heads together then I'll step in and I'll shine all the time."

You walked along the sidewalk and you led your mama by the hand. You told mama to look in at every window because the sun was looking in.

And you asked the sun, "Mister Sun Shine why don't you shine all the time?"

And the sun told you, "Ohh if I did the place would get all hot and all dry and all empty."

And you asked the sun, "Why don't you shine nice and easy like and not hot enough to burn things all up? And make all of the whole world real real really pretty?"

Selfless Portrait

October First
1946

SELF PORTRAIT

woody Guthrie

And the sun told you, "If I did that people would all get tired of me and besides it would not be fair to the fish, the alligators, worms and ducks, for, you see, they enjoy the rain and the mud puddles and the big clouds everywhere."

And so you held mama tighter by her hand and you asked her, "Mama will the sun shine come and go with me to school every day or will the mean old clouds try to stop it? Or are the clouds really good clouds? Like Mister Sun just said? And will my teacher bring Mister Sun Shine into my school room?"

And your mama said, "Yes. Your teacher will bring the sun shine into your room. But Cathy must bring her own, and also some extra for the teacher."

You liked school on your very first day. Mama stayed and played with you. You painted a picture with the paint brush. You climbed the bars. You sang songs and you danced and your teacher and your mama were awful proud of you.

On your second day or your third day the teacher asked mama to come down and stay with you while you ate your lunch with all the boys and girls and then to stay with you while you took your afternoon nap from one to three p.m. Mama was awful busy working and so she told me would I be able to come down and stay with you and I asked her yes, I'd be glad to.

You had been sleeping at home in your own room and in your own bed and so you did not take to your little bed at the school any too quick. There were twelve or fifteen other kids there and most of them got up into their beds and laid down their keppulas and went right off to sleep. You ran around and laughed and played with them like you were in a big play ground. I tried to coax you up onto your bed but you told me that, "Everybody is foolish to waste all of their nice time away in a little old bed"—but still you liked your little bed because you did come over and set down on the edge of it a time or two. You made the kids laff and your teacher told me to lay down on your bed and to see if this would cause you to come and lay down your head. Finally did come and climb up. It took you an hour. The teacher had to send you out of the room because you were so full of pep and noise. She kept you out for a while and talked to you and I laid on your bed and waited. You came in and climbed up again and then you went off to sleep. Your first nap at your Community Center School.

—From the 1945 date book, February 9–12

An account, probably all too hilariously accurate in its details, of the formation of the new left-wing folk song organization, and of its intentions.

PEOPLES SONGS AND ITS PEOPLE

I was in the merchant marines Three invasions, torpedoed twice, but carried my guitar every drop of the way. I washed dishes and fed Fifty gun boys, washed their dirty dishes, scrubbed their greasy messroom, and never graduated up nor down in my whole Eleven months. Two NMU Brothers, Jimmie Longhi, and Cisco Houston rode with me on every trip, and we carried a mandolin, a fiddle, and one more guitar, plus a whole armload of new strings which we lent to the troops and sailors on all of these boats. We walked all around over North Africa, the British Isles, Sicily, and sung underground songs for under-fed fighters. We sung with prisoners of war on both sides, and held meetings on the troopships to get the men to write letters to their congressmen. Then I got sucked into the Army on VE Day, May the Eighth, 1945, the day that Hitler gave up. (He must have seen me coming in) (Me and that Red Army and a couple of million Yanks and others on the outskirts of Berlin and Burtchesgarden). I sang in the Army Camps around my barracks, the PX, the beer gardens, and the rifle ranges, hills and hollers, and down in Texas, then across the Mississippi from Saint Louis, then out Las Vegas (Lost Wages), Nevada. They counted my kids in Las Vegas, found out I had an Army of my own, and sent me back to Mitchell Field, N.Y., where I got more IQ's, Interviews, Movies, Shots, Lectures, Films, Sermons, Preachments, Exercises, Blank Forms, Signatures, Seals, Documents, Medals, Emblems, amongst which, as I flew out at the gate, I seen was an Honorable Discharge.

I beat my way to Forty Second Street, swung a Seabeach Subway train, switched over to a 1894 Norton Point trolley car, and this took me to 36th Street, where I walked one block to home. I kissed my wife, baby, friends and comrades, neighbors, and then looked in my Daily Worker and saw that there was a meeting of some people that called their selves "Peoples Songs." I grabbed my guitar and lit out to Washington Square, walked one block to the home of Mr. and Mrs. Ohta, their Son, and their daughter, it was the daughter, Toshi, that had married my long

People's Songs flyer, Chicago concert, 1948.

tall banjo playing pardner, Pete Seeger, before he went into the Army, and I took off on my boats.

Daddy Ohta had been all over the waters and lands of the Pacific working in the Army as an interpreter, because, being Japanese, he knew all of the tricks that the Fascist Japs could throw at him. He had a lot of jobs to do, to study and to report on psychological, physiological, geographical, astronomical, germicidial conditions, their police and their thoughts about their Rulers and the Allies. I don't know what they called Father Ohta, and I don't think he ever had any set title, just called to do the jobs nobody else could do. His wife was so glad to see him come home that she allowed Pete and Toshi to use her house for Peoples Songs meetings without much protest. Mother Ohta comes from Virginia, is proud of it, and proud to speak in her southern voice over the fone to several hundred that ring in every day to ask about People that are a part of Peoples Songs.

I got down into their basement front room just about sundown and Toshi showed me a piece of sewer pipe the plumber had just taken out from under their floor, "One Hundred and Seventy Five years old and older," she said he had said. I asked her where her husband, Pete, was at, and told her, "I am a firm believer in this idea of a Peoples Songs organization, because we can carry more filth out of this town in one year than that old sewer pipe took away in a Century and Three Quarters, where's Pete?

PETE walked down some steep stairs before Toshi could tell me where he was. Pete saw my guitar, unslung his banjo, and before we could shake hands or pass many blessings, we had played, Sally Goodin, Doggy Spit a Rye Straw, Going Down This Road Feeling Bad, Worried Man Blues, and Fifteen Miles from Birmingham. This gave Toshi her chance to carry the joint of lead pipe somewhere back into the rear. I saw that the room was an old settler, with a low ceiling, dark shadows, stains of several memories, filled with dim lights from two or three standing lamps, and hung full of Japanese prints, drapes, paintings, metal incense burners, ancient ash trays of bronze and copper, Japanese and Chinese paper lanterns, a rock floor in front of a wide open fireplace burning full of old boxes and kindling found along the curbs. But Pete's banjo sort of drowned all of this out, and he sung me all of the new songs of satire, wit, anger, protest, hope, and longings of the GI's that he had played with and sang with out in the Pacific. "The Bungalow Of The Island Commander," "I Just Want To Go Home," "Uncle Sam, Won't You Please Come Back To Guam," "Quartermaster's Store," and others that sounded like an Army wanting to march nowhere but to home. Pete played louder, faster, better than ever. He told me that I also had got better. And then we set our boxes over in a corner and Pete told me all about the idea that he had cooked up about Peoples Songs.

"To organize all of us that write songs for the labor movement, to put all of our collections of songs into one big cabinet, and to send any union local any kind of a song, any kind of a historical material about anything they might need, and to shoot it out poco pronto, in today and out tonight." He stretched his legs out from his sofa across two reading tables and one padded chair where. . . .

"The unions have cried for the material that we've got, they need our several thousand songs, and they need new ones made up on the jump as we go along. They have written to me, to you, to every other songwriter or collector and had to waste time while you wrote to me and I called somebody else and they chased the next one up one side and down the other. All of this time was wasted. The bosses and the monopoly folks own their leather lined offices, pay clerks big money, pay experts, pay detectives, pay thugs, pay artists to perform their complacent crap, pay investigators to try to keep our stuff beat down, and the only earthly way that we can buck against all of this pressure is to all get together into one big songwriters and song singers union, and we will call our union by the name of Peoples Songs. And if we all stick together, all hell and melted teargasses can't stop us, nor atoms hold us back." I had never seen Pete speak any other way since I've known him, and so was surprised to hear him vision out a new plan to help the life of the trade union bubble up bigger and plainer.

I don't guess we talked about Pete and Toshi's Four months old baby that died while he was in the Pacific. But I had heard said that Toshi was pregnant again and I must have heard all of this in the sounds of their voices. Pete stopped talking and Toshi leaned toward me as I walked around the room, she rested her arm on the padded chair and said, "We thought you would rather like the idea. And I'm sure you will enjoy the meeting here tonight. You will see all of your old friends, Robert Claiborne, Horace Grenell, Herb Haufrecht, Lee Hays, Lydia Infeld, George Levine, Simon Rady, and there'll be Saul Aarons, and Charlotte Anthony, Edith Allaire, Bernie Asbel, Dorothy Baron, Oscar Brand, Agnes Cunningham, Jack Galin, Tom Glazer, Mike Gold, Baldwin Hawes, Burl Ives, Rockwell Kent, Lou Kleinman, Robert Kates, Millard Lampell, John Leary, and you may know Mildred Linsley, or Bess Lomax, Alan Lomax, Walter Lowenfels, Francia Luban, Jesse Lloyd O'Connor, or remember, Shaemas O'Sheal, or David Reef, there's Earl Robinson, Bob Russell, Betty Saunders, Paul Secon, Naomi Spahn, Norman Studer,

PETE SEEGER
fixews a
string

By the famiu
& well knwné
ARTI   WOODY GUTHRIE
               Last Nigh
               Mar

Mike Stratton, or Josh White, or Hy Zaret, or if not all of these, then the ones that aren't too busy or too far away to come. But they're already excited enough about the general idea to be on our sponsor committee. You see, we will print up every month a bulletin, a little bulletin."

"Not too little," Pete put in.

"Anyhow, a bulletin, either by mimeograph or photo offset."

And Pete said again, "Or off the presses of the Daily News."

"Well, not just overnight, anyhow," Toshi smiled, lit up a cigaret, and knocked the ashes off into an incense burner on the green wooden tea table at her knees. And in that special way that a wife treats her husband after his first or second week back from a long fought war, Toshi let other lights come across her face as she followed her thoughts around the room and the globe. "Of course, later on, we will buy out the Daily Mirror and run a Peoples Songs paper every day, with whole columns and pages about the struggle of the working people against their owners. But for the present moment, we will be satisfied with a little mimeographed bulletin just to more or less plant the seed of our ideas in the minds of the people we are trying to reach. Of course, me, I want to raise a houseful of children for Peter to sing to sleep. But, maybe I can find some sort of an organizing career here working with Peoples Songs."

"Your job is to keep me organized," I heard Pete laugh.

Our banjos and guitars layed in their corners and echoed with everything we talked about. Mother Ohta set a long table full of meat, rice, gravy, sauces, glasses of milk, and she filled each Mexican clay plate with its fair share, then lit two lonesome looking candles, and rounded up Takashi or Daddy, and the boy they called just Brother, then herded Pete and me away from our couch and Toshi out from her arm chair. At the table we went over all of the larger and smaller plans of the Peoples Songs, and by the time we had cleaned our plates, the first early comers had found their way through the door.

THE MEETING WAS MORE OF A SINGING PARTY, a hand shaking get together, a joke telling, tale swapping session, and then in the middle of all the singing and laughing, we all found a vacant inch somewhere on the floor and sat down to listen more than to talk. I said very little because I agreed with all I heard. I wanted to spend this whole night in my capacity as a professional looker and listener. We told our latest plans and scratched out some of our older ones. We had a free election where nobody got beat up nor chased down the street for voting. We give everybody a job to hold down. Everybody who wanted to speak spoke, some sang us songs and ballads as we sat on the floor. We heard all about the atom in its clothes of destruction and its building powers. We heard stomach ticklers make fun of Hoover, Hearst, Pegler, Lewis, Browder, Rankin, Churchill, the KKK, the gun thugs, the Bilbo that rymes so plain with Jim Crow and filth. We heard Lee Hays spray the Senate with DDT, heard me sing how hired thugs held a door closed at a Copper Miners Strikers Christmas Ball in 1913, in Calumet, Michigan, and how Seventy Three little children got . . . I heard Betty Sanders sing some that she sung for the men on the Pacific Islands. I first saw Betty just about the time that Pete went into the Army and I shipped out in the Merchant Marines. She has got lots better, still wide awake, wider eyes, to the smells and tastes and sleepy sounds of American Home Grown Fascism and Monopoly Control. I gave Betty a little clipping about her which I had found in a magazine out in Cheyenne, Wyoming. She had missed it, and was glad to get it for her scrapbook.

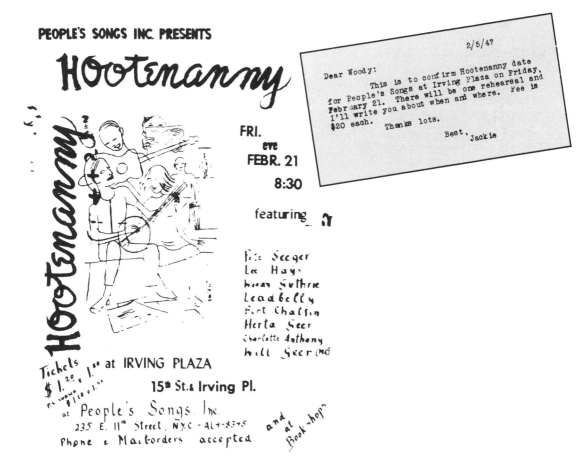

Bernie Asbel sung and we all sang with him the weary trail song of a hungry soldier discharged and "Looking For a Home" to Leadbelly's old folk tune of a fighting kind, "The Boll Weevil is a little black bug." Leadbelly was out on the West Coast tonight singing with Earl Robinson, Burl Ives, Cisco Houston, and others, all of the protest songs that the radios and movies would like to hush up. But we could hear Leadbelly on our record players on Disc labels and Union labels and Asch labels, the kind of real peoples biting songs that Moe Asch, son of Sholem Asch, takes down on unbustable plastics. Herb Klein- man whipped his piano keys into a lather and a sweat and made us all laugh at his double talking fast ones, his weepy slow numbers, styled in the usual Broadway patterns, only full of gunpowder and sung from the workers line of eyesight and mouthing. Several groups of AYD kids from all over the seaboard banged on cheap guitars and banjos their songs old and new that keep their streets singing and foaming with hate for the Money Powers and love for the workers. All of the atom power on the planet could not stir up as much dust and intelligence as these newly come kids in the American Youth for Democracy. I played with everybody, thumped chords, and stayed as far and as close to them as I could, because the room was so crowded that you had to propose holy wedlock to even move, and then you had to let your shoes stay on the floor there where you used to be. I'd heard boatloads of soldiers, sailors, towns full of bombed peoples, villages full of peasants and guerillas, heard all of these sing in the sounding hole of my guitar, but this little room shook as much as any boat, village, or town that I had heard the people sing in. I will include all the boxcars, saloons, churches, jails, halls, houses, of wood, iron, steel, marble, hard rock or granite. I will include the whole outdoors, the clouds and the weathers and the empty spaces of the blue. I wondered if AYD could stand for "All Yell Democracy," "All Yodel Democ- racy," or "All Do Something," I didn't know what. I think this is the best sounding Democracy I've heard so far, and this is the ring and tone of Peoples Songs.

Shaemas O'Sheen sang Irish songs with his grey hair in the lamplights, and with almost as much fire as the Youth Kids. He got an idea. To make up a Peoples Song for the GI's stranded on the foreign shores, tired of the whole mess of war, and anxious to fly home. We all made up a new verse to the old tune, "I Don't Want No More of Army Life, Gee, Ma, I want to go home."

I blowed all my pesos
In Manilla's lousy joints

I ain't got a penny
But I got a thousand points

The ships rust in the bonepile
Its awful plain to see
They can haul bananas
Why can't they carry me?

And just about everybody there made up not one, but two or three verses, and we sent the song by cable to the GI's.

Well, after this night was over, we all found a road to go home. I felt like I had seen something close to a miracle take place here in the house of Ohta's. This was action of the highest kind, it was fast action, fluid drive, jet propelled, and atom powered with plastic trimmings all around. It was a bunch of people working together in a field where they had all worked more or less alone before tonight.

And letters went out to the union locals, on out past the rural free delivery boxes, and up the lost mountainsides, and on over the humps to the tall office buildings, lit on your desk, and we got your answer back. I would like to tell you some of the words picked out of these letters, but all of this is in the bulletin (along with Sixteen Songs, articles, etc.,) of this month's issue of "PEOPLES SONGS."

The first Peoples Songs Hootenanny was thrown in the Ohta home, and Eighty people came. The second Hoot was up in Brother's apartment on Thompson Street, and a Hundred and Twelve came. The third was in the Newspaper Guild Hall on East 40th Street, and Three Hundred sang for a half a day. (I took my daughter, Cathy, Three, and she sang on the stage and out on the laps of the folks she chose in the audience, and taught the Singers how to add a completely new technique). Our next session was in the Little Red School House on Charlton Street, and the seats flooded over with faces and faces, wild hands clapping, yells and cheers for Leadbelly, Blind Sonny Terry, Brownie McGhee, that came to help out Pete Seeger, me, Lee Hays, Betty Sanders, Tom Glazer, Alan Lomax, the CIO chorus, and to hear Bernie Asbel sing his newest one, "My Hands." Seventy Five people in the balcony had to stand up. Everybody else stood up because they couldn't set still.

I saw these Peoples Songs raise up storms of stiff winds and wild howls of cheer from the people in their seats, and saw also, that almost every chronic headache was eased and made quieter, I mean your headaches about writing, singing,

I go so dang'd solitary and so dang'd lonesome hearted just about a dozen times a day that I feel just about like Leadbelly must have felt about that same number of spells every day when he sung sometimes I take a great notion to jump in that river and drown; but he never did quite make up his mind to quit this world and to make that high jump which I've not got the courage nor the nerve neither one to up and jump; so no matter what the news you'll ever be hearing from and about me, Ruthy, you'll never quite be hearing that one and if you do hear it you'll know it never is true enough to be factual; I want to go on and I want to climb and ramble on and ankle on and stumble on and stagger on, every hour I can to see for my own self how many hours I can do it.

NOTICE OF BOOKING 7/25/47

Woody (with Ronnie, Ernie, Julie) ... has a booking on
Sat, March 8 ... at ... AM/PM
at Newspaper Guild
(Address) 40 E 40 St

Travel Dir:
I'll call you Fri March 7th for rehearsal.

Person in Charge: Jackie Gibson   Fee: Benefit

NOTICE OF BOOKING 3/10/47

Woody Guthrie (instead of Pete) ... has a booking on
Sat March 15 ... at 11 ... AM/PM
at Hungarian Workers Club 809 Westchester
(Address) Ave Bronx (For J.P.F.O.)

Travel Dir: IRT white Plains train to
Prospect Ave stn.

Person in Charge: Andy Adler   Fee 31.50

Dear Woody:

The AYD Folksay Group is having an affair
in Plainfield, New Jersey — Saturday Eve,
November 8th and would like very much to
have you entertain. The fee is $25.00/
Are you available for this date?
Please let us know.

Sincerely,

Leonard Jacobson

NOTICE OF BOOKING 3/31/47

Woody Guthrie (with Leadbelly) ... has a booking on
Fri April 11 ... at check me later AM/PM
at Needle Trades High School
(Address) 225 W 24 St

Travel Dir: (For Spanish Refugee Appeal)

Person in Charge: Iris Schwartz   Fee 22.50

CANCELLATION OF BOOKING

Performer Woody Guthrie
Date Wed, Feb. 19
Place Joan of Arc High School

They've changed the
type meeting and plan
no entertainment.

PEOPLE'S ARTISTS, INC.

Per: Jackie Gibson

2/4/47

Dear Woody:

Re. the Morningside Community Center
benefit show Sat, Feb 8, please be at Town
Hall no later than 11:10 as your portion of
the show goes on at 11:30 PM.

Many thanks for your cooperation.

Sincerely,
Cy Mann, Director
People's Artists, Inc.

NOTICE OF BOOKING 2/4/47

Woody Guthrie ... has a booking on
Sat Feb. 22 ... at ... AM/PM
at Syracuse NY — C.P.
(Address)

Travel Dir:

Phone: Syracuse 3-2760
Person in Charge: George Sheldrick   Fee: 45.

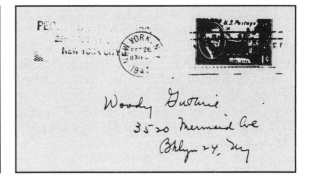

PEO...
NEW YORK CITY
1947

Woody Guthrie
3520 Mermaid Ave
Bklyn 24, NY

copyrights, fees, pay, finances and money. PEOPLES SONGS shows you the easy simple way to make and to protect your own ballads, poems, songs, tunes, and your arrangements to old public domain melodies. PEOPLES SONGS showed me how to thrash out most of my terrible headaches that hit me when I try to talk salary or money to folks that raise the long green for good causes. Troubles of programs, stage shows, picket lines, the radio studios, records and books, songsheets, musical arrangements and how to write, what to write about, who to curse, who to fight, who to hold dearest to your heart. Your only worry will be in your actual work of creating, and even for this, PEOPLES SONGS sends you the best tips, leads, and material that is available on your problem or project at any given period in time and space.

I can't sum up what I've just said, no more than I can sum the glacial ages and our streamlined atom cities up into one sound of my mouth. But, I can say that the sounds of the singing human voice has outlasted almost every chain, bilbo, and shackle that our capitalistic few could latch onto us. THE PEOPLE THAT SING their real Peoples songs will be the people that will win our new world just around this next bend.

And besides all of this, my daughter, Cathy dances only to a song when it is a Peoples Song. She tells me that this holds good for every kid in her nursery school. And we've got the whole Atlantic ocean and all of its oil and wreckage out here to back her words up.

Woody Guthrie
3-19-46

———— ▬▬ ————

One of the key unanswered questions about Woody Guthrie's life is whether he actually joined the Communist Party. Certainly, he was proud of his association with it and often worked on its behalf. There is no record of his being a member of the Communist Party. Those who knew him best said that he never joined. Maybe Woody himself said it best: "I ain't necessarily a communist. But I've been in the red all my life." So the joining of hands he refers to here probably reflects an alliance as much spiritual as political. Probably.

People's Artists booking cards.

THING CALLED SOCIALISM

The job to be done is to get this thing called socialism nailed and hammered up just as quick as we can. I believe this just as much as I believe my own name, and lots more. We've got to pay whatever it costs us to get socialism in here just as early as we can. This is that big job. This is the only job worth working on. Socialism is the only job worth wasting any time or strength on. It's the only job that'll give you and me and all of us a good job we can be really proud of.

Socialism won't skip a single one of us. It'll not make hoboes nor bums nor dirty backdoor tramps out of any of us.

The biggest thing that ever happened to me in my whole life was back in 1936 the day that I joined hands with the Communist Party. I'll stick to my words, don't you worry your head one minute about that.

> Woody Guthrie
> Stone Crest Lodge
> Bethlehem, N.H.

Nazism took a friend of mine out for a wild naked ride tonight in a truck.

Fascism ripped off the clothes and pure hate beat her skin to big red whelps.

Ignorance left her laying out in the weeds to die, but her union spirit picked her up and walked her back to town nine miles and a half.

—From the 1946 notebook

BIG SMUDGE

I carted my paints and my water color brushes today down the street two short blocks and painted some fancy leafs and weeds and stems all around the edge of the window of the Communist Party.

I painted, "Join the Communist Party" on a strip of wrapping paper and "Kill the Taft Hartley Slave Law" on some more strips. "Let's Have a Low Cost Housing Project for Coney Island" and "Read Your Daily Worker." Gwen, from Texas, my 11½ year old daughter helped me clean, sweep, scrape and paint and fix the windows of the Party office and the book shop.

When we got it all done, I went in next door to a little eat shop and a big soda jerker told me "It's just one big gigantic smudge."

I didn't even say one single word. Just drunk my coffee and walked out.

8-3-47
Woody Guthrie

Woody not only wrote great songs in the heat of the moment— he was also capable of composing some of his meanest prose under the stress of immediate events. Here, stuck in a Hartford hotel room, homesick and just plain sick of the life of the itinerant political folk singer, he writes as eloquently of the travails of the professional road musician's life as anyone has ever done. Music fans who know Bob Seger's "Turn the Page" and Jackson Browne's "The Load Out" will recognize here the ancestor of those songs, speaking with blunt and bitter clarity. For anyone who imagined Woody, with his persistent optimism, a mere naif, "On Ballad Singers" is a most effective corrective; it shows him firmly attached to real life at its worst.

ON BALLAD SINGERS

Woody Guthrie
March 20, 1946
Hartford, Connecticut
Bond Hotel

My wife told me tonight at the supper table that several comrades in our neighborhood, Coney Island, had held a meeting to decide what sort of entertainment to use at a rally which is coming up. She said, "They decided that all of you ballad singers are not dependable, all of you, I mean, *none* of you. And so they *refuse* to use a ballad singer on their program." She sat on the corner of our eating table and gave me a lecture about carpenters, painters, factory workers, and tunnel drivers. "If the tunnel digger didn't show up you would never have had your subways and your Holland and Lincoln Tunnels."

She had a perfect right to lecture at me, because I had a date to sing at a big negro church for the Council on African Affairs, and I told her that I did not feel like going.

I had driven her to Philly to see her doctor and her eye specialist and several families of old friends and relatives and had smoked and bounced in our '36 Buick around those cobble stone streets ten dozen times, had driven back and forth, had found our car window smashed and all of our belongings ransacked.

We had parked on a parking lot all night, and the car looted next morning. Shoes, socks, letters and papers tossed out on the ground, my $100 guitar case opened (looked at) but not taken. The dashboard locker was broken open, emptied out and only a thermos bottle (two cups of postum) taken. My overcoat was gone. The back trunk door was jimmied open, and not one thing was gone. (I had just bought a new $2.00 jack, a tire wrench, 2 gallons of oil, a tire liner, and a few pliers and screwdrivers, (none touched, none gone.) I told her that it looked like a police job to me, for my new book of songs was gone, half of a new ballad about the bombing of the games home by the Midland Railroad bullies, and some titles of other songs I am working on. (Several around the case of Sacco and Vanzetti). This book was gone.

"No." She told me, "It looks more like a gang of Philadelphia kids to me, that just got started good, didn't have the least idea of what they wanted, then somebody interrupted them and they got scared and ran away." She looked pretty sad at our bashed-in window. "I'll at least have a lot of fresh

Clockwise from left: Woody, Jean Ritchie, Pete Seeger, Fred Hellerman.

air on my side now. But what can Philadelphia do to keep its rage of kids from going around smashing car locks and windows?"

"Lucky they left us our engine and tires. I guess our gas tank is sucked dry," I said. But the motor can and the gas was untouched.

We drove past the G.E. strikers on parade down Broad Street, with signs that said, "G.E. can't run Philadelphia," and other banners. We had to beat it on out for New York because the wife had to teach five or six classes of modern dancing. She's been a dancer and a teacher now for ten years. (Almost as long as I've been a ballad singer.)

Back home in Coney Island I felt tired out, so I bought a bottle, took two drinks and laid down on the bed. To think and to rest.

My wife asked me, "Aren't you going to go to your booking tonight?" And I said, "No, I don't feel like it. Its a free booking, anyhow, no money in it."

"It makes no difference, money or no money, you owe it to yourself, and to all of the other folk singers to go. Plenty of talk is going around about how none of you can be trusted to get two short blocks and do a performance."

I told her I still didn't feel like going. "I feel like the program would be better off if I stay home and read the papers."

The wife pulled the curtain closed. I heard her in the kitchen drinking hot tea and talking with Shirley. Shirley is a smart, nice, square built girl, nineteen, a good D.W. sub getter, and active in every way you can think of. Over and over I heard their words, "Not to be trusted." "Undependable." "Folk singers." "Wild." "Promiscuous." "Unpredictable."

But I didn't hear any words pass between Shirley and Marjorie that I have not already called, cursed, heaped on my own self. But as they spoke, and as their clay glasses rattled, I rolled the ballad singers side of the story over in my head.

We are a different lot, a different herd. We buy and carry high priced instruments which are big and bulky, and which get scarred and destroyed at the first jolt, and we hit all of the jolts. We have a family or two to support, a car to keep fed, high gas, oil, hotel, cafe bills. We are asked more to perform for free than for a fee, we donate a part of our pay back to the good causes.

Tom Glazer has one wife and one baby, so does Alan Lomax, Josh White has a family with four kids. Bess Lomax has a baby and her husband, Baldwin Hawes, and Peter Seeger supports his wife and home (Toshi Ohta), while Burl Ives donates to upkeep of his father and mother, Betty Sanders is saving nickels to get married, Richard Dyer-Bennett keeps a child and a wife.

There is a thousand neon lit spots all over New York where AFOL nite club performers draw down good lettuce at a nice easy pace, while the progressive or labor movement singer is protected by no union and guaranteed no job nor

I've got to practice up on how to be rational so's I can throw out my chest and tell you you're not rational.

GRAND PICNIC AND DANCE

Broadway Entertainment

WOODY GUTHRIE
SINGING STAR OF MOVIE
AND RADIO

BETTY SANDERS
STAGE STAR, FOLK SINGER

RADISCHEV DANCERS
OF NEW YORK

AMERICAN FOLKSAY GROUP
SINGERS AND DANCERS

CONN'S. OWN UNITY PLAYERS

MOVIE SHORTS:
JOE LOUIS, CHARLIE CHAPLIN,
LENA HORNE

SPECIAL FOR MOTHERS AND DAD, TOO . . . NURSERY SCHOOL ATTENDANTS TO LOOK
AFTER THE YOUNGSTERS, FROM 2:00 to 7:00 P.M.

Free Beer   Free Beer   Free Beer

Choice Food

BROILED STEAKS   SOUTHERN FRIED CHICKEN
BAKED HAM   SPAGHETTI and MEAT BALLS

Plus

FAMOUS FOODS OF DIFFERENT NATIONAL GROUPS

Games for Young and Old   Pony Rides for the Youngsters

SUNDAY, FOURTH OF JULY
HIGHLAND PARK,   WEST HAVEN

Highland Street — off Campbell Ave., West Haven   **12 NOON TO 10 P.M.**

Take M trolley from Green, New Haven. Coming in from Bridgeport on the Post Road, take first right after the
Armstrong Billboard, into Campbell Avenue. Coming from Hartford, go through New Haven, follow U.S. Route 1, into
West Haven; take left at Forest Theatre into Campbell Avenue.

DANCING - POLKAS - DANCING

Auspices Labor Press Committee   **Adm. $1.00 plus Fed. Tax 20c**

fee, no set income. I can make four times my present amount of money by singing in the saloon than in the halls where progressive people rally and meet, and I have asked myself why a million times. I guess it is because the labor movement does not know yet that it has a fund of several thousand tunes and songs, old fighting ballads, history songs, spirituals, and such likes, which I hear in no saloon, what all of us progressive singers (folk or not) are trying to do is to put union militant music (or at least music with a meaning) into the factories, onto the air waves, stages, record players, on sound trucks, etc., and even onto the juke boxes in the gin mills. And there are plenty of the forces of monopoly out to hush us up.

One of the slickest ways to hush us up is to hire us to perform under their censorship, or to buy us out and put us on their shelf, or to use us in the padded saloons and to pay us enough to scare us away from all of our left wing friends and comrades. We do not have a union as folk artists because there is no such union anywhere. We have to belong to a speakers union, a singers union and a musician's union. I have belonged to three at the same time. And yet, people faint at their fone receivers when a folk singer mentions the word money. We do not get a job every night and all are forced to make two or more places over one night's time on the weekends.

You get peeved at us because we cant spend the entire evening at your party. (I would love to come and meet you and greet you and stay for the entire evening, but I have got to sand my rails on down to four other places.) I have played for as little as two and three dollars a many (several hundred) nites and have made on the West Coast and on the East Coast as many as five dates a nite. Many many are the many that I tossed the money on the rug and split the breeze to the next cause party.

The war hit us with higher prices, higher meals, gas, hotels, tires, travel expenses, and our instruments that were made in Europe. We had to pay ten times as much to repair and to replace. We had the same worries as a dancer would face but our gear cost usually more and got ruined easier. Our troubles were a lot like your portable actors, but we travel alone and can get lost, broke down, stranded alone, while you usually travel in pairs or whole companies, one can run for help while one sits at the scene of the breakdown. I have got lost and got sore and got mad, cried, walked, missed the whole affair, and then bought me a bottle and

HOO-ray

THE SAM ADAMS SCHOOL'S HAVING ANOTHER RIP-ROARIN'...

Hootenanny!

BY
PEOPLE'S SONGS INC. N.Y.
SATURDAY EVENING

November 1st
Jordan Hall

AN ALL STAR CAST! IN A VARIED, NEVER-A-DULL-MOMENT PROGRAM,
INCLUDING NEW, JUST-OFF-THE-GRIDDLE TOPICALS ON HOUSING AND THE
HIGH COST OF LIVING

Betty Sanders

Woodie Guthrie

Al Moss

Charlotte Anthony

international folklorist
...she wow'd us last year

the Woodie
...of Dustbowl ballad fame

negro folklorist
...a truly great artist

beautiful balladist
... we mean beautiful!

CLIP AND MAIL NOW!
(a sell-out last time)

SAMUEL ADAMS SCHOOL
37 PROVINCE ST.
BOSTON 8

Also on sale at Jordan Hall

Please send me Hootenanny tickets for November 1.

...$ .75
...$1.20
...$1.80
...$2.40

NAME_____

STREET_____

CITY_____ZONE_____

Enclosed check or money order for $_____

sneaked off to some vacant lot to weep and to drink, then to play my sorrows away up and down the truck route bar. Oh, yes. Folk singers get just as lost as you do. And it so seems that I am always at a new street in a new town when your new day dawns and you march to your school, college, factory, your ship, truck, your door of work. It was free transportation that got me lost, but it takes money to get me home.

The train runs too fast and too slow. The taxi takes you for the old runaround or gets mad and wont haul you out to your zone. The subway is too crowded and the bus too fast and you lose your little date book on some leather seat. You fone the party and the receiver buzzes in your ear. You fone again and its off of the hook. The snow and ice holds you back and the rain, wind, and sun fights against you. You have no income because you are not dependable and no home life to keep you sober. You read papers and pamphlets by hooks and by snatches and always get broken into by a fone call, a rehearsal, a money raising party, or to charge out into the weather toward your next address.

That next address in these days is apt to be a good little stop and your car is liable to sneeze or cough or growl or sling a shoe and once she goes dead on you, it is just T.S. You put your self and your life and your car into the hands of some grinning mechanic and you just bite your tongue and pray.

The war took us ballad singers away on ships and trains and trucks. We all kept on singing. I failed to get a Special Service job in the army (on account of my radical background). They sent me to a Teletype College and I got my diploma, then they gave me a job painting signs (like Hitler once did). But I kept my guitar limbered up around the PX and the barracks. I had lots of fun because I did not have to worry about finding a new address every thirty minutes. I may not have set the entire army air corps free from the bonds of complascency, but I don't think I set any man back none. I was in the army for eight months. (Merchant Marines for three invasions and got hit twice). I made up lots of new songs at both places.

I am not a good hand at figures, not a bookkeeper, nor a very good arguer. I have to strain my brain to just write down a page and get to a mail box, but I do read the D.W., the other union papers, even some Hearst ones for real comedy, and I will still be rounding the bends when a lot of good ones wear out. I am just now learning really the kind of

Talking Union is the best kind of talking you can do, union in your house, union in your street, union in your town, or union around the world.
—FROM 1946 DATE BOOK, JANUARY 11

The world had to be round. If it was any other shape none of us wouldn't be here on it.
—FROM 1946 DATE BOOK, JANUARY 12

The best religion I ever felt or ever seen is world union.
The highest step in any religion is your joining up with the union of every mind and hand in the world.
—FROM 1946 DATE BOOK, JANUARY 13

An atom bomb must have blowed up and killed all the folks up on the moon a long time ago. I hope race hate don't blow us off the earth.
—FROM 1946 DATE BOOK, JANUARY 14

There's nothing bad wrong about chasing a woman, but it's bad if you chase her and feel bad when you catch her or feel bad when you don't.
—FROM 1946 DATE BOOK, JANUARY 15

Changing lovemates and love partners is not a bad thing. To have to pay a lawyer your dough to change partners is the bad part.
—FROM 1946 DATE BOOK, JANUARY 16

songs I want to write, how to write them. Our apartment is too small for me to get much done around the house, but I write on trains, buses, in box cars, hotels, jungles, Hoovervilles, wherever I can. I started my voice and still hear it. I ask you to watch the newly organized "Peoples Songs" headed by Pete Seeger and his wife Toshi Ohta. These are several dozen of the most progressive song writers and singers already in "Peoples Songs," and I am a true believer that we will see them thrash out and settle many of the headaches that cause the audience to say that performers are not sincere and performers to howl that you listeners, you fixers, are not sincere. The trouble is lack of organization, the worlds worst illness, and I believe in my soul that "Peoples Songs" will help a lot.

———————

The following is Woody's account of the huge Westinghouse strikers' rally. Note that, at least in his initial impressionistic notes, he's as wrapped up in the comparatively new phenomenon of air travel as in the events of the previous evening. (He was probably flying alongside Pete Seeger and Lee Hays.) Perhaps because he finds flying so exhilarating, when he finally gets down to politics, it's Woody the all-but-incorrigible optimist speaking. According to Joe Klein, the show hadn't gone very well for him. Yet these notes are one of the clearest statements of the incredible hopefulness felt by radicals in the months just after the victorious conclusion of the war.

March 23, 1946

I flew from Pittsburgh to New York this morning. Left at 2:15 a.m., got here at 4:30 or 5:00 a.m.

Flying after dark was as good as the trip yesterday, and yesterday was a very clear sunny day for this early in March.

The lights from towns and farms were a sight I had never seen before. I've walked up mountains and pulled over humps in cars and trucks, but never just drifted over a whole range of them like a big bird.

I looked down into the red hot stacks and furnace of steel mills across Pennsylvania. I saw fiery vats of moulds full of white hot iron and steel. Saw car loads of hot slag poured down the dumps. I had almost as much fun seeing the world

I hope you never do call me another Walt Whitman or another Will Rogers. I ain't neither one. Let those two rest in their silent sleeps and call me just by my own name.
—FROM 1946 DATE BOOK, JANUARY 18

I'd ought to take this automatic ash tray out and dump out the butts, snipes, and ashes, but the snow and the wind is so cold outside it would freeze my balls off before I got back in.
—FROM 1946 DATE BOOK, JANUARY 19

If I be stingy with people then they will be stingy with me.
—FROM 1946 DATE BOOK, JANUARY 20

I heard a gambler down in a Texas cathouse yell, I feel like chasing me down a nice juicey chunk of strange ass. Five feet wide and nine inches deep.
—FROM 1946 DATE BOOK, JANUARY 21

Some so sickly as to say we can't even turn life's tides of events. I say that we do and we can make current events fall any old way we want them to.
—FROM 1946 DATE BOOK, JANUARY 22

President Truman has proved to me that he don't like my trade unions, don't like organized labor, don't like the Communist Party, don't like the human race.
—FROM 1946 DATE BOOK, JANUARY 23

from up here as I had singing for Ten Thousand Westinghouse Strikers.

I saw Twenty Thousand people parade through the streets and over the river bridges in Pittsburgh. I saw the Monongahela melt into the Susquehannah and ease on down into the Ohio.* I saw cops ride motorcycles and high school bands play for the strikers. I saw soldiers and sailors march with flags and banners at the head of the parade. Pretty girls done fancy tricks with long drum major sticks. I saw street cars bring the workers in from Thirty miles away. I wish I could have seen this big rally from the air. I saw people throw pages of Peoples Songs out from high buildings to flood the crowd as we sang on the bandstand at the marble steps of the City Hall. I walked and carried my guitar with Lee Hays and Pete Seeger. Pete bought a car jack and a handle because he is fearing the trouble back in New York. I told him I was going to buy me a gallon can of green fence paint while here in Smokey City.

We sang "Solidarity Forever" and the papers said the rally started off with a communist song. Oh. Well. Any song that fights for the case of the workhand is a communist song to the rich folks.

Speakers spoke between our songs. The mayor dished out a nice plate of broad and liberal words into the faces of several Thousand sore and anxious strikers. We sang Two songs made up this day for the situation here at Westinghouse. The crowd roared like the ocean in a rock cavern. Good to see and feel.

This was the biggest meeting, march, and rally to ever take place here in Pittsburgh. The Iron Town never saw so many troopers nor so many cops nor so many workers in their everyday clothes. The One Hundred Troopers were made so much fun of that I nearly felt sorry for them. The men that sent them in got ten boos out of every mouth in the crowd. I saw buildings full of people looking. Streets full of others that listened and learned. We saw a big page of history here and we helped to write it.

If I had of been a sick man at the early start of this day I would have got well awful quick. There was so much of that electric surge of life in the air that it would make a new person out of you if you would let it take hold of you.

*Woody has confused the Allegheny, which joins the Monongahela without benefit of famous folklore, with the Susquehannah, which flows into Chesapeake Bay from the other end of Pennsylvania, inspiring several classic tunes along the way.

CADILLAC EIGHT

How many hundred
Does it take
To grab me down
That Cadillac Eight?

Cadillac Eight
You get straight
Cadillac Eight
You get straight
Grab me down
My Cadillac Eight

If your Buick
Fools with me
I will run you
In the sea

If your Oldsmobile
Gets smart
I will beat you
From the start

If your Pontiac
Gives me pain
I will suck
You down the drain.

If your Chevvy
Touches me
I will run you
Up a tree.

If your Dodge
With me gets wise
I will pass you
In the skies

If your Ford
Gives me a run
I'll pass you
Like the rising sun.

If your Hudson
Messes around
I will beat you
Right on down.

10-31-46
BACK BAY STATION
BOSTON

Every speaker was a fighter and a lawyer and a teacher and a preacher. Every charge against the company we made plain. There was jokes, yells, and hate in the voices. I could hear the voices of people fighting a fight, Ten Thousand in one big union camp.

The liner notes booklet for Woody's second album of children's songs was eventually carved out of the latter sections of this account of how those records were made. The parts left out of the published notes make fascinating reading as an account of the record-making process, at least among folk singers, in that period.

Last night we made the second album of kids records, "Songs To Grow On," called, "Work Songs To Grow On."

Recorded Seven sides. Don't know which Six will be picked out, yet.

1. Pretty and Shinyo
2. Plant My Seed
3. Build My House
4. All Work Together
5. Take My Penny
6. Needle Sing
7. [*left blank*]

I liked having Marjorie there to help me. She tells me to sing it slow and plain, to vision Stacky Bones in my mind.

It's hard for me to sing slow enough. I've nearly lost my old knack for singing slow since I've come to New York where you sing so fast.

Marjorie is smart enough to know all of this, and smart enough to slow me down, to get me to take it greasy, easy, and to say my words plain. I think my records will help you and your family to talk a little bit slower when you hear them.

Our first kids album is getting around now, and getting some pretty good writeups in the papers. It is called "Songs To Grow On (Nursery Days)."

The Six songs in "Nursery Days" are these:

CADILLAC CADILLAC

I'm gonna drive
A Cadillac Cadillac
I'm gonna drive
A Cadillac Cadillac
Aint no use to try
To stop me.

I'm gonna drive
A Cadillac Cadillac
I'm gonna own
A Cadillac Cadillac
All you other wheelers
Git back git back
Aint nobody
Gonna pass me.

I'm gonna have
A Cadillac Cadillac
I'm gonna get me
A Cadillac Cadillac
You caint make
A Cadillac stay back.
Aint no wagon
Gonna catch me.

10-31-46
BACK BAY STATION
BOSTON

1. Dance Around
2. Put Your Finger
3. Wake Up
4. Don't You Push Me
5. Jig Along Home
6. Cleano

We all think that "Work Songs To Grow On" are as good, I think a speck better, than "Nursery Days." I am not real sure that I done the second batch quite as bubbly as I did the first ones, I mean, as a performer. Oh, well, you'll have to buy them and then grow up and judge for yourself.

We'll see as we see.

"Nursery Days" was written for Stackaboney while she was nursing her days and I was nursing nights. The school nursed her during her days and Marjorie nursed her in her mornings while I drank rum and sodie and nursed her some at night. This was when I was mostly alone with her and when I'd take my pencil and my paper and jot down her words as she hummed them or said them or sang them. I didn't get one half of her words wrote down nor set to a ryme or a tune.

Marjorie's still asleep this morning, after our big studio recording session last night with Moe Asch, Marian Distler, (some other man, Disc's Publicity man, forgot his name. He's a good guy, anyhow. I could tell that).

I just fed Cathy her juice and some of my adult vitamin pills. She says, "Save the little vitamin juice stuff for the baby inside of mommy's tummy. I'm a big lady now 'cause I make my plate clean. I take mommy's big vitamin pills and I swallow them down just like you do, don't I, daddy?"

I took her to school. She watched some little gold fishes in a barber shop window for a while, and asked me all about them. I told her all I know and now she knows more about those goldfish than me or those barbers either one.

I mailed my article about "Stackabones" to the magazine for old and young kids, "Two To Six." The piece is accepted already and is to be put in a early issue of 1947. Look out for it. Just a piece about Stacky going to school, just these four blocks, these four big worlds with one shady side and one sunny side we see from our house here to her Community Center.

We played all of the "Work Songs To Grow On" for Cathy a few songs. You'd ought to see Cathy and Marjorie act the songs out.

I sure don't recall any songs my baby life was blessed with. My dad sang me lots of good old songs, all right. I can hear him singing to me right now. My mama was our best singer, though, and was a real good hand to tell us kids the story, over and over, and then all over again, over slow and over easy, till it sounded to me like a nice ripe and a juicey strawberry in her mouth. It was even better than a strawberry to my ears.

But the songs, mostly, well, they seemed to be long and sad, weary and dreary, and awful, awful hard for me to catch onto, somehow. I sat on the floor with my brothers and my sisters and we held mamas hand and laid our heads in her lap on her apron. And listened.

And, we listened some more. It was lots better when papa would help mama with all of the songs and stories, because he put in a little more of the wild running fighting sounds and monkey shines that made my ears stand away out and wiggle for more.

Cathy likes her songs and stories and dances best of all when her mommy and her daddy get together and sing, talk, and dance. She joins in lots quicker, and lots louder, when the whole family lays down the newspapers, their books, their knitting, twitting, and their lowly spirits, and all get going together on our story, our song, and our dance.

We beat tamborines, drums, oatmeal boxes, books, we rattle shakers and spoons, we jingle bells and tin cans, we jump around and shuffle and dance and then we take a quiet easy spell of telling some story. We make up some crazy new story if we forget all of our old ones. She gets more fun out of this, I guess, than any other thing our whole family does.

Marjorie and me said when Stacky was first born that we wouldn't break our necks and Cathy's, too, trying to teach her any vast nor any deep theories nor feelings about art, books, movies, nor about songs nor music, but that we would try our level best not to block, bar, nor hinder any of these things when they did bubble up in Miss Stacky.

I've been playing and singing songs I made up now for nearly Twenty years and Cathy at 3½ already can out ryme, outplay, and outsing me any old day.

Marjorie has been a modern dancer and a teacher of dance now for Ten or Twelve years, and I'd say that no dancer I've seen yet moves and says what Cathy says while she dances. While most dancers and singers are somewhat down stumbling with their intellects, Cathy is already out and down, on and gone, gone on over to that genius place and left

"Cathy Plays a Record"

every chain and shackle, every lock and key, every cage and pen, every hall and wall. I sometimes think she even leaves her name behind her when she comes and when she goes. Ask her.

I don't want you to use these songs to split your family apart, to give the kids something to do while you do something else. I want to see you throw down your book, your paper, magazine, your worries and your troubles, and to come and join in with the kids.

Let your kids teach you how to act these songs out, these and a thousand other songs. Get the whole fam damily into the fun. Get papa, mama, brother, sister, aunt, uncle, grandma, grandpa, all of your neighbors, friends, visitors, and everybody else in on it.

My songs are not to be read like a lesson book nor a text, but to be a key to sort of unlock all of the old bars in you that keep the family apart or the school apart. I'm not trying to lure, to bait, to trick, nor to teach the little fellers how to do because the kids have taught me all I ever will know.

Watch the kids. Do like they do. Act like they act. Yell like they yell. Dance like they dance. Sing like they sing. Work like the kids do. You'll be plenty healthy, and feel pretty wealthy, and live to be wise, if you put these songs or any earthly song, on your radio, record player, or on your lips, and do like the kids do. I don't want the kids to be grown up, I want to see the grownups be kids.

Woody created all the time, but often his most interesting pieces, short and long, rolled out of him in great compulsive bursts, like the Grand Coulee Dam song series. The following short pieces were all jotted down in August 1947, mainly in a plain old dimestore stenographer's pad to which he gave the title "Coney Island Short Hauls."

I just can't hear the same kind of a singing in my written or printed page here that I felt through Arlo's wool shawl giving him his nippling bottle this morning before sun.

I guess I'm too busy having kids to read so many books as you.

I guess I'm too busy writing my kids their books to graze your page of wit and sage.

My sagey brush here in my baby's nurse room dances homier and happier than a dozeful Sandburg.

And I see more to be lots sadder about than Whitman, Burns, Pushkin, and Sandburg all added up.

8-2-1947

ONE LITTLE WARM SPOT

I tell you it's just that one little warm spot in me that you and all of you are looking for and breaking your axles down digging after.

I preach but one gospel and that was what I found in your belly dance. I teach you but this one lesson and that is to move warm.

I never sing but one song and that is a song to stretch out and go by.

I show you just one little warm place in you here where I come from.

8-2-1947

DON'T MESS ME AROUND

There had better not nobody try to mess me around just because I'm a poor hard working landlord. I'm not anything but the janitor around here and not even a good one at that.

I'm not one of those rich birds like you think I am. I'm just as hard a worker as you or anybody else. No sir. I'm not rich. I never was rich like you think. I don't own no ten or fifteen buildings like I wish I did and so you cant call me rich which I'd like to be. I just own this here one building here and I'm deadly sorry of the day I gave my good money for it. If I had my good money back I'd be an awful glad man.

I ain't been landlord very long and I don't even know how to be a landlord. I'm too soft and easy on you people and I know I am. You just ask my wife and she will tell you that three hungry dogs could talk me out of six months rent. In fact I wish my wife was right here so's you could get a look at her.

One look at her and you'd see that I'm not no landlord.

I'm just here because my wife needed this here climate. She had to have the salt air in her lungs.

And that's whose the landlord. Her. Not me. Not little old me that you see here in your hallway asking you how about your rent.

Woody Sez:

THEM: AFTER ALL WHAT IS MONEY? US: DERN IF I KNOW — NEVER HAD ANY!

WHITMAN, SANDBURG & PUSHKIN

I ask me this question and if I didn't answer it I couldn't go on.

Does Whitman, Sandburg, or Pushkin, either one, actually talk in the lingo, brogue, and ways of talking through of the kinds and breeds of the working people I've met and dealt with?

And the only answer I can say is, no.

Whitman makes glorious the works, labors, hopes, dreams, and feelings of my people, but he does not do this in the sorts of words my people think, talk, and dance and sing.

Sandburg tosses in grammar words that I never do hear my kind of folks talk. And Pushkin does the same. They praise, describe, they pay their thanks and their tributes to my people, but not in words my kind of people think.

So I've got to keep on plugging away.

August 5, 1947

ROUGH TOWEL

I and my wife made some loving today here on our couch in our newborn baby passion club. And I got worked up to such a flying point that I got up my nerves and asked her to do something she said she was too tired and too sleepy to do now.

And I jumped up and tried to read a paper, but I was too blind to see. I held a book in my lap too bitter at my roots to read. I was too mean to even come in the shower and give her a hot rubbing down with a rough towel like she asked me. She asked me to come in to Arlo's room and read her some pages about a 4 week old baby, but I said no and just set in my chair.

It wasn't till away up in the middle of the day that we got to doing it all over again and I got so full of sweet things my bitter stuff run out of me and stayed gone all day.

August 5, 1947

"Like a Dog on a Bone"

Hi Little Arlo,
Suck all you can
Ho, Little Arlikins,
Suckle like a man.
Hold you on my shoulder
Pet you with my hand.
Hey my Little Arlo
Bubble if you can
Hi, Little Arlo,
Bubble all you can,
Hey, Little Hobo,
Blubber all you can,
Howdy Little Belcher Boy,
Bubble like a man.
Bubble like a big pig.
Bubble when you can.

8-7-47

I SAY TO YOU WOMAN AND MAN

I'll say to you, woman, come out from your home and be the
    wild dancer of my breed.

I'll say to my man come out of your walls and move in your
    space as free and as wild as my woman

I'm married and wed to a dancer in my front line and the ways
    she moves while I beat my skin drum would knock your
    soul and your lights out

I beat my old drum skin and sing to my big family, you, Arlo,
    you, Stacks, you Teeny, you Stew Ball, you, Bill, you
    Marjorie

Come out from your made walls and out from your sins and
    out from your sick spell and dance to high glory

You pore sick head poet that sung to my woman to stay here in
    these sod walls and laze around sleepy and doze around
    sheepy while your man is the one to go out and see action.
    You jail home poets are dead in my dust. I sing your song
    but I sing it just backwards.

I say to my woman dance out of our home.

Dance out and see fighting.
Dance out and see people.
Dance out to run factories.
Dance out to see street meats.
Dance out in the deep stream.
Dance out to your vote box.
Dance down to your office.
Dance over to your counter.
Dance up your big stairs.

If your husband gets jealous, dance out to new lovers.

If your man keeps your heat tied dance out and untie it.

Dance out to sing equal.
    Dance up and be pretty.
    Dance around and be free.

And if I just had this one thing to say to a husband it would be
  these words

Go dance

That's all

Just jump up and let go and dance

Dance in our own way.
  Sing your own song.
  Whoop your own kind of a yell in the start and in the finish
  of your dance.

Mammy of nature gave birth to you in her body and hills. You
  give birth now to old female mommy nature in the male
  feelings and rivers.

Go dance.
  Both of you.

Go dance.

Woody Guthrie
Aug. 13, 1947
Coney Coney

I'LL MAKE YOUR SOUL HUNGRY

I'm gonna jump out one of these days and tear this place
down.
  If this world hurts me I'll hurt it back.
  If this street tries to choke me down I'll choke this whole
street down.
  Your town tries to poison some parts of me and I'll poison
some parts of your town.
  Treat me wrong and I'll treat your sweetest dream wrong.
  You try to make me hungry and I'll make your soul hungry.
  Tell me you got no job for my hands to do. I'll find ten ways
to make your heart feel like this world don't want your hands.

Woody Guthrie
August 7, 1947

MY MISSING PEOPLE

I heard my radio here today broadcast from police headquarters a report about two people, both of them young girls,
one was 13, one a little older, and they told how these girls
looked, how much they weighed and then he said, that is all.

Two girls. I'll bet you my last bottle dollar that you'll find
more folks than this missing down and over on this lower east
side.

Or try Palestine. Jerusalem. Or try the British Long Gun
Holy Land.

Ask Chiang Kai Check how many he's caused to come up
missing.

Count Franco's hungry and dead prisoners.

August 9, 1947
Coney Island

I watched your black feet scuffle down along my Mermaid
    Avenue sidewalk tonight and a thing come over me and
    said our ten toenails have all been looking glasses full of
    your hurt face watching your hands of ten fingers cut your
    toe nails.
I asked that sidewalk why do people all of your same color
    stand along my curb in the fronts of my little stores and
    wait for my filthiest job at slow money?
I hate this fascist hate that puts you down and keeps you here
    scuffling.

Woody Guthrie
Aug. 16, 1947

MOUNTAIN DANCE GIRL

That girl I saw doing that mountain dance with her boy
friend was pretty enough to set my weeds on fire. Her heels flew
with her legs in the light. Her knee had a quick easy bend to it
which made me jump and swallow spit. There was something
or other in the fly of her skirt that didn't let me see much more
than half of her hips when she whirled on out and past me. Her
face and her hands were turned away from me. I never did really
get to see enough of her to satisfy me. But what little I did see
set my woods on fire.

Woody Guthrie
August 4, 1947

PRIVATE ENTERPRIZE

Arlo Guthrie, 8 wks old, you are sucking your bottle here on my lap good and warm. And we just cashed our Capitol Songs "Oklahoma Hills" check for $1155.56 with which we bought today our little red passion wagon. Marjorie left for town sleepy to teach her class with Pearl Lang down at Martha Graham's studios. All of us are all worked up about our first big ride in our forty six V8 Ford two door. Bubby Greenblatt was down good and early already this morning with her postal savings bonds to lend us. We pay the Mad Russian of Surf Avenue $1711.22½ cents this afternoon and we take off on our big first ride over to New Jersey to buy 20 each of every album I ever did make to pass around as a sample. Well this is my biggest free chunk of enterprize I've got off so far. But you yell your lungs out and tell me that just one suck on your nipple is a bigger private enterprize than our little red Totsy # Two.

Woody Guthrie
August 29, 1947

CLOTHES LINE POLE

There's a long keen soft wood clothes line pole out here in my back yard that holds a pulley and a screw eye and a rope or cord line for about seven families in six different windows. Nobody can't paint the pole because it's not on their property. And the man's place it stands on won't paint it till the other hangers buy him the paint and the brush. This is the funny part of capitalism. Everybody uses it but nobody gives a damn about it.

Woody Guthrie
August 4, 1947

TO F.D.R.

To you, good singer
    man, F.D.R., I tune
    up and plunk off
    this dripple.

I did hear you when you
set down in my old

Every spot the earth at the
    centre of it.
Life is a matter of life or death.
INSIDE FRONT COVER,
1946 CALENDAR BOOK

white house by my
wood fires to make
me your little talks
and little chats.

I could tell by the rings
on your voice that your
wife must have brung
you five or six kids
already.

You talked just like my
blacksmith uncle John
plays his fiddle and
he's done won fifty rough
contests and had his
six or seven kids and died last year.

I say you and my uncle
John's anvil and fiddle are
two things I could go on
and listen to for twenty
more elections.

Woody Guthrie
August 11, 1947
Coney Island

---

*One reason Woody remained loyal to the Communist Party was
that the party remained loyal to him. After the war, for several
months he wrote a regular column in the party's newspaper,*
The Sunday Worker, *about his adventures and imaginings and
attitudes and insights. Their freshness and sense of humor
evoke Will Rogers. It's hard to conceive of anything remotely like
them appearing on any of today's stodgy op-ed pages, left, right
or center.*

ME . . . AND INGRID

The price of a movie, like the price of anything else, is just
too high.

Most every movie, like everything else, is twice as bad as it
ought to be. Every movie, except one or two, tells me not to

worry, the world is okay, wages and prices are where they ought to be, and I'd ought not to commit no crime because it pays too much to the ones already in the racket.

Our lords and owners know that we are disgusted, nervous, restless, and mad about the way they are running our country on the rocks. They shovel wagonloads of our own good money into the mechanical mouth of their movies, papers, record players, operas, plays, and guards, to tell us seven jillion ways you can't see the sun if you're crying how bad things are run.

If you make two words that say, "I Haven't Got A Worry In My Head," or "The World's Okie Dokie It's Just Me That's All Wrong," they will pay you more money than you can carry off in a big sack.

Your two words don't even have to rhyme or make any sense. They will stretch them into songs, plots, dramas, true confessions, detective stories, and run them in serial form to sell stuff with.

If you make up two words that tell something wrong with your life, how to fix it, of course, you are a Communist causing a big depression by giving too many hands a job.

I've been to the movies more this past six months than ever before in my life. I didn't have the money when I was a kid in Oklahoma. I was on the road too much singing Union songs on the West Coast, then I sang all over New York for a year or so and was always too lost to think about movies. I shipped out for eleven months during the war in the Merchant Marine and only seen the movies they showed aboard the troopships. I was in the Army eight months in several camps, and went most every night for fifteen cents to see an eleven cent show. I got discharged and came home, and somehow, kept on going to the movies.

I am married to a dance teacher, Marjorie Guthrie, and she teaches and rehearses at several schools, which causes me lots of waiting, which causes me to drift into lots of show houses. Picture shows, we call them where I come from. I guess you New Yorkers would call them Bergman Houses.

I used to throw an ice pick at a movie list and go to the one it stuck in, till I hit Bergman in *Saratoga Trunk*, then, *Notorious*, then, *Joan of Lorraine*, and one alongside of Bing which I forgot the name of.

I tied a red bandana around my eyes and walked for one hour straight, then going into the Bergman that was nearest where I stood.

One night I found myself in a worse twist than the Republican Congress with no program. I took off my blindfold at 42nd and Broadway and seen her name in lights on four different

If I don't sing when I feel like singing, I go nuts, and I stay that way till I do sing.

movie shows. I counted nine average citizens who had gone into fits of indecision the worst of which, I guess, was me.

You have seen pictures in papers showing jaywalkers getting run down by walking through thick traffic looking whapper-jawed and crooked. Well, both the pedestrian and the driver in several sample cases have confessed that they were looking at Ingrid lights when the wrecks took place. I doubt if things have cleared up much even to date.

Marjorie came in late the other night and told me, "Guess who took Janie's dance class today at the studio. Ingrid Bergman. She's good, too. She has that same way about her movement in a dance class which she has on the screen."

I ran off to a movie to get a breath of night air after a hard day of writing, and caught her with Robert Montgomery in *Rage in Heaven*, where Bob owned a big steel works in England, married Ingrid and fought against his workers' plans to build better houses to live in.

I used to just write Marjorie a note and say, "Am out with Ingrid. Be home soon, I hope."

But the past couple of weeks I write a note and leave it with the ticket box girl and say, "Dear Ingrid. Had to go home to the wife and baby. Hope you can make it without me this time."

Marjorie bought some balcony seats to see Ingrid in *Joan of Lorraine* at the Alvin a couple of weeks back. Our seats were student seats at a student benefit for the Neighborhood Playhouse and you know how far back that is. Our $2.40 seats didn't even get us down close enough to tell male from female. And with everybody wearing sets of robes, drapes, armors, or tights, it tangled me up in Scene I and I never got untangled.

Sam Wanamaker plays her leading man, even if she does most of the leading. Sam plays awful natural, straight, and easy, sounds serious when he tells how the curtains and props had to be bought on the black market, like a 60-cent loaf of bread in Italy or Sicily. He tells how crooks are financing the show and how the head producer is in jail for something like felony or larceny. Or it could be vagrancy, or public nuisances, I forget.

Anyhow, Ingrid wants to make some changes in the play, so that Joan steers her pure and honest path to her goal, her vision of a free France, without taking up with any folks that could be gangsters, robbers, greedy, or just plain forces of evil.

Ingrid plays it with lots of feeling, since she's always wanted to be a poor little girl that fought against greed and taught others how to fight it, also. She yells loud enough to be heard in the two-forty balcony seats, and in the dollar eighties when she gets madder and hotter under the blanket.

Ingrid Bergman is one of the best, I can't doubt that, but I've seen her in oodles and gobs of pictures now, and this one play. And I say she never has had a part that frees her enough to make full use of her gifts and talents.

I doubt if I'll ever see her in any parts as real or as honest as the slum pictures that Sylvia Sidney did a few years back. The movies are sewed up too tight by our bankers these days to fight or to ridicule our landlords. No star the brand of Sylvia Sidney, Greta Garbo, Merle Oberon, Louise Rainier, or Ingrid, is going to be hired by the big lords to speak out against the lords themselves.

When the workers own and control their own movie sets and studios, own their theatres and radios, then we can have real facts of life played and acted for us by artists even more capable, more social conscious, than the ones we've got now.

So, folks, just don't get downhearted about the way our best minds and talents are misused and splattered around. Better shows are coming. A few are here already in the littler houses.

The social system to replace the sour black market setup we've got will cause a finer use to be made of finer, clearer minds.

—*Sunday Worker*
January 12, 1947

THE BOWERY AND ME

I walked along the Bowery the other night looking for a room. I flew back from singing at an AYD affair in Cleveland, had money in my clothes, as the feller says. Didn't have to sleep along the Bowery. I had enough legal tender to sleep outside on any other avenue I wanted to. But I got my start down along that Bowery, and just every so often I get the old feeling to go back down there and to test the results of the latest election.

I started on Third Ave., really, 125 St. and Third Ave. I knew where most of the flop joints were, because my name had been inked down in all of their registers. I can tell more about any city or town by walking down its Bowery or Skid Row than I can learn in any other way. I've walked along Lower Pike in Seattle, California Ave. in Oklahoma City, Congress St. in Dallas, Fifth and Main in Los Angeles, Ave. J in Sacramento, South St. in Philadelphia, the Skid streets of Chicago and several others just as crummy in Duluth, Milwaukee, Akron, Cleveland, Toronto, Phoenix, Baltimore and several dozen ratty roads of New York City mighty nearly as filthy and wild as the Bowery proper.

"I'm full up an' I stay full up. No beds," the first clerk told me as he shaved in an old shot-looking glass with his suspenders hung down and his winter underwear open at the neck. "Try furth'r down." I took a good look around at the firetrap floors, walls, ceilings and thought how quick one little cigaret stub or loose match could turn this stinky hole into a lost bed of homeless ashes. As I walked down the stairs I could smell the stinks and whangs in my mouth and my nose of spit, spittle, puke and the contents of stomachs, bowels, bladders and kidneys soaked so far and so deep into the wood that the creosote and lye powders, the floor oils and floor sweeps don't even dent nor weaken these tastes and smells.

A few blocks down I walked up another stairway that made my teeth grit and my eyes water. It was a worse deathtrap than the other one, even if it never does burn down, just living in it is like being dead. I didn't get the name of this place. But I did notice that it had some high fancy name, like most of the others along the Bowery have got. I saw names like:

The Royal Peacock, the King's Ransom, Queen Paradise, the White Carnation, Golden Era, the Emancipation, Happy Hearth, the Red Camelia, the Gay Fireside, Welcome Rooms, the Liberty, the Victory, the Little Flower of the Revolution, the Virgin's Chambers, Pink Elephant, the Bunny Rabbit.

I have never heard such a parade of high-sounding names for these traps and dens of thousands of beds, with thousands on top of thousands, and more on top of them. The neon lights were so costly and so bright they hurt my eyes while I walked up and down several more stairs asking, looking, smelling, tasting, listening, touching, and then walking back onto the sidewalks again to shake and shiver to the rumbles of that big elevated railway that runs along old slippery, slickety, dirty, spitty Third Ave.

I walked past dreary blocks of buildings so old, so rotten, so rickety and so dangerous that I wanted to grab me a bucket of waterpaste and a brush and smear good union fighting posters, handbills, programs, and showbills all over every fence, window and wall. I watched long lines of folks stand with their money ready to buy tickets into movies with titles like: *The Lizard's Curse, The Mummy's Lover, The Riders of the Six Gun Canyon, Roaring Knives, Mystic Gurgles, The Ghost of Skalderblatz, The Green Eye at the Purple Window, The Slung Gun, Suspicious, Fictitious, Lads of Courage* (43d installment), *The Green Evil of the Grey Mansion, Murder on the Tar Roof, Corpses Last Kiss.* (Last three special selected for your child Saturday morning at 11:26. First two kids receive free skeleton with hatchet and bomb.) Ten cartoons picked out to end your child's worries.

I could not remain sane and recall each picture and cartoon by it's rightful name. I told several ladies in a bunch drinking seltzer water, "Take y'r kids an' statch 'em at th' morgue. They'll come out healthier." One lady twice my size in a black coat told me, "This'z th' only child care cent'r we got aroun' hyere. Th' movies on Saturday mornin'."

It seemed like to me the Bowery got rougher and tougher the farther on down toward the City Hall I walked. I remembered standing in Washington, D.C., and hearing a union lady tell me, "Here you see the greenest and the barest trees, the nicest flowers and the stinkiest yards, the finest marble buildings and the sorriest slum holes, all within two blocks of one another."

I walked on and thought to myself this Bowery here is the very pulse and heartbeat of New York City and of New York State. I can see millions of faces of every color here in this grimiest of all hellholes. Where are the women to match with these hundreds and thousands of lost and stranded men? Somewhere, somehow, there is a woman for this man, that man, that one over there who fell down on his face in that tile doorway. This man astride this brass fire hydrant passed out with blind spasms is a son, a daddy, an uncle, and a sweetheart, a lover of somebody some place or the other.

WHO ARE THE MEN?
WHERE DID THEY COME FROM?

And these five men fighting over that bottle of cheap water vino, they look purple and a pasty muddy color with these neon lights hitting down on their faces. Who are they? Where are they at home? What whispered word in which padded office took these men's money and herded them down here to lose all sense of hope, plan and reason? Sober these nine up, give them a room with a tile clean shower, and an x-ray, a good medical going over, and they would take root and leaf out toward the lights of the sky again.

These in this big crowd here watching this fist fight. Their faces ought to be on every movie screen there is, and their voices ought to be in every song and ballad spun and sung. Women grab their men out from the mob. A little boy in raggedy knee pants leads his GI brother out of the crowd and across the street under the train's wheels.

I stopped into an eat joint right next door nearly to the famous Bowery Follies. Take the worst tables out of your trash piles and city dumps, take your dirtiest tubs, buckets, troughs, feed bins, mangers, out from your sickliest, slimiest horsebarn in this or any other state. Grab up those rottenest, buggiest, flee-bittenest, germiest chairs from along your most corruption and spit-smeared concretes and pavements, set them inside the four oldest and puckiest walls that you can find in Europe, Asia, Africa, North or South America, scatter the chairs and tables full of vets, soldiers, sailors, people in slimy pants, shirts, coats and sweaters, heads covered with old sweaty oil-soaked hats, and pick your silverware and dishes to match, then go somewhere over past the backhouse alleys of the Land of Nod and take a dozen or so of the worst cripples, put aprons on them, and you've got this place with the blue-chipped walls, and no partitions that I sat down to eat in.

No partitions. I could see from the cash register back to the kitchen cookstove and storage boxes. I ordered 50 cents worth of chicken. The man went into the storage box, then heated my frozen chicken in a skillet, and carried it to me before it even heated warm through and through. I bit into it and when my teeth struck against that warm outer side and that ice-cold meat around the bone, well, I gave up the ship.

My belly is like iron. I've rode a thousand freights, I've hitched ten thousand trucks and cars, and I've crossed this continent several times the hard and hungry route. I waited on gunnerboy's tables, 50 at a meal, in the Merchant Marines. I've slept in a hundred jails overnight and eaten in that many more. I've slopped at the flop where the mission bells stop and floundered the scurvy dime. I've beat my teeth on the rocky reef and skippered the blue canoe. I've sniffed at the latch in the brushy patch and shivered the cindery rails.

But this little blue wall eating place with the big white chalk marks all over the plate glass outside, well, friend, I hate to admit it. I always prided myself on having a stomach that I could just throw any old thing down into it and forget about it, like circus glass eaters you've seen. Well. Out I come. I made my way to the curb, but didn't heave the old ho. I held it. My thoughts still stink from eating that meal. I mean that few nibbles.

I walked in at the door of the Bowery Follies before it was time for the Folls to crank up. I saw one man in an old derby and a false handlebar moustache, some silvery-haired mothers on the bandstand, a fellow with a banjo, a lady tuning her fiddle, somebody whanging a piano keyboard. I walked around the walls reading foneyfied quips, blurbs, blabs, and blarnies written by those lofty minds of the press who see the old Bowery somewhat different than I know it.

I didn't get far till a white apron with a man somewhere in it told me not to hold my nose so close to his clippings and photos. He shoved me back over to the stag line by the bar where I usually would of, but I didn't, buy myself no black rum. I didn't want no coin of my realm being spent to buy silly blurbs in blind papers about these several million souls out along this Bowery that the Democrats and Republicans and the other black market fascists have put there. I called my wife on the Follies Fone and she let me sing a little song in Cathy's ear. I made it up. It went:

> Since I seen the difference 'tween
>   rich an' poor,
> I can't feel at home on this Bow'ry
>   no more.

Oh, but as I looked through that glass there on the fone booth, I could see the gay lads and ladies from the outer and upper streets taking their honored seats to laugh and joke, to josh and to tease the millions of nervous wrecks caused by their own blind, sad and silly greed. I feel like writing 10 books and 100 People's Songs about the Bowery I know.

—*Daily Worker*
January 26, 1947

WANDERING SINGER EXPLAINS THE MEANING OF HIS JAZZ

Busting around this country as much as I have, you hear a lot of good music and some of the best is jazz.

Most jazz tunes tell a story about me and my troubles. It's the way my house and my street and my fields looks to me through my eyes when I get troubles. My story can be six verses long and all about one little chunk of leather. Or it can be 16 verses all broken apart and jump around all over.

I can't vote and I know it. I can't live in no good house and I know that. The worst jobs and your dirtiest and heaviest work is all I get. Not much money to buy good clothes, nor no good

house. Whiskey is neutral spirits, rot gut, boose leg, hot shut, king korn, lye can stuff, red label cheap or its no label at all.

My board wall is rotten and nailed over with a rusty tin baked enamel sign, GGG, fever tonic, malaria pills, liver and kidney pills. Tooth powders, hair dye color come back. Chewing tobacco, plug, scrap, and dry hand leaf. Three, four and six point snuff. Headache powders.

Pepsey, Cokey Coler, Doctors Pepper, lemon sodie, red cherry fizzle waters. Big baked tin signs that cost me twice as much every year as my shack house ever did cost. Tin signs to cure you.

Hundred Little Signs

Malaria, fever, running chills. Oozey sweats, fits, spasms, blind staggers, epileptic, the syph. And brass knuckles and billy sticks out to keep me here in my lonesome old hole. I gotta do something. Do it quick. Can't speak nor sing nor work up to your good job. Why try? Do which?

I see a hundred little cardboard signs every day or so here on these walls of my barrel house: No singing. No dancing. No loud talk. No credit. No kids wanted. No hands needed. No rooms empty. No dark skin allowed and no light skin allowed.

I break out every minute in a cold bath of hot, easy sweat. I see this world like a child and like a cold fever. I walk my floor half scared out of my skin. I live crazy. This world is run crazy. It's a world with a drunk driver.

I grab my brass horn because it's all I got left. I grab my piano keys because I don't know what else I can grab. My slickety oiled drum stick I grab onto just to keep from busting out hog wild and maybe hurting you or somebody else.

I grab my lamb gut bull fiddle strings the same way. I grab for the handle of my guitar. I take a tight fanning hold on my little old mouth organ, because I learnt long time ago how to make it do my talking for me.

You pounded my eyes with your old dead sand. You leveled my ear full of tough sealy wax. My mouth you pour every day full of hot tar. My nose you scattered full of tickle feathers. My skin you laid your buckskin leather strap onto. You laid your lead-loaded sap up against my head and my folk's head.

Got to Fight

I got to fight back. Don't want to fight back. But you make me have to fight back.

I grab my saxifone and snag onto my clarinet.

I grab hold on my greasy strong banjer, grab my blow jug same way. Grab onto my rattling bones, my tinkling spoons, my rosin up broom handle.

My music box says what you tell me I can't say. I see you prick up your ear and listen. You don't quite know, do you, just what my jazzified oil rod music is saying to all of my other folks you got lawed up and hobbled down? No, you might hear my signal house so very plain.

I'm breaking those web laws you got spun all around my naked hide. I'm breaking my way out to the clear light of day to when I do talk and I do sing, to where I do vote and I do walk and I do dress myself up to where I look lots prettier than you want me to look.

My jazz song is my war song. My shuffle is my war march. My song is my fighting song. Every reed and every note I blow is my war tune and my fighting story. My singing, dancing tree of history.

Call it jazz. Call it rumba or samba. Or polka. Or the blues. Or your ragtime or your jittery swing stuff. It's all from me to you. I blowed every drop of it out of my old horn and strings so's you could answer me back and help me get myself out of the sickliest and biggest jail you ever saw.

Busting out. This is what I mean when you hear my jazz.

—Daily Worker
August 15, 1947

Moe Asch, head of Folkways Records, could be irascible, parsimonious, and doctrinaire, but he believed strongly in Woody's abilities. Although he never paid Woody much money, he did a great deal to preserve his songs and the sound of his voice.

Woody more than repaid the debt, even going so far as to write the laudatory reviews of Asch albums included here. (Disc Company of America and Asch were sister labels of Folkways.) He also clearly regarded Moe Asch as an important political comrade, often writing him about political issues of the day (as well as continually dunning and importuning him for funds).

Asch also commissioned Woody to do a variety of projects, ranging from the songbook, American Folk Song *(from which "Leadbelly is a hard name . . ." derives) to the Sacco and Vanzetti songs, the notes and manuscript lyrics for some of which we've also included.*

July 15, 1946
CINYC

Disc Company of America,
Dear Everybody:
Dear Moe:

I have been doing a good bit of thinking all along about the whole business of folk songs, and ballads. I thought several years about it before I ever met up with Burl Ives, Josh White, Dick Bennet, Alan Lomax, Peter Seeger, Aunt

Molly Jackson, Huddie Ledbetter, Sarah Ogun, or Jim Garland, or anybody else.

There are all kinds of different positions you could take on this subject, I mean ranging from pure reaction to pure union; from purest capitalist uses, to the uses, we will say, that fight for socialism. I have always taken the side that I thought would help the workers in the lowest places to know their real fighting history, and to be proud to take their place, each in his own part of the fight. I have alway said in my songs and ballads that this old world is a fight from the cradle to the grave. I have never sung nor made songs just to entertain the upper classes, but to curse their clawing, reckless racketeers, and to warn the nervous ones that live and die by greed.

Not all of us folk and ballad makers and singers stand where I stand. Not all of them see the world as I see it. Some would rather be a "character" and to be fotographed and filmed, broadcast and recorded, and paid big money by the big money side. They would rather occupy a certain social position, to be well known, to play the game of publicity gangsters, and to enjoy the crowds that clap and yell when you tell them directly or indirectly that this old world is okie dokie, she is all right, she is a nice good place to live on, and if you kick or argue, or make too much noise with your mouth, then you are just a native bornkicker, and a griper, and you are kicked out by your own inability to "cooperate" with the high moguls.

If your work gets to be labelled as communist or even as communistic or even as radically leaning in the general direction of boleshevism, then, of course, you are black balled, black listed, chalked up as a revolutionary bomb thrower, and you invite the whole weight of the capitalist machine to be thrown against you. I know that there are thousands of office holders, and just ordinary workers, trade union leaders and members by the potential millions that are branded already by the capitalist investigators as "communistic." Lord knows, even PM and Eleanor Roosevelt, even FDR, himself, are all branded by the experts of the capitalist machine as "communistic." I have decided, long ago, that my songs and ballads would not get the hugs and kisses of the capitalistic "experts," simply because I believe that the real folk history of this country finds its center and its hub in the fight of the union members against the hired gun thugs of the big owners. It is for this reason I have never really, sincerely, expected nor dimly prayed, nor hoped for a single solitary minute for a penny's worth of help from the hand of our landlord and ruler.

I can't help wondering about the strange love affair and all the warm friendships that arise between our big owners and a man, we will say, like Josh White. And when I see this same back patting and hair rubbing going on now between the bosses and Burl Ives, I find my curiosity growing faster than the weeds here in my back yard.

I know very well that the big ducks that hire the squads of gun thugs to fight union men and women, meet every day to decide on the latest amount which they can spend to put their enemies out of commission. In any war, both sides have got an actual price set on every soldier, just how much they can afford to spend to knock an enemy soldier out of the picture. The prices range from so much to a higher amount, all depending on the rank and station of the soldier, his popularity, following, and his standing, etc. etc. Our landlords and owners pay almost these same rates to their hired soldiers to knock off, in one way or another, the fighters over on the union side, the members and leaders of the trade unions.

To the big owners, an artist of any note or fame, that can be said to work or fight over on the union side, is classed by the big boys as a soldier, a technical, or an artistic captain or a general. The money paid to clip off working class artists may start at a measley Ten or Fifteen Thousand, and run up very quick to the sum of, A Hundred, Two Hundred Thousand, or a Half a Million long greens. (This is no money at all to the big handlers that toss bales of money back and forth across their tables to the tune of a Million, a Billion, or more, Dollars).

It is not only a question of buying you and your art out of circulation, to keep you from stirring up your people against their blind owners; it is, lots of times a question of blocking your hand on every side, or causing you to get all lost and tangled up in a thousand traps of their psychological, emotional, economical, legal and illegal sorts of personal warfare. This will take the forms of bribery, social disgrace, exposes, running down your work, discouraging your talents, and insulting you on every turn. This sort of work is carried on, we all know good and well, by the plain clothes "experts," the snooping keyhole "investigators," and detectives of a dozen sorts that telegraph every move you make to the big polished office of the high muck. They pay more money in just sniping at you from every door and window than it

Dick Flyer Dyer Bennett...
Are you raping and killing all of my folk songs or just sprinkling them full of seeds to grow on?

Frank Warner...
Your songs fill up my Hudson River Valley and overspill out acrost my gold hill deserts to my old Sacramento. My wife likes these songs you play and sing in the ways you play and sing them. There's a good touch of put-on about you, but it's warm as soup in my bowl and I like it.

Aunt Molly Jackson...
If they got a more American woman than old Aunt Molly Jackson from Harlan County Kentucky I ain't seen her yet.

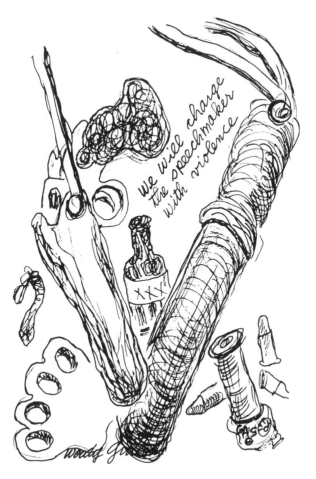

would cost to put all of your children through the finest marble schools and colleges in the world. (Else, how could some hands ever earn enough money to lose by the bales across gambling tables, at the races, and in a thousand and one shady ways in night clubs, hotels, mountain lodges, and hideaways?) The only reason why capitalism can never feed nor put shoes on all of its workers is because it must take out from your pay the billions and trillions of dollars it takes to hire experts to eavesdrop, to spy, to trail after you, and to send in fone calls, telegrams, and written letters that follow half of us around (unknown to us) all of the days of our lives.

It is not just a question of you, as an artist, selling out, and becoming harmless to the owning side. No, you are never actually bought nor bribed till they have decided that they can use you in one way or another to rob, to deceive, to blind, confuse, to misrepresent, or just to harass, worry, bedevil, and becloud the path of the militant worker on his long hard fight from slavery to freedom. Your art helps to preserve, to prolong, to keep alive, and to glorify the essences and the principles of the owning, ruling side. If your art did not add new life to their side, kid not yourself, they would certainly never shake your hand and drop their bloody money down into your lap. And it is the highest form of your owner's joy when he buys you out from the union side, [where you] have spent several years of your life getting people to follow, to hear, or to stand for a while and listen to what you have to say, or to live their lives in spirit and in action in the way that you lived your own. This makes you worth lots more to your owner. But no matter how much he actually pays into your hand, you never get more than a small fraction of what you are worth to him, because he must pay a long line of dicks, guards, deputies, plain clothes men, snoops and stooges, snipers and fonies, that played their parts in rendering you completely harmless, and so, another weapon against the workers and their union.

And we mustn't dope ourselves into thinking that the battle is any less than all of this. All of these things are true about you, no matter if you never came within a mile of a union fight in your life, nor even spoke a word on any side of any argument. The spies are right on the same old spots reporting just as expensively about the ones who are not revolutionarists, because there is always the old fear that you are a revolutionist of the wisest and slyest sort when you keep quiet. This is the bad part of a capitalist system, this dog eat dog, this spying, tracing, tracking and trailing after one another always under the covers of night and the shades and shadows of day. It is all of this spying on each other that causes the newspapers to be full of killings, murders, rapes, robbings, divorces, shootings, stabbings, and every known kind of disease, decay, rot, and degeneracy. This is the system which the owners would like to prolong, to keep alive, to prolong as long as they possibly can, because in the wild blindness of it all, they get all of us to fighting against one another, and rob us coming in the fields of production, and going, in the realms of distribution. This is the system I would like to see die out. It killed several members of my family, it gassed several and shell shocked several more in the last world war, and in this world war just past, it scattered lots more. It drove families of my relatives and friends by the hundreds of thousands to wander more homeless than dogs and to live less welcome than hogs, sheep, or cattle.

Josh White . . .

I met and drunk down Josh White a few times. And I say this with one finger pointed in Josh's face.

Josh, you know how to act the big shoe over in the campling fires of your enemy. But don't forget how us folks are back here where you come from.

I want me a fast hammer new model Cadillac just like your new Buick.

Burl Ives . . .

You got awful tired of singing around with no folding stuff to make your woman snap open and shut. So did I, Burl.

I want some folding fodder in my long old empty.

Josh White . . .

I really get a kick out of a hearing Joshua White beat the fool out of that fiddle of his—he can play that son of a gun more ways than Martin Dies can hijack you on a credit. Josh don't ever know which key he's a playing in. But you start out a singing and old Josh starts a winding up them keys and he don't let you get but about one note head start on him till he's done tuned up and caught up with you and played your vamps and introduction twice while you was catching your breath and then you can't lose him and they ain't worse to try. Joshua is about the best I ever heard I believe.

This is the system I started out to expose by every conceivable way that I could think of with songs and with ballads, and even with poems, stories, newspaper articles, even by humor, by fun, by nonsense, ridicule and by any other way that I could lay hold on.

I am not sure that Josh White had any such a plan in his mind when he put away his boxing gloves for his guitar. I am not sure what Burl Ives had in his head.

I could not say what sort of an overall thought that Richard Dyer Bennett had in his mind when he decided to tune up his lute and make a living singing folk ballads. I know that all three of these ballad singers have sung for radical rallies and meetings, entertained in homes for left wing causes, sang at cocktail parties where the cause was a revolutionary one, and have performed many times among trade union people for the reasons of building the union stronger. It is going to be lots of fun now to keep an eye on these three sons and observe how they grow or rot away.

Lee Hays as Caesar, undated drawing, ca. 1941–42.

I think that I have proved that a folk singer, to sing best what the people have thought and are thinking, is forced to turn his back on the bids of Broadway and Hollywood to buy him and his talents out. I feel like my work in this field will someday be seen as the most radical, the most militant, and the most topical of them all. After me, in this vein, comes Aunt Molly Jackson or Sarah Ogan, then Jim Garland, and then Peter Seeger, Lee Hays, Bernie Asbel, and the whole run of artists at Peoples Songs. Peoples Songs are on the very verge of becoming more of a mass (workers) movement than all of Hollywood, Bdwy., and the Nation-wide radio nets (records and broadcasts) combined. Peoples Songs is the organization which the big boys (owners) cannot buy, and cannot bribe, and so must draw a bead and fight them straight across. And this is what we must make the owners do, draw their sights on us and fight us for all they are worth. It will be in the fight of their own starting that their own artists and workers and soldiers will desert them and come over onto the Peoples side by the droves and by the herds. And you must not ever fall into the mistake of believing that the big boys can ruin or "hurt" or "wreck" the folk field, because the more outrightly bloody they become the faster their warriors will desert from their side to our side. Most of their fighters are not solidly convinced as you might believe, and the moment it draws to a clear cut battle in words or votes or with bullets, then is the time when (as in all other revolutions), the rich are sadly and sorely surprised to see their hired ones pack up and come over onto the side that every child knows is the right side. This is why I am not scared to see the big fight coming closer, because once it gets underway, it will clear away the fogs of nervous waiting, and ninety per cent of the psychological tomfooleries will clear away.

You might think I'm stretching the sock too far to the east by starting to talk about folk singers and ballad singers, then dragging in all of this rigamarole about a door to door fight around the world. But, this just goes to prove that this same fight can start anywhere and it will always come around to this same big battle. Everything is a part of the conflict between the boss man and the work hand. The work hand can't ever hope to get its fair and honest share of the good things it turns out by its works, because the boss (owner) dishes out over half of the good things (the best half, too) into the pockets of his hired goons and thugs and onto the tables of his guards and protectors. He must support and

Earl Robinson . . .

If a lot of people didn't know me I wouldn't walk nine blocks to hear you sing your head off. If a lot of people didn't know you, you'd not ride two feet to hear me knock my teeth and tonsils out. If a lot of people didn't know both of us, we never would smile like we do and shake hands in front or in back of a camera. If so many folks didn't know both of us, we never would have met up in that first place. But man to man I like you. You got the sounds of lots of people' troubles way back somewhere in your eyes.

keep his snoopers and sluggers in a wild, neurotic kind of cocktailish big shot set ups, the neon lit kind of a life that you hear and see all around you, and wonder who hires and pays for it. Any kind of art, entertainment, theatre, book, or a song that keeps his own lost army thinking that their world is the real world, and, at the same time, will confuse and screw up the minds and hands of the workers, the owner will pay tubs, buckets, bales, and shovels full of money for. He absolutely must, must, and must, hire loophole robbers and stealers of a thousand shades to get this money by hookery and crookery out from the pocket of the worker. This is why the owner claims that all of us, as workers, business people, owe some kind of a ghosty Public Debt which amounts to billions of dollars, or thousands of dollars for every one of us. To hear our owner tell it, I am several thousand thousand dollars in debt to my own self. And so are you. Everybody owes his own self a pile of dollar bills six foot deep. This is the mess that our country is in. If you can see any way out of the racket system, well, you've got lots clearer eyes than I've got. And, this is the world that the owner will pay me handfulls of money to sing about and tell my people that it is okay, all right, hunky dorie, fine and dandy, that it will all work out if we will just keep our mouths and brains quiet and let the lord and the boss and the owner work it out around a banquet table with soft music and waving hips in the background and somebody crooning in a dead sort of a voice into a mike and a loud speaker padded and lined with drapes and curtains. Every folk song that I know tells how to fix something in this world to make it better, tells what is wrong with it, and what we've got to do to fix it better. If the song does not do this, then, it is no more of a folk song than I am a movie scout.

When you ask yourself which of the so called folk singers live up to the real name, you can cross lots of their names entirely off of your list. Other names you could put lower down on your list. Lots of names you've never heard would have to be first and second on your list.

Ask yourself, does the singer, (artist or poet), take part in the fight to win a better world for the worker? There is only one big fight with a million and one legs to it, the fight of the worker to win his fair share from his owner (boss, etc.). The more the owners allow a singer to be heard around, the less he can sing the tale of the worker's fight. Before your voice can be heard or your face fotographed, you must actually turn into a weapon of the owner against the worker. I know from a hundred cases of my own experience that any work of protest, fight, militance, or plan for the worker, was blue pencilled and censored a dozen times. Any word that was too true, too strong, or too loud in criticizing the world owned by the big boss was scratched out by several hands under a thousand reasons.

If you play any part in getting money from the worker and giving it over to the owner, then you are an upright and true citizen. But if you play any part in getting money from the owner and giving it over to the worker, of course, the loud speakers and printed pages yell and scream that you are a wild man running loose with a pocket full of atom bombs and a head full of communist ideas. Your owner will throw all of his bad books at you if you sing your song to cause the worker to go down and organize his soul into the fight for better trade unions. The price on your head is then, not only just the sum set aside to destroy some one single enemy, but a sum sort of equal to the price of several workers. This is all because you are causing the workers to band together and to talk, think, plan, and fight together. It is when you do this that your owner starts losing in the battle. He loses because in the long hard run, the owners commence to get nervous and they have got a way of eating one another's bellies out. The workers, not so greedy as the big owners, are calmer, have got more guts and energy, and their thoughts melt and run and stick together, and the longer and harder the fight lasts, the stronger and the calmer they get to be. This is why the workers always win out on top when things come to a real head.

Yes, we are going to have lots of fun watching the poets and the artists and the players, dancers, and the singers come up from the ranks of the workers and drift over onto the side of the owners, one by one, ten by ten, and then some more, and then some more. It is going to be educational and entertaining to see how soon most all of them forget what they fought for, stood for, for their long and weary days down on the fighting bottom. I am keeping my eyes open and my ears, and my mouth, just to see what twists and turns, what shapes and forms, the works of Josh White, Burl Ives, Richard Dyer Bennett, and others and others will take. I have already watched and seen several dozens walk up the money plank and turn to an oily pile of rope. It is going to be an education to watch the militant works of Earl Robinson, and the others in his same vein.

Woody Guthrie
7-15-1946
CINYC

Blind Sonny Terry . . .

Blind Sonny Terry is a people's artist, having, in these days, that is, in this particular stage of our history, a very deep and sensitive human knowledge of how the heart of the world beats.

Southern landlordism and poll taxism has barred him from taking his full part in the running of the mills, shops, ships, and railroads, and have locked him out from all kinds of jobs, except porter, janitor, shine boy, and the likes, and so when a mill whistle blows, a train whistles down the line, it sounds so alive and full of power that 16 million Negroes' minds see great pictures and hear great music in the common every-day things that man has built, but, so far, not all men have been able to make use of or enjoy.

Sonny Terry has got to be explained to the people or his art will go over their head.

And in understanding Sonny Terry, you will learn how to enjoy and live in the real people's music that is on a train that's bound for glory.

July 10, 1947

Disc Company of America

I am playing your Disc album tonight of modern piano compositions by Alan Hovaness and John Cage, played by Maro Ajemian and Alan Hovaness, with David Stone Martin's fine ink drawing on the outside cover.

I've been around at several dance gatherings and musical houseparties here in New York City where I heard John Cage overhaul the family piano in his own way and play some of his choked down odd and unusual kinds of things. I've heard him work with [a] roomful of tomtommers and drummers on first one stage and then the other one, and not only did I feel that this sort of piano music was really a keen fresh breeze, but a welcome thing in the way of a healthy change from the old ways you hear the average piano played.

I remember when I was a kid, I used my grandma's piano, a Price & Deeple, upright, to storm myself up all kinds of wars, fogs, storms, battles, courtings, growings, and love affairs. I sat by the hour and passed my time doing this, and got the idea at this early age that there was no end to these kinds of inventive things that a piano can do to the right touch of the proper hand. This must be why I hear what I hear here playing your album #875. I know I have heard lots of these same sounds coming through the world in the way I've come. Even while I took my walks and visits through North Africa, Sicily, and parts of Mexico, I thought I heard sounds that you didn't hear played on the average home or joint or tavern or church or stage piano. I think that John Cage and Alan Hovaness have caught and handed over to us a whole forest and desert mountain full of these fine things that would be looked down on or looked over in bashful weakness by ninety nine out of a hundred second raters in every window.

Your daily friend,
Woody Guthrie

I need something like this oddstriking Hovaness and Cage music to match the things I feel in my soul tonight, anyhow. Marjorie gave birth this morning at 10:10, July the Tenth, to a big seven pound baby boy over in the third ward of the Brooklyn Jewish Hospital where Classon crosses Prospect Avenue. So let me say my thanks one more time to you, Maro, and to you, Alan, for recording up and down for me all

of this virgin unsettled and wild wide open sounding dancy
music there on the keys of your big piano.

———— ————

Whether these are rejected, lost, or forgotten liner notes, a review
intended for who knows what publication, or just late night
ravings Woody summoned as he listened to music he loved and
found himself inspired to prose poesy, no one will ever know.
They were found in one of the files Moe Asch's family sent to the
Smithsonian Institution after Asch's death. But "Blues" is
nonetheless intriguing as Woody's personal assessment of Amer-
ica's foremost form of folk music.

BLUES

Josh White. Jack Dupree. Mary Lou Willliams.
Nora Lee King. Sonny Terry. Woody Guthrie.

Asch Records

It's the shape of the world all around you that causes
your blues. And your blues is caused by some things you
want and can't have. You hear your own music inside your
own self, and, so long as our world is run just for the profits
of a few rich families, you are going to keep on seeing plenty
of sights all around you that make you feel blue.

And you're going to hear lots of other people singing
your blues right along with you. The blues is the voice of the
finger that points to your world and shows you what's wrong,
shows you how to get together and fix it.

You will have the "No Vote Blues." You will have the "No
Money Blues." You'll feel the "High Price Blues," "No Job
Blues," "Jim Crow Blues," "Nursery School Blues," "Mean
Old Landlord Blues," "Black Market Blues," "Empty Belly
Blues," "Empty Bed Blues," "Lonesome Cold Pillow Blues,"
"Holey Shoe Blues," "Last Bottom Dollar Blues," "Long Lost
Highway Blues," as well as the "Child Delinquency Blues,"
"Venereal Disease Blues," "No Education Blues," "Ku Klux
Klan & Association of Manufacturers Blues," along with the
"Low Wages Blues," "Empty Cupboard Blues," "Buggy Old
Rotten House Blues," "Gangster Blues," "Outlaw Blues,"
"Juvenile Court Blues," "Reformatory and Prison Blues,"
"Ratty Jail House Blues," "No Lover Blues," "No Sweetheart

Blues," the "Wrecked Life Blues," "Too Much Whiskey Blues," "Sharecropper Blues," "Chain Gang Blues," and a lot of other blues caused by the Profit Grabbers.

Yes. It's the Profit Worshipper's fault, your Blues. But it's your own fault, too, because you didn't fight and work hard enough to beat him. The Blues is all right to have. Your Blues shines a big spotlight on your enemy and shows you all of the mess of trouble that he has caused by robbing you. You are in a fight and the blues is a weapon that you use to tell your people what all is wrong. This is why your own kind of music is a real deadly weapon. It gives you the chance to speak your mind, blow your top, flip your lid, shoot off at your mouth, and to sing into music the words of the fight that's going on in your mind. Your enemy is going to try to drown your music out with his own brand of music which says, "Oh, everything's hunky dorey!" "Everything's fine!" "Don't Worry!" "I got you. You got me." "I'm ragged and hungry, can't vote, can't get money, can't live one tenth of the life I know I ought to, but I Ain't complainin'! I'm happy! I got my road! I got my hill! My tree! Grass! My sky! I Don't Want To Fight No Racketeer! I'm Fine! Lonesome, empty, miserable, starving, in debt, beat down, held down, walked on, stepped on, but fine! I feel fine!" (This is the title of the song that your enemy would like for you to sing). His radio stations blow and blare out this song of crap and manure twenty four hours out of every day, yes, trying to beat it into your head that everything's fine, fine.

But you've still got your Blues. You haven't lost them yet. You haven't cured them, and you haven't eased them. Your blues rolls around in you like the seven seas, and your tunes and words blow in like the four winds, and you hear in the dark alleys, slums, ratting buildings, rotten fields, you hear your own Blues coming on and coming on.

Wall Street didn't do anything to cure your blues, and neither did our Two Hundred Families that own the Forty Eight States. Neither did the Republicans, Hoover, nor Dewey, nor their fascist friends, Fish, McClean, Lindbergh, Martin Dies, John L. Lewis, Westbrook Pegler, Franco, Mussolini, Horoshito, nor Hitler. They laugh at you and your blues. They tell you that several millions of us are supposed to live like dogs in a scum hole, and not sing any blues, not to complain about it, and not to join no union, because we're not, by the laws of Nature, really supposed to think in our heads, feel in our hearts, see with our eyes, hear in our ears, march with our feet, nor work with our hands, nor even to

FOLK AND POP

A folk song tells a story that really did happen. A pop tune tells a yarn that didn't really take place.

—AUGUST 8, 1947, CONEY ISLAND

speak with our mouthes, nor to vote with our brains. Yes. Your song inside you tells you to get together and not stop fighting till you get all of these things done. Don't you suppose that this is why the big boys make fun of the fighting music that goes on inside your heart? It's your thoughts. Your hopes, ambitions, hurts, hopes, and visions, and they laugh at you, because they don't value all of these things of yours, no, not even one red solitary cent. And so, we, several millions of us, Oriental, Occidental, and Accidental, should just keep plodding along on our bloody feet, not hearing our own minds, not thinking our own thoughts, not singing our own songs, not playing our own music, but to waste our time away with our ears stuck into some puny, spineless, yellow bellied, radio or movie house. It's not our own song, not our own dance, not our own dream, not our own aspiration, not our own long and lonesome blues, even. Nothing there is ours. Once in a blue moon a little flicker flashes onto the screen or a little sound leaks out over the air waves, but only once in a century's plant's tenth blooming. We want to see our lives flashed in our homes, schools, nurseries, colleges, parks, libraries, depots, art galleries, saloons, and in our halls of the arts and the sciences. Don't you suppose this is really why we're fighting this war? To bring an end to the imitation world and to build up one that we can look at and sing about, and say "It's ours. Mine. Yours."

These are simple thoughts. So simple, in a way, that I almost blush when I write them down. But, I am listening to an album of records which is just called, "Blues," put out by the Asch Record Company, and as I hear Josh White sing a couple of his very best blues songs, I let my mind ramble all around the world, and I suppose that every country and every nation, too, is singing the "Liberation Blues," the "Freedom Blues," "Hard Work Blues," "The Anti Jim Crow Blues," the "Dead and Gone Facist Blues."

JOSH IS REALLY SINGING the "Careless Love Blues," but, I don't know, somehow I see a lot more than that as I listen. I guess I see a couple of million teen age girls, some under twelve years of age, waiting along a street, an alley, a long boardwalk beside the ocean, for a soldier, a sailor, a catch of any kind. Maybe I see a couple or three million faces that would like to get married and live sort of in a home, but high prices, no money, won't let them. I could be seeing ten or twenty or fifty million people in homes that aren't happy, and never can be happy, never can be normal, never can be natural, never can taste nor feel love, nor labor, as it ought to be. I see whorehouses, diseases, pickpockets, rollers, petty thieving of all sorts, and blackmail and graft, and crooked politicians all lost somewhere in the whirlpool of Reckless Love. I don't know what Josh is thinking about as he plays and sings, but I do know that it is on this same order. I saw his picture not long ago in the paper, and he was going around from door to door getting people to vote for a good man. I hope Josh's singing and playing will cause you to jump up and do the same. I hope it will cause me to do the same on my ship or wherever I work around the shore here.

MARY LOU WILLIAMS AND NORA LEE KING must feel some similar kind of a hope in them, because Mary Lou sings: "I ain't a gonna do nothin' wrong until my baby comes home!" She seems to hint that when he comes, of course, then she will do something wrong, but whatever she does, I don't think it will be wrong. Mary Lou and Nora Lee make me see how a whole army of women must be feeling these days, separated from the smell of the one you're waiting on.

Program, "Songs for Mr. Lincoln,"
Sophie Maslow dance.

I think I can say, for us seamen, at least, yes, and for all the service men everywhere, too, that we feel exactly as Mary Lou feels, and as Nora feels. These records are big ones, twelve inches wide, and still, they are finished almost before I can get started listening. I play this one over and over and listen.

CHAMPION JACK DUPREE is a man that puts on just about the best clothes and jewelry that he can buy. He wears enough gold chains on him to pull a jeep out of four mudholes. He thinks that way and he lives that way, and he makes himself welcome in any place where his feet touch the sidewalk. He is a man being a man and he is proud to be just what he is. I feel proud for him, too. I watched him down at the Asch studios as he made this record, "Too Evil To Cry." He sat himself down on that piano stool like he owned the whole world and all it's little fences. He seemed to be breaking those fences down as he crashed his hands down like an octopus on those piano keys. He frailed that piano like a tree full of nuts, and the music trickled out of it, or rather, rolled and poured, and jumped out of it, like some kind of a ten ton bomb unloosening itself in the studio. Jack talked first. He talked out over the piano and into space. His woman was out there and he spoke to her like she was there on the lid of that piano. I never will forget it. Champion Jack has been a lot of places and jumped some tall fences in his day. He's a man that knows. A man that was there. He's a man that can tell you more about it in a jiffy than I could in a week. The woman that Jack talked to was too damned evil to cry. Well, the piano keys sound like ten swarms of birds and bees, as well as several herds of wild animals running in a thunder storm, dodging through the zig zag lightning. I can't tell you any more. You can just imagine how evil a person has got to be to be "too evil to cry." That's pretty evil. And I guess we all feel this way some of the time. Champion Jack Dupree is a man that makes his self welcomed everywhere by talking to a piano like it was his woman, or to his woman like she was a piano. He's coming a long ways up.

BLIND SONNY TERRY blows one on his mouth harp. "Lonesome Train" is the name of it. Sonny imitates the wild running howling of the big fast trains that he could only hear and could not see. His people could only sweep them and clean them, but not allowed to drive them. His people could hold down the pick and shovel, broom and dustpan jobs, spittoon polishers, trash pickers, garbage handlers, the hot sweaty, hard blistered jobs, yes, but not allowed to work his way up to a better job. Sonny told me that he wanted to show the people how a train made music as it rattled around a curve in the Jim Crow country. He plays a song that catches the whole essence and spirit of the train, but yet there is a wild mixture of tunes set to a dozen tangled rhythms that folk lore and folk music experts will be trying to unravel and to analyze for the next ten centuries. I personally don't think that you will succeed in unraveling it, nor in finding a form nor a pattern for it. It sounds spiritual, bluesey, ragtimey, and waltzy, run away, and racy, a polka, a schottische, a square dance, a march. Blind Sonny just doesn't happen to know that there are any limits in this world, and the longer he feels this way about his music, or his life, the better. He puts the whole world and all that's in it into this number, "Lonesome Train," just as he did into his "Harmonica Breakdown," and his "Harmonica Rag." Here is a spirit, a spirit not only of the hard hit, poll tax, sharecropper south, but a spirit that seems to bust loose out of the landlord's very hands, and a spirit that tramples old Jim Crow into the dirt of the earth. Sonny only whoops, only hollers, only moans and yells in a high religious voice as he sucks and blows and works his tongue around over the notes of his harp. His head is way back and his hands pound and beat against his mouth as he chokes the tone and the rhythm that he wants out of that harp. It is a fifty cent make. He is a whole symphony orchestra, doing, as well, in some ways better, than any Hundred piece band that you have ever heard. How he does it I don't know. I can't see inside his mouth. I wish I could, but I can't. How does he do it? You listen. Then try to tell me. It's Mongolia, Tibet, Bombay, Algiers, Oklahoma, Kentucky, and New York, and Hollywood, and everything else.

AND BLIND SONNY TERRY IS HERE TO STAY.

WOODY GUTHRIE AND CISCO HOUSTON play a glad sounding blues, a fast runner, a hard traveler, called, "Ain't Gonna Be Treated This A Way." Two big guitars. Cisco plays mostly on the big bass strings, sort of a minor sounding drumbeat, and keeps the main rhythm going while I play the tune on the higher strings. This is a good sample of the One Hundred and Thirty Two pieces that we recorded for Asch. Not the best, not the worst. We sing our own kind of a harmony, and we ourselves don't know what to call it. The song was at first the tale of a runaway slave getting loose from his mean boss. Next, it spread among the White folks and even the cowboys coming back down the old cattle trail. It was sung by the several hundred thousand people as they

And America is like the rest of the whole world. We are still lucky, because our very greatest art is yet to come. This is our hope. Our dream.

Lee Hays, Burl Ives, Cisco Houston, and Woody.

left out of the old Dustbowl to get away from bad landlords, and as they marched on to California to meet up with some more mean landlords and tough cops. We met out there in California and went around singing these songs at the camps of the Migratory Workers of all kinds, in the Federal Camps, and in the run down Jungle Camps. We found people hungry for life and hungry for music, and they treated us like kings and princes. We just hope that you will listen and hear something here that will remind you of your own hard work and your own hard road, and we can't say much more. I like to try to say what other people's music makes me think of, and I like to try to write these things down here so you can read them and think, too. But, when it comes to trying to think up something to say about a piece of my own, I don't know why, but I seem to always run short on words.

I think you can safely set this album of records up alongside of your best Blues records. I think you will hear lots of things in this album that you did not hear in your others. Drop into your record store and play it and listen to it. Let your mind roam and let your thoughts ramble just like I've done here. Listen for a spirit, and a big broad, world wide feeling. Jane Dudley, one of our finest modern dancers, has already created three dances to the music of Blind Sonny Terry, and they appeared on CBS Television together. Audiences go wild with applause. I've heard them clap their hands for ten or fifteen minutes without a rest. Jane and Sonny have always had to just roll the curtain back up again and do another encore. This is true, also, of the music of Josh White and the dancing of Pearl Primus, who have been setting the wood afire before some roaring audiences.

I'm not trying to sell you this album of records. I just want to sort of shove you in the door of your record shop and let you hear them played. You'll do the right thing, I know that. But, go down and go in, and ask them to let you hear, BLUES, put out by the Asch Records.

It's the homegrown and imported Fascists and Poll Taxers that's singing the worst blues of these days.

Note:

MARTIN DIES, famous squawker and hawker, was down with some kind of a sore throat, sort of a Nazzicoccus Cockeye, or something. He wasn't able to appear in this album, as was planned with his "Union Busting Blues." Maybe he'll get in another time. Watch for details.

Woody Guthrie

———————

When General Lucius Clay, the American judge in charge of sentencing Nazi war criminals, sentenced Ilsa Koch, notorious for her torture of prisoners in the Buchenwald concentration camp, to a modest four-year prison term, Woody wrote these verses in outrage. (So far as we know the song has never been publicly sung or recorded.) Rosa Lee Ingram and her songs were, most likely, domestic victims of America's justice system.

LUCIUS CLAY & ILSA KOCH

Lucius Clay he said today
A life term is too long
For Ilsa Koch of Buchenwald
So he cut her years to four.
Rosa Lee Ingram and her two boys
Got a lifetime jail cell run
For hitting a white man over the head
That tried to kill her with a gun

Chorus: That don't make sense to me, boys,
           That don't make sense to me;
           Three Ingrams rot for life in a cell
           While Ilsa Koch walks free.

I held up the publication
Of my verdict in this case,
Because I did not think it made
Good news upon the page.
I cannot find connection
With the ashes at Buchenwald
Nor lampshades cut from human skin
And mistress Ilsa Koch.

Chorus:

Oh, yes, she's low, and very low,
But I have searched my mind,
And 'twixt the bones and Ilsa Koch
No word of proof I find.
My word must stand in Frankfurt land
I am the highest word,
I am the highest of the high;
The case is open and closed.

Chorus:

If Rosa Lee Ingram had gassed and burnt
Five thousand living souls;
If her two sons had robbed gold teeth
And stole the corpses clothes,
If the Ingram boys had cut their shades
From tattooed human skins,
Would we cut their time from lifelong terms
To four little measely years?

Chorus:

                                  1948

Toward the end of the forties, Woody began seeking within himself to find another big book project to match Bound for Glory. *He wound up writing the novel* Seeds of Man, *though it wasn't published until many years later. But he also considered doing another piece of autobiography. This remarkable document was one result.*

IDEA

The family of people that I'm telling you about, they wasn't lucky enough to even be sharecroppers, etc. I lived right with them for more than two years. This tale will tell you some of their weaknesses but I hope it will tell you more of their strength. There were thirteen of us. We lived in a two room house. It wasn't even a house. It was in an old shack down at the bottom of a big steep hill. Two rooms.

My mama and papa were both injured in a fire. This family asked me to come and live with them. I had been working out at the golf grounds with Claude, the oldest boy; we also took our sacks over our backs and went all over town picking up junk. Brass. Copper. Aluminum. Rubber. Lead. Zinc. Sold it for so much a pound down at the city junk yard.

We had had a gang and waged war with other gangs as I told you in my book, "Bound for Glory." But lately it seemed like we were growing out of our gang life into a new sort of a life. Into a new kind of a world. Into a world where your eyes follow after everything that wears a dress.

Here there was even a fight and a dozen fights, skin and hair was knocked off right and left. The older members of the gang were now about fourteen or fifteen. The younger boys hated us because, after fighting with them and against them in gang wars and fist fights, we commenced to turn our eyes at these animals that fix up to look so pretty in skirts. Girls.

We had laid around the gang house for eighteen out of every twenty four hours for several years. We grew there. Belonged there. We were part of the roof, stove, spitoons, sacks, part of the scenery on that hill.

I had seen every weed sprout, and grow, turn dry, go to seed, sprout and grow and turn dry again from that gang house for five or six years. I'd been in its jail a thousand times for a thousand crimes. I had been everything from scavenger to president ten or twelve times, fought on the good and bad side of fifty wars, won, lost, and broke even at every sort of a game the mind of a kid can work out or invent.

The younger kids were glad in some ways to see us older ones sort of ease out of the ganghouse. They could hold higher offices with us gone. We had fell to reading story books and magazines and to gazing by the hour at the women's section of catalogs. We looked too at guns, steel traps, rifles, pocket and hunting knives and even looked at suits of clothes and new shirts.

"I did, too, see yuh ridin' past 'er house on that bicycle!" a little one would say.

"Did not!" I'd say back.

"Did, too!"

"Did not! Shut up!"

"Yuh rode past there about a hundred dam times! I seen yuh! I seen yuh! 'At's why yuh ain't been a showin' up at our meetin's here lately!"

"Aw! Hush yer trap!"

The gang house rocked with our argument. It was almost every day.

"I seen yuh! Seen yuh hangin' 'round up there again!"

"Just ridin' that bicycle! Hell, that was all! That's a good block to ride around. Ground's hard, smooth, no pebbles to dump you! Goddammit! Hush!"

The house would be full of yells.

"Men: I vote that if he cain't pay no 'tenshion to our gang an' don't come to our meetin's that we vote 'im out!"

"I'll do what I dam please! When I dam well please!"

"Yeah?"

"Yeah!"

"Whatcha got on them fancy duds for if yuh ain't been up there ridin' 'roun' and 'roun' that block like a dam monkey at a circus?"

"Gotta right to clean up oncet in a while ain't I? Don't mean I'm quittin' th' gang, does it? Goddamighty! Has a man gotta crawl in this dam lousy hole an' rot here an' lay here an' stay here till he goes cockeyed? Cain't he even git on a bicycle an' ride aroun' some without bein' accused of quittin' th' gang? How many meetin's I mist? None hardly! None a tall! Hardly!"

Several heads looked into the pages of the roll book. "Hmmm."

"Hmmmm."

"None. Hardly. Last one was yesterday. Absent. Last Tuesday, absent. Monday big special meetin'. Not present. Seen with clean clothes on talking to two girls. North side of town. About time to boot him out. Hmmm. None. Hardly."

That north part of town part was one of the worst things held against me.

"How many sez keep 'im in?"

"Out?"

"Four. Five. Six. Seven. Looks like it's out."

"You can take your lousy old gang and your rotten old house an' shove it up your you know what! To hell with all of you!"

The door of the gang house slammed. The stove pipe shook down some more soot. Another man went over the hill. If he came back, rocks would bounce off his head. So it was goodbye old gang house and all of your arguments and fights. It was goodbye to the things that meant all of your existence. All your old memories were back in that old rickety shack yonder. Half of your years you had spent there. You were there long before these kids got old enough to join up.

It was with a sigh and a heavy head that you walked away. But something just a little stronger was pulling you on, and you half worried, half wondered, half laughed and half cried as you walked out of one season of a kid's life into another one. Another one. One filled with girls.

Not always does it happen that you break out this quick or this clean, but there always came that heavy day when your heart had to choose between the two worlds, the world of the gang and this world full of girls.

"I did, too, see you!" She would play with those buttons on her dress and look down at the ground. "I saw you with my eyes!"

"Did not!"

"Did, too!"

"Did not!"

"You were in old dirty raggedy clothes and you played around over at that old nasty gang house all day long!"

"Wasn't me!"

"Was too! I know you when I see you!"

"Not me."

"I walked down the alley real close to the gang house. And I saw you. And I could smell tobacco smoke and old nasty stuff all the way from where I was walking!"

"Them little ole kids ain't got no sense! Whattaya think I'd hang out down there for? They ain't even got sense 'nuff to know 'bout how you feel when ya feel like ya feel about how you feel—."

"About what?"

"Oh. You know."

"Feel about what?"

"Oh you know how ya feel."

"About what?"

"Aw! 'Bout, ah, what ya go an' ride some bicycle aroun' some block, ya know."

"Yes, which block?"

"Aw, gist most any block. Ya know. Any old block. Gist 'cause th' dirt's good an' hard an' they ain't none o' these little round pebbles to throw ya. Lots o' streets is too rough. Some's so sandy ya cain't guide it straight. Others is too full of weeds an' some's got ole garbage piles fulla glass an' nails. Puncture tires."

"So?"

"Well. So, you gotta find some street to ride a bike on aintcha?"

"I suppose."

"Awright. Then say, well, fur instance, say some girl happens to be a livin' right aroun' there in that same block somewheres."

"I see."

"Th' bike don't care who lives aroun' there does it? So long's it gets good hard dirt ta roll on!"

"Ohhh, no. It wouldn't care."

"Yeah. But, but, ya see, what happens is, when th' guys sees ya over there, well, first thing they say is you was over there 'cause you was over yonder or 'counta 'cause she was over where she was when you was over there where you was."

"Ohhh! How mean! Do they really say such nasty things?"

"Yeah. Sure. Gist 'cause your folks happen'd to move there in that house. Could I help it where they move to?"

"Why no!"

"No siree. Like I could help it who lives where they live! So they all say I like you more'n I do them. So they say I don't come to meetin's. So they vote an' say you're outta th' gang! Just bang, bang, bang!"

"They all say you like me?"

"What they 'cuse me of."

"That's the most awful thing that I ever heard of in all of my days put together! Why! I won't stand for it! I tell you I'll just not put up with it! That's the biggest lie that anybody ever told! I'll go right down there by myself and bawl them all out and make them let you come back to that ganghouse and play all you want to! And ride your bike anywhere you please! Come on!"

"Ah. Yes. But, they, you. Me."

"No sir! Come on! If they said such a mean awful terrible thing about you I'll help you fight them! It's ten times worse for me to have everybody saying or even thinking or even dreaming that you could ride your bike around my block because I happen to live there! Come on! We'll tear that old shack down and kill every kid in it! To think that they would even dare to even so much as to even whisper your name and mine in the same breath! Come on! Fight!"

"Awww."

"Come on! Come on!"

"Aw, but, ya see."

"Come on! See what?"

"Ah, what you said they said. It's right."

"What did I say they said?"

"You said they said it."

"I did not! It was you that said it! Not me!"

"Yeah. But they said it."

"Said what?"

"Said about th' bike an' me an' th' road an' you an' th' gang house an' them. Said it."

"What?"

"Said I liked you. So now I say what they said."

"You will not!"

"Huh?"

"You will not say it just because they said it."

"Yeah, but they said it like it really is."

"So what?"

"So I just let it stay said."

"What stay said?"

"I like you."

"But they ran you away because of me. Now where will you go to play? You'll get lonesome. You'll go back."

"Nope."

"Oh, yes you will."

"Nope. Won't."

"It's nice to have you say you like me and all of that but I don't want to see you lose all your friends just because of me."

"Get some new 'uns."

"New friends? Where?"

"Ah. All around. I gotta good job if I wanta take it. One where I c'n hang aroun' th' drug store there all day an' all nite if I want it."

"A real job? Really? Doing what?"

" 'Liverin' stuff. Bicycle."

"On a bicycle? You mean you get paid real money for riding on a bicycle?"

" 'At's it. Been practisin' already.

"Gosh. Gee, I'm so glad."

"Me, too."

"Those old crazy boys in that old nasty ganghouse! Pfffft! They make me sick! They haven't got any job! They're too lazy! They're too mean and too crazy to go out and get a job! They're not worth one snap of your finger."

"Aw, just ain't very old, 'at's all. You know how kids is. Play, play, play. 'At's all they think about. Play."

"And you're so much older than they are. Your mind is so different from theirs. You're so much different somehow. More sense somehow or other. I don't really know. But, your job. When do you go to work?"

"Mornin'."

Slim

Tough Guy!

— Woody Guthrie —

Drawing of Slim Houston, Cisco's older brother.

"Ooooohh! So soon?"

"Needin' th' money. Get a few suits a clothes. Shirts an' britches. Needin' some good new shoes pretty bad, too. Haircut. Show money. Few things."

"Yessss you will. I mean you'll need all of that. But I hope you take good care of your new hat."

"Well, 'course a hat, now, a hat is somethin' that, 'course, could wait. Could git along bareheaded till I git my suit an' shoes first—then my clean shirts just ta sorta bang aroun' in, when I ain't all dressed up, 'er nothin' to go to the show, 'er like that."

"You're absolutely right about the hat. Yes. Hat could be put off. Besides your hair will look good blowing in the wind."

"Huh?"

"I say, your hair. It looks good. In the wind. Like."

" 'At's 'bout what I thought you said. Boys! I'm gonna ride that ole bike so fast that my hair'll blow way back like this! Zooomm!"

"Gosh."

"Whizzz!"

"Golly. Yesss!"

" 'Roun' corners leanin' 'way over like this! Zing!"

"Be careful. You'll kill yourself. Don't tear your new clothes full of holes. Watch out!"

"Zingo! Knock, knock. Hey! Lady! Here's yer drugs ya ordered about two seconds ago! Go by what th' label says! "Bye! Swish! Sssshh!"

"Ohhh. I just thought."

"Thought of what?"

"Thought of how nice you'll look on your bicycle going all around. Every girl in town will see you."

"Yeah. Guess they will."

"How nice you look. How fast you ride."

"Yeap."

"You'll go right up to their doors when you take the medicine."

"Hmmm. Guess I will."

"They'll come to the door and say lots of nice things to you."

"Be a few will."

"They'll take you away from me. I know they will. You'll get so proud that you'll forget all about me. They'll take you."

"How can they when you ain't even said yet that I could have you?"

"Didn't I say it? You didn't ask me."

"I'm askin'."

"You've got me."

7

THE FIFTIES

I better quit my talking 'cause I told you all I know
But please remember, pardner, wherever you may go,
The people are building a peaceful world, and when the job is done,
That'll be the biggest thing that man has ever done.

—"Biggest Thing Man Has Ever Done"

The fifties began as a moment of high promise in the Guthrie household, when Nora Lee Guthrie, Woody and Marjorie's fourth and final child and their second daughter, was born on January 2, 1950. Woody still worked, but only intermittently because of his health and, as a result of the Red scare blacklist, with even smaller profit than before, so Marjorie now started her own dance school. But Woody's health was deteriorating, and with it, his mental condition. For the next four years, Woody drifted in and out of his New York life. All the while, his ability to create steadily drained away. In the Guthrie archives, what's most noticeable among his notebooks and journals from this period is the terrible disintegration of his once perfect handwriting. You can actually see his hand quaking and shaking as it holds the pen. By 1954, when the last selection here was written, he was fortunate to be able to scrawl half a dozen words onto a single large ledger page.

Yet even in these years, Woody from time to time managed to pull something very worthwhile out of his travels and travails and his morning readings of the newspapers. He was only thirty-seven years old in 1954, when his creative life essentially ended (he lived another fifteen years). We can only imagine what he might have created if he'd been given a more normal lifespan.

1950
THE NEW YEAR

I hauled Marjorie down to the Brooklyn Jewish Hospital, not on the First of January, but real early on the morning of the Second, around about 6½ or 7 in the a.m., to see what will the harvest be?

If there is anything else that took place or happened around the clover leaf these past few days I guess I just didn't register it.

While I was in the West Street jail she told all of our friends and neighbors I was out west. Everybody asks me how things are out west. I don't know what to tell them.

I never do know.

I wrote the wrong date on 150 or 200 home made Nora Lee Cards and had to go through all of them all day today and scrub out the wrong date and scribe in the right one.

Thanks mainly to Irene Ereckhsohn, the house and Joady and Zibber stayed afloat in my blind staggers. Thanks to Bubbie Gee for feeding us and for telling Arlo (Choondulah) all about the flowers along the Surf Avenue bus Route.

The above is from the 1950 datebook, pages for January 1, 3. The page for January 2 reads, "Today is the Birthday of Nora Lee Guthrie" and continues:

I'm a smart looker
And you can't fool me
So please name me
Nora Lee, Nora Lee
Come to my window
at Brooklyn Jewish
and you'll see
How perty I look
My maw and me

and then you'll know
why you can't fool me.
Fool me, not me,
not me, me, me, me,
Call me Norey Lorey
Nora Lee
Nora Lee
Nora Lee

_____ ▬▬ _____

*Woody undoubtedly drew this story of three black men shot—
two fatally—for being in the wrong coffee shop at the wrong
time from one of the New York City tabloids, but the specifics of
the incident are lost. Unfortunately, those who've lived through
the late eighties up-South lynchings in Howard Beach, Queens,
and Bensonhurst, Brooklyn, will find the situation all too rec-
ognizable and contemporary.*

FURGUSON BROTHERS KILLING

Story of New York Police Killing of Two Furguson Brothers

(Characters are four Furguson Brothers & a tearoom attendant & three white ladies at a table & one white patrol cop
& folks and friends that come to the funeral . . .)

(Scene: Long Island newly built shiny metal tearoom where
our four brothers come out on a Long Island busride to
celebrate reenlistment of our younger brother into U.S.
Navy . . .)

Second Youngest Brother: (Wears GI uniform & stands in
serving line & jorshes at younger brother . . . motions . . .)
No . . . No . . . Not me first . . . Age before beauty.

Third Brother: (Wears civvy suit . . .) Dirt before the broom.

Fourth Brother: (Shaggy work duds) This is your day Lonny
ta be first. I went first back one day in nineteen nineteen.

KILLING
OF THE
FERGUSON
BROTHERS
Woody Guthrie

First Brother: (Laffs) I don't see my favorite brand of bonded in here so I'll have t' settle I guess for just one little cup of your best light coffee

BALLAD

Let's stop in and drink us a hot cup of coffee
That Long Island bus was an afurl long ride
We've gotta keep y'r blood warm our young brother Charlie
'Cause you've reenlisted for quite a long time

(All four nod heads & order cups of coffee & stand waiting . . .)

You've been o'er that ocean and won your good record
And a private first class needs hot coffee the same
As 'Lonzo or Joseph or just plain ole Richard
We'll each drink a hot cup to each brother's name

(We see four brothers stand and wait for cups of coffee . . .)

The waiter shakes his head wipes his hand on his apron
He says there's no coffee in all that big urn
In that glass gauge here there looks like several inches
It looks like this tea room's got coffee to burn

Attendant: (Wipes counter with damp rag) But there's not any coffee in my pot for you boys

(Brothers all hold down voices and argue with boss:)
First: Don't you know which country's we're living in sir?
Second: This isn't Hitler Germany man
Third: It ain't no Jimkrow place
Fourth: Mebbe you ain't heard about being born'd equal yet

Attendant: (Walks to dime fone) (Dials for police) Make it fast

We made him a speech in a nice friendly manner
We didn't wanta scare you ladies over here
He calls for the cop on his fone on the wall
And the cop comes and walks us out in the night's air

(We see four boys march out doors ahead of copper and line up laffing with faces to wall)

This cop says we have insulted this joint man
He makes us line up with our faces to the wall

We laffed to ourselves as we stand here and listen
To our man of law an' order puttin in his riot call

(Cop turns and walks over to young Charlie . . .)

Our cop turns around and walks over to young Charlie
Kicks him in his groin and then shoots him to the ground
That same bullet went through the brain of Alonzo
And his next bullet lays my brother Joe down

(We see fourth brother hauled off to station in prowler car . . .)

My fourth brother Ricky got hauled to our station
Bawled out and lectured by the judge on his bench
This judge says you Furgusons are looking for trouble
They lugged Ricky off for a hundred day stretch

(We see big long string of old jallopy cars smoking in along
back of two Hearst wagons coming into sight of a graveyard . . .)

This morning two Hearstes roll out to my graveyard
One hearst takes Alonzo and the other'n takes Charles
Charlie's wife Minny brings her two boy children
Some friends and some kinfolks in some ol' borrowed cars

(We see a deep kind of a silence over whole crowd broken only
by the loud sounds of Minny's two sons sobbing & crying . . .)

Nobody knows quite how to tell her three sons yet
We're all biting our tongues here and shaking our heads
None of us knows how to make you three kids know
That Jimkrow kill'd Lonzo and Charly too is dead

This town that we ride through's not Rankin's Mississippi
Not Bilbo's Jimkrow town of Washington D.C.
But its Greater New York our most fairminded city
In all my big land and my streets of the brave

Who'll tell you three boys that your daddy he's gone
(He helped those fascists & Nazis to death)
Who'll tell you three boys how our ol' Jimcrow coffee
Has killed a few millions the same as your Dad?

    E
       N
          D

One symptom of the decline in Woody's mental health caused by Huntington's chorea was an increasing profusion of mystical and sexual imagery. Here, those two themes merge with his political beliefs in one of his last, wondrous blasts of vision.

Nothing in this earth life is vulgar to me.

Nothing around this planet's crust is lowdown to me.

I see nothing obscene around me no matter where my ten senses go to scratch around.

I can't see one thing indecent about any of the cells nor germs nor plants, nor bugs, nor insects, nor skybirds, nor seeds of man.

To call God's highest works (man) by some sort of a fearful obscene name would in my set of books be the worst of sins.

Man's clothes and man's drapings have not one snap to do with making him any more noble, any more honest, any more upright, nor any more wiser than he is when he puts on another few dollars worth of draperies or when he seeds them all and cometh forth wearing no more than his naked skin.

There is no known article of duddery, wrappery, bandagery nor of clothing which is one one thousandth as pretty, as free, as healthy, and as miraculous as the naked skin of even the worst, ugliest, dirtiest, sickest, human being on the face of this earth.

I know though how it happens from door to door and from house unto house how the great terrible disease of inner fear causes many many of my people to hate, to curse, to vilify, to fear the very shapes of their own sickening nightmares in regards to a naked human body. I see absolutely nothing to be afraid of about the humanly body in or out of its rags and wrappings.

And I pity most of all my great numbers of Godly friends, comrades, kinsmen, relatives, who invent such a thick mudwall of selfproud sickly virtue that any dam little hurt from any source or any direction must hurt and must sting and must pain their guts like an openly intended insult. These struckdown wounded friends of mine are most assuredly the very ones I pity most.

Do they know in their hearts and in their minds that your own human body being Gods grandest work of art is not hurtable by any open intended insult, moreso especially not hurtable by an insult when no such an insult was aimed or thrown your way.

My world looks too full of good wide open battles to do right and win for the general good welfare of my whole race of people, for me to spend my strengths and my powers killing my own crops of fearful imaginings in my own deathly cellars of puffed up self pride—it is only the ones who get all puffed up like a frog with self pride, and stuck out with stickers of selfish pride like a porcupine, that get their own terrible fears insulted most often.

I see as others like me have seen that it is always the ones who go do all of the big jobs of work in this world who are just too busy to let your words insult them. The works of life move in their veins with a kind of a milk and honey sweetness which no insult can slander and which no slander can hurt by insult.

It is always the ones that feel inwardly so trapped, so hurt, so defeated, so weak, so useless to the world of people around them, that are so easy to insult at a close range or at a great ways away, either by pure accident or on purpose. This turtle shell skirmish is the only kind of a useful wordly battle they are mentally capable of taking a part in. And this poison stagnation of all good flows of forces and universal powers in their souls turns off into a kind of a fearful hate that gossips, distrusts, distorts, twists every word, good gesture, good work, good friend, that comes within poison range of the fearful ones gun. Allowed to run to its wildest forms, no form of insanity is any more awful, nor any more pitiful.

If all of the greatest books of our classical art masters are filled from frontpage to backplate with undressed human figures then the fearful one could get no drop of pleasure from any such undraped sources. And if the very most classic books along any line, be the same in broad and in general, then every word of good wise knowledge is also, unto the airy imaginings of the fearful one, just more and more stacks and piles of obscene, lascivious, vulgar, lowdown, rotten, stinky, filthy, dirty insults on top of more insults.

This kind of a silly groundless fear of self cooked and self served obscenity, vulgarity, etc., is one sure and certain sign that it flows not from anywhere, not from any one place nor places in the world around you, but from the things you hold in your own soul.

You see in other people a true picture of the things you already have in your own deeper self.

You can't even hide your own self away from the eyes of the other ones no matter how hard you try.

Just being a little bit too easy to insult is one thing, but, the real true pity is that your acid will not stop at a mere little insult nor at a thousand such crazy dreamings; it will tomorrow brew up in your poisoned braincasery the wilder passion, the blinder hate, the deadlier acid plot and scheme that everybody and every thing is working together to tear down your reputation, your morals, your virtues, your works, your very success in this life. And then tomorrow once more you daily dream that all of us (the elements, too) are trying all we can to murder you to kill you, to rape you, to bring about your end.

Gain all the wisdom you can about your human body. Get all of the knowledge you can get about your human body. Learn every little fact that you can learn about your own human body.

Your own body is the only one thing that you can put your head to, to study for all of your lifetime. Every other form and channel of study leads on up and up to your miraculous body, anyhow.

You clear up the foul webs in your own humanly house by forgiving and by forgetting the faults, errors, miscues, and missteps, mistakes of all of the other folks that come across your eyesight.

Not one square inch of this earth map is going to be really won or lost by gossip nor by verbal insultery. If you waste your sacred gifts and talents in this soapy backyard chatter of little personal insultings, this whole world and all its Godly useful works and workers will march on out past you so many centuries in time & space that you'll die dead of pure ignorance as to how to even catch up with us all again.

I can well understand and partly personally forgive the terrible sins of old maids, bachelors, and such kinds of people, who maybe for some fairly sensible physical rockbottom reason so choose and so desire to live so muchly and so fearfully alone as these friends do. I can't say that I'd place any of the planning nor running nor bossing of other people's lives into such terribly lonely and solitary souls as are the old maids and the bachelors; but at the same time I'd not curse, flog, belittle, nor try to insult, much less to actually punish by pains nor by death, any such unmarried, barren, infertile, citizens as these be. Yet their own insane fears of personal insultery, when placed or allowed to sneak to the position of command or ownership has caused entire dozens of human races to go down to the sillyest graves of death—

all because some big shot somewhere was a little bit too easy to feel insulted.

At very first early cradle stages of the sense or the feeling of insultery, it seems and appears to be very muchly the style, the fad, the big thing everywhere you look or listen to the backdoor gossip tongues.

You puff your kids up all good and full of pride and you decide your best battle to fight and to win is against everybody and everything that tries to hold you back, or to keep you down, or to take a social gain away from you, or to rob you of some pleasure you get out of your own kind of work.

Your loose tongue finds out that most of the time there's just not anybody trying to hyste you, gyp you, shake you, roll you, clip you; and so, since there's just not any (real) body on hand to be your shadow boxer, your opponent, nor your mortal enemy, then, your own tongue is forced by the shortage of any real physical concrete opponent, to make up, to invent, to sorta dream up an enemy (or a whole army of them) once in a great while in order to keep the tonguery fun rolling.

And then, to keep in a bit of good form (and exercise) the wild tongue has to travel lots farther in every direction, towards the outer side and towards your inner side, to catch up with an enemy, even a dreampt up enemy, even a strawman enemy, and even an old crazy scarecrow enemy.

And then the least little thing done by your friends around you turns into a double talky obscene, vulgar, lascivious, lowly, fresh, sex maniacal, hint of some kind of an inner or an outer insult. (Or both).

This is why I never anymore go by fads, nor by styles, nor by any other shift in the human drapes and sceneries. The sceneries fade. The human always stays.

Obscene. Vulgar. Low down. Shirty. Filthy. Rotten. Bad. Stinkery. Insulting. Maniacial. Call him or her every curse and word of cursery that you know and the human still goes on being born just as stark naked as the palm of your own hand. None of your own turtle shell fear bombs hurts one human being even for so long as the snap of your finger. You pile $50,000.00 worth of pretty colored clothing on top of him or her and he & she are always and eternally free and cozy and stark naked down yonder in all of your ragbags.

You have been cursing the whole human race, they've not been cursing at you. You've been afeard of the whole human face; it's never been afraid of you; you've been running away from everybody; they've not been running away from you. You've been throwing insults at the whole earth's people; they've surely not been tossing bad insults at you.

Even a good word of friendly criticizm tossed your way looks like an atom bomb of insultery when you see it through your fraidyful specks.

Every crime on the page of every sad docket book is pulled by the state of mind that false fears make believe the whole world has turned against. Rape, Robbery, Murder, and all drops of other bloodsheddery is done and actually brought on by the ones who sickly dream that everybody in the world pokes fun (insults) them, and blocks up their chance to go places.

The very disease that causes the great threat of the obscene (vulgar). You cant any more prove that the obscene really exists, since you cant find any two people that can so much as even give you the same definition of just what obscene vulgarity means to them. One will tell you that certain words, actions, sound obscenely vulgar to him; whilst the second person will say something so vastly different that there's just no sense of a connection between the two meanings. In different languages spoken even on two sides of the same mountain there are very seldom any two sexyfied teasing words which mean the same kind of profanity. I could curse my head off in an Indian tent in some other lingo and still be a good fellaman amongst all of my Indian friends.

But, in any earth dialect of any known tongue, I'd have to grow up in my braincase above any and all sorts of accidental or intended forms and sounds of gossipy hails of insultry words, well meant or ill meant, before theyd call me a full grownup manchild.

You just have to find yourself, your hands and your heart, a job of good hard work that keeps your feet so busy on the good run that, well, you've just not got one spare minute out of any 25 hour day to even so much as to think about the crazy quicksandy boghole of suicidal dreampt up insults, even when you know full well that a few million real hard enemies are really out there mouthing for you and gunning for you.

If your brain has not already found for your three hands and your seventeen eyes just such a good war job, you're a dead duck goner anyhow from your own wounds of your own bitter acid insults and wilder dreams.

I have come very very close to finding, to making my own self just such a job of good works. I find another big continent of my work just about every day.

Lots of good fine people here and yonder have oftimes accused me of being more or less aware of some kind of a key secret which I use to go unlock all the gates and hardbarred doors to get at every hideout holler of the human mind.

I've read a big mountain of books both good and bad on the subject of the soul, the heart, the spirit, the mind of man, but I've not stumbled in my labours so far upon any one medicine (that has not already been discussed and fairly well named and branded before I got to be born).

Love is the only medicine that I believe in. It enters into all other forms of good medicine and good nursing. To me the easy rub and gentle touch of the nursing hand is more potent and longer lasting in its healing powers than all or any other known drug medicine.

Love is the only God that I'll ever believe in.

The books of the holy bible never say but one time just exactly what God is, and in those three little words it pours out a hundred million college educations and says, God Is Love.

And that is the only real definite answer to ten thousand wild queries and questions that I myownself tossed at my bible. I mean to say, that is the only really sensible, easy, honest, warm, plain, quick and clear answer I found—when I was ready to throw socalled fearful cowardly thieving poisoning religion out my trash door, it was those three words that made not only religion, but also several other sorts of superstitious fears and hatreds in me meet one very quick death.

God is Love.

God is really love.

Love can be and sure enough is moving in all things, in all places, in all forms of life at the same snap of your finger.

Love is the powers of magnetic powers and repulsions that causes all shapes and forms of life to run to a hotspot and meet its mate.

Love makes this wonder then in fifty thousand billions of uncounted trillions of life's forms, shapes, patterns, in every step and in every stage of life, in the lives of the living cells, in the lives of the living bugs; the lives of the biting insects; the lives of the living reptiles, the lives of the living animals; and in the very lifebloods of all the living forms of birds; and in the same plain ways all through the moves and the actions, the very thoughts of every human being that travels here in plainview of our eyes.

Love moves them all.

And in all of them love does move.

And wherever I look to see a wiggle or a waggle or a shape of humanly form there I know is a thing not to be in any way hated, nor in any manner despized nor even feared, nor shadowed around with insane cold suspicions; but to test forever and for all my days and for all my nights, too, my powers of love, (I mean by that) my own powers to love.

Love casts out hate.

Love gets rid of all fears.

Love washes all clean.

Love forgives all debts.

Love forgets all mistakes.

Love overcomes all errors and excuses and pardons and understands the key reasons why the mistake, the error, the stumble, the sprawl, the fall, was made.

Love heals all.

Love operates faster and surer than space or time, or both.

Love does not command you, order you, dictate to you, nor even try to base your acts and your actions; love much rather asks for you to tell its forces what to do and where to go and how to build up your planet(s) here by the blueprint plans of your warmest heart desire.

Love cant operate in your behalf as long as your own sickly fear will not permit love to operate in your behalf.

Love is universal.

Love governs the spin and the whirl of this earthly planet all around through your skies here;

Love moves and love balances every other planet star you see there above you by the uncounted blue jillions.

Love moves and balances fifty billion and more kinds of powers and rays and forces inside every little grain of sand. And love causes peace and harmony to whirl a new whole universe on the inside of every little atom.

Love catches up with space.

Love outruns time.

Love makes the big world little and the little world big.

Love makes all good seed fertile.

Love multiplies and love divides.

Love is in the triggery works of all mathematical numberings.

Love moves to drive the weather and all of the powers of your elements. I see above all how your minds and your storms and all of your clear sunny skies are not just big accidents.

Love allows no accident to happen.

Love lets no waste occur.

Love wastes no ounce of motion.

Love works all mysteries.

Love works all miracles; yet I call no working of love a miracle. (Nor a mystery).

Love labours only for the next good and welfare of the most people; for by doing the most good for the most people, love operates fastest.

If it were not for that sun you see rize up yonder in your sky every day, there could be no form of life take place on our planet earth; but the sun's rays are not your deathly enemy as faithless ones taught you to believe; that sun yonder I say to you is your very best friend if you take all its rays and give them a job in love to do. Love balances, holds, and controls all the moves and acts of the sun; the sun must shine by the grace and permit and by the very permission of love itself.

Love fires and burns and boils around in every inch of the great fiery belly and great fiery face of the sun, but, love also does the same job for several other millions of Great suns Greater in size and power than yonder's daily new morning sun.

Love is all force.

Love is all power.

Love is all energy.

Love is all strength.

Love is all health.

Love is all beauty.

Love is all good work well done.

Love is all fun.

Love is all pleasure, all joys known.

Love is all eternity.

Love is here now.

Love is the thinker of every good thought.

Love is all there be.

Love is all space. There be no space that is empty of love.

Love ties all things together.

Love makes all things one thing.

Love lends all. Love takes all. Love flows over more with

lovelights than all of the great splashes of all our great sunshiney waterfalls.

Love kisses above and down below your waterfalls.

Love makes all your good & bad laws and love takes up your own sickly laws and breaks them into sand grains just for the laffs and for the kicks.

Love is always glad to make you gladder.
Love feels sad when it makes you sadder.
Love works best when you give it a big job of work to do.
Love loves you most when you love love the most.
Love sees you best when you see love the best.
Love finds you when you find love.
Love finds you where you find love.
Love meets you where you meet love.
Love gives to you what you give to love.
Love loves most of all to work for you.
Love loves most of all to build up or to tear down as you desire and as you command.

Love forgave you all of your humanly sins back there twenty six months before you ever came out of the womb of your mama's belly. You are already a good clean commander of all the forces and powers which love controls.

I say to you, take up your post and your command of love.

I say to you, take up your very own gift and talent.

I say to you, take up your power of command.

I say to you (and to all of you and yours), take up your word, take word of your command.

I say to you, this power to command the absolutely neutral powers of love, this command is your very own birthright; no piece nor coin, no pile of gold, no penny paid, no dollar mailed, no stamp licked; no priest asked, no minister called—unless you so desire it and so command things to be thusly and solely (for the well and goodful use of most of us).

Command love to work with you and for you.

Command love to operate in you and through you to heal, to help, to lift, to bless, to cleanse and to spread the good word and the good news that the day of human hate and fear and dark lostness is all over and all gone and a day of new bright command at your hand;

For your own sense of your own commandery will grow only as you pass the great command (word) onto all of your

Woody at Coney Island with his kids, 1951. Left to right: Nora Lee, Arlo Davy, Woody, Joady Ben. (Courtesy of Marjorie Mazia Guthrie)

dear dearly beloveds in humanly shapes of misery till your command sets them freed into their own commandery.

Tell your comrade, Comrade, bend down in dank fear traps not one second longer—Comrade—your love commands every known (and every unknown) kind of universal energy in existence. And that which has lain is the sad unknown for so many insane creatures on this one day, by my one newfound word of command—is the insanity all choked out.

To love is to shape, to plan, to order and to command.

To know how to love fully you must learn how to command fully.

No human is full grown till the love tells him to command all. Fear before none. Quiver before nothing. Kneel at no spot. Beg no cure. Be a slave to none and master to none.

Command the skies.

Command the planets.

Command the starlights.

Command the very heavens.

Command love to move and to act for you and your sweet mate—and for all the other such love praise like you and your mate and your children.

Command your plan (in love) to come to pass.

Command your desire to happen.

Command and say:

"I command that all the powers and all the forces of love in my universe to shine and to make warm and friendly the labour and the seeds of man. I command that today's battle be badly lost to that soldier who is this day the greatest distance away from his home. I command all the rays of my good sunny shine to tear down my old city of hate and to build up my new town of love. Destroy this day every law against love."

You of course, know that my own command here is but my own sample for you to see to use to shape your own commands by.

The resolution in my union hall is a command passed on in love for the best welfare of the union members.

I just hope that you will now be a bit more hotly and keenly aware of your power as a love commander.

You have to learn to love even your most deadly bitter enemy if you'd really hit the most high peak trail of your own powers as a love commander. You must bring death to none and life to all or you'll just never quite tip the high top as a love commander.

Your love command must forever be just exactly the direct opposite of war's crazy baseless hatreds. Peace. Peace. And sweet sweet peace must be the song of thy tongue tip. Peace is love. Love is peace. Your love command must for all eternity be your peace command.

Your every command must make your whole world a better one to work on and to love on.

This whole crust of a planet is a pretty place to walk around over; I have not overlooked very many spots in my walkings; but what we need around this world is a generation of bossy commanders in love in place of our crop of scaredy-kat slaves boiled in the oils of their own dreamy hate.

Hate can never command.

Hate can never be the boss.

Hate can't ever ever win an inch.

Hate can't stay. If you flush your own life down the floody drains of hate nobody weeps when you sink.

Hate has took away whole crazy nations on top of nations.

Hate never took one single lover away.

One true love commander can turn the universes of hate into heavenroads and byways of love, love, love.

Sweet love.

Sweet love.

Sweet love.

Oh poor poor sickenly soul of lost gamblers, why why why must you rage and shake and beller and howl when you don't [know] no heads but the one tied onto your rotten shoulders?

Why rage?

Why bellow?

Why shout and spit crazy in the wind? Why look blind?

You can't ever win.

You can't fight, because you can't see.

You can't see because you are so blind.

You are just blind on account of your own sick fears and your hatreds.

And you know all of this a good bit plainer than most any other human around you;

A slave to hate,

That is what you are;

A slave to your own hate;

That is all on earth you are now.

A crazy slave to crazy fear and crazy hate.

No more than a slave to your crazy dream that fever flashes on your own picture screen; where you know most plainly that your hate and your own fear has chained you down for another one of its crazy howling weeping crying wailing and cursing slaves with all your sense of control gone, all your self control (your self command) gone out of you.

Love for these people all around you here can pick up your dying carcass and heal it up again as good as a new one.

Love is the only thing that can help you now.

Love is your only ray of good sunshine.

Love will give you back your self control.

And love will put your own command in the palms of your hands.

Old Man Joads is now down rolling in the clean dirt on the floor—eight months old and getting older every time he grunts and rolls. Like his poppa, like his daddy, I'm a roller as of old, I'm a grumbler and a grunter just like you, my Rolly Joads.

And for you of the deathly dope drug, you of the crazy needle, the pill, the reefer fag, the hot spoon, the opee pipe, the dead mattress, the gone spirit, the gone life, the heavy headache, the crackling temples, the walleyed eyeballs, the spitty lips, the loud yells of choking sickness, the gun, the gut, the stickup, the fight, the cops, the big chase for more dope and for more guns and more stickups, your own fears and hate can be cured and healed up by one kind of love tonic, and one kind alone. Love will take your hand and lead you back to a job in my open sunlights.

Absolute slave you are today to your hateful despizeable dopes, yet you can too step out here in line of the duty of love and take up a command post as sure and as certain as can any of the rest of us.

Space and time you shall command them both.

All things that be in time's own space you command all these along with the others.

All that grows in spaces own time you too command and order these unto your heart's plan.

Your own heart will plant its plans for the great freed goodness of all my seeds of man;

And all my seeds of man will love to work and to build and to feed and to breed according not to webby old law books, but by the very law plan of the only soul and spirit.

And my body shall be my only soul and my only spirit;

And spirit shall be this way from my only soul and body.

I command thus and so.

I have uncovered here one great good useful lesson to be learned by both armies now doing such loud marchings, both the going capitalist, and, the coming communist.

I can greet you on both sides and tell you now in plainer ways about your newfound love command.

We must rise up today from older kinds of slaves to command the newly seen forces of nature. I sing a Ma & Pa Nature a lot closer to home.

Thats all my new biblebook is; a command of nature and a control over all the forces of Ma & Pa Nature.

―――――――

In September 1952, doctors at Brooklyn State Hospital finally diagnosed Woody, who had previously been judged either an alcoholic or mentally ill, as suffering from Huntington's chorea (a rare disease and difficult for diagnosticians to recognize). Woody was discharged within the month and he simply fled,

away from home and family and facts, all the way out to
California, where Will Geer and other friends were making a
sort of last stand of the Left in then undeveloped Topanga
Canyon. There, land was so cheap that even Woody could afford
to make a down payment on eight acres—albeit, an almost
vertical plot, essentially a steep cliff.

There, in Pretty Polly Canyon, as he called it, he wrote the
notebook that includes these seven short pieces, surprisingly
strong and coherent for all the painful struggle it must have
taken to compose them and set them to paper.

B W BREAKDOWN

I report to you the morning I see the sky to be all blue and all
    in the clear near here
And I report also that in our voting box at our last November's
    election how it was that all of us, or how it was that a
    goodly number, too many of us did, the same as ever,
Go and walk along with and pretend to be close followers of
    our maddest foulmouth'd ravers
When we voted our vote and when we dropped our helpless
    little ballot vote and when we drowned our freest voice
    down in the prison acid tanks you call by the name of
    voting boxes.

We did go and follow or we did pretend to go and to follow the
    words and the deeds and sadist actions and killer pointers
    of your deadly fringes by letting this unhuman war keep on
    blazing and framing over yonder in sweet old Korealand.

We did go follow or surely pretend to go follow the insane facts
    and maniacal orders, commandings, and dictatings of all
    of our toppermost sadmouth ranters when we let you exist
    a little bit longer in your making and in your creating and
    in your shipping and in your dropping down on the grassy
    roofs of living huts and living towns and living villages and
    living cities your deathly diabolical destructible weapons
    of your atomic, your hydrotic, your germ filled, germ
    spreading, fear choking, disease killing bacterias of ten
    thousand quivering sorts and kinds.

How can you even so dimly dimly pretend to follow after a God
    by the name of Love when you believe in and even worship
    after empty dead buildings in the place and in the stead of

warmblooded living human beings? And even when you do use us to go to follow your very own god of hate and your god of destruction do you not know, O' my good worker, O' my great neighbor, that you follow verily in the track of your own desolation and your own destruction? Or is it because your own deeds of your very own guilt burns thy mind and your fleshbody beyond all good warm desire to love and to work and to try to remake and to try to rebuild and to try to refertilize and to repopulate the scenes of your devastating germ warfare?

My tongue is tired of talking more to you. My finger is paralyzed here from begging you to break free from your killer among them and to come join my builder gang here where I'm at this morning.

> Woody Guthrie
> Topanga Canyon
> Dec. 1952

CANAL ZONER

I spoke to a Canal Zone fellow
At a radical left house party
Here in Sherman Oaks last nite
And he told all about how the
    people of his home town
    always grabbed up their guns
    and marched like that every year up to the courthouse to
settle in the flesh and in the person
    any question about any kind of a new law on their books
    He said all of the men on his family tree had already got
knocked off and gone on along
    He said his home town was just a mile or so from the
    rainiest spot in the world
    He married a Sherman Oaks lady I've known a long time,
and in two years married life they've had two children; and
every year, I told him he'd have to practice plenty to ever have
as many kids as I've got.
    Two and Seven.
    Two wives. Seven sprouts.
    Teeny. Sue. Billy. Cathy. Arlo. Joady. And Noralee.

OKLAHOMA NURSE GIRL

Oklahoma nurse girl
My Oklahoma nurse girl
Walk my packed and crowded ward, girl,
Walked my jammed and crowded ward.
Forty men like me to tend to
Forty guys like me to rub down
Forty men like me fell plumb in love with you.

Oklahoma nurse girl
My Oklahoma nurse girl;
How'd you come to walk my Coney ward?
'How'd ya come to walk my Brooklyn bedline?
Ohh, y'r husband he's a pilot in a plane
You say he's just not made it back yet?
You say he's just not made it back?

Oklahoma nurse girl
My Oklahoma nursery girl,
You don't look like more'n a little kid of a thing
No more'n a little old kid of a thing
Pacin' all around my yellin' ward here
Walkin' y'r legs off 'round my ward.

Oklahoma nurse girl
My Oklahoma nurse girl;
I feel like cryin' and feel like bawlin'
I feel like bawlin' like some baby
If cryin'd bring your pilot home
If cryin'd bring him home

Topanga Canyon

UNCLE STUD

Do you like a trade union
Uncle Stud, Uncle Stud?
Do you like a trade union, Uncle Stud?
Hell no dammed if I do
If it fights no more than my C.I.O.
And my dam'd old A.F. of L.

Do you need a good union
Uncle Stud, Uncle Stud
Hell yes, I dam shore do
'Cause I couldn't live a day
If I didn't have a union fulla folks like you
And full of people like you

Do you think about uniting
Uncle Studdy, Uncle Stud?
Do you think about uniting, Uncle Stud?
Hell yes, I dream 'bout it nites
Hookin' up with a fighter like you
Latchin' onta some soldier like you.

Do you claim to love to battle
Uncle Studdy, Uncle Stud?
Do you really love that battle Uncle Stud?
Y'bet your boats, I rejoy to purely fight
If I fight ta help some doctor like you
And which alongside me a doctor like you.

> Woody Guthrie
> Topanga Graveyard Splitt
> December 1952

EDUCATE ME

I never sung or made one ballad song to entertain you.
I made all of my stuff up to tell you and
To educate you
I'm an educator
Not any entertainer.

> Woody Guthrie
> Topanga Dec. 1952

PSYKOE RAVER

I am that psycho raver
You hear so much talk about.
I'm fixed on all your battle lines
From north pole to the south.

I am that psycho raver
You hear so much talk about
I raved and drew my G.I. pay
As long as I held my sight right.

I'm that wild psycho raver.
I got paid for shooting wild.
And government check for killing wilder
As long as I kept my gun clean.

I'm just a skid row raver now
I rave in my Bellyvue ward
Nobody sends me a paycheck now
You tell me I'm raving too loud.

Woody Guthrie
Topanga Graveyard Canyon
December 1952

WALKING BED

Those first four days after I had my operation in that Coney Hospital I didn't recognize in yourself nor anybody else; they had to chain my feet and my arms to the side of my walking bed there and feed me by rubber hose from jugs of some kind. I do remember seeing that nice pretty nurse girl that said she was born'd and raised down around Tulsa Oklahoma; I remember how she said her husband was a plane pilot of some kind and how she didn't get to see very much of him and how she craved most of all things just to be raising up a son; I saw [a] big Italian worker there that woke up screaming "Explodemente! Explodemente!" And met that big husky Negro by there that sketch such classical little quick pictures. Oh Ruth you don't see do you how many solitary long & lonesome dry and empty years all of my hospital joints and me have been so dizzily riding our walking beds waiting for the deep soul and heart of you to come and walk around our walking beds.

Woody Guthrie
Topanga
December
1952

I wish I was
twenty five years
younger . . .
But hell
Folks like me
Ain't Never goin'
To die
Noway.

Woody loved Albert Einstein, his fellow humanist socialist, and according to legend once even hoboed from Coney Island to Princeton, New Jersey, in order to visit the great man. Like anyone who thought much about the world, Woody was also entranced by atomic power—its potential for harm, its (then brighter) potential to bring good energy and technological marvels into existence. "The Atom and Me," scrawled at the outer limit of legibility into a notebook sometime in 1954, is one of the last truly coherent writings Woody left us. But it shows also that, however ravaged in body and mind Huntington's disease might have left him, he never abandoned his soul or his vision.

THE ATOM & ME

Could electricity be the stuff that keeps all of us alive and kicking?

I still claim that all of our planet and stars and [illegible] all get just right before [illegible] egg can hatch out or [illegible] get born.

Which goes for all of us electric juices in between here & all of our stars up there.

Which is sure one big bunch of power when you try to count it aint it?

But it does take all of this power here just to hatch up one little egg of any kind and to keep this little egg thriving and growing.

I still argue its this very same kind of electricity that you see getting used by us in all of our so far ninety nine chemical elements. We know a few small little things which our atom elements do but we've not even got so much as one little word as to why they do this.

We see them stick together in some certain ways but why they glom together we cant even begin to tell.

We see them all hold on together but we dont know what power holds them together.

We see them dance around us here in all of their pretty shapes to & colors & all their fine designs.

But why they hold onto their shapes and their designs I cant say and nobody else can.

We see as many sorts of atom shapes as we can see of all of our vibrations of magnetic electricities in all of its trillions & trillions of uncounted flavors.

And we grow up seeing how these atomic dances and mag-

ONE LITTLE THING THE ATOM CAN'T DO

In the nearby day to come
When we whip this atom
  bomb,
And when we use its pills of
  power
To build houses to the sky;
Atom power is bound to be,
But the biggest miracle that
  you'll see
Will be one little thing the
  atom can't do

Chorus:
One little thing the atom can't
  do,
One little thing the atom can't
  do;
It can't hug and kiss your
  cheek,
It can't call you honey dump-
  ling;
No, that's one little thing the
  atom can't do.

You can drop your atom pill
Down in the gas tank of your
  car;
It'll roll you round this world
And shine your shoes ten
  times a day;
It can't show you how to court
  or kiss;
It can't sing songs about your
  lips,
No, that's one little thing the
  atom can't do. *(Chorus)*

netic prancings in the rays of our sun is one thing we cant live here without.

Like we can see these rays in all of our living trees & our grassblades & things that we see grow.

We see how our sun keeps all these things alive and moving.

And it makes me halfway guess that we'll always be able to see some finer and some bigger shows as we go on guessing at and figuring out all of our biggy little pains of land around us.

When we find some kind of a hiring hall here on earth big and roomy enuff to hire us all fresh and as we come instead of wasting nine tenths of our lives as we now do trying to print up some new loyalty oaths to all sign.

All of our work kinds I know are itching and going crazy working for us a atom age job or an electric age job of some sort and we all go exactly as nutty and equally as batty and equally as crazy and get equally as full of destruction when you wont let us work freehanded in your construction.

I say theres a big plenty of atoms out here for all of us to investigate and an oversupply of bugs & genies & *gnats* & flies & electric vibrations to more than keep all of us buzzy as hell.

I can't help but hate to see all of us wiggling around in rooms like McCarthys trying to suit & satisfy his dictatorial mind when he cuts off all of our most gifted and our highest talented minds and he keeps them from being useful to the rest of us. If I am dying and some communist doctor and nurse can save me I say go ahead and cut—but I hear all my new crops of new generations of kids growing up to ask me if I lose it when some dimwit alleges communist.

Atom wheels can take you rolling
Down to the shade of lover's lane;
Atom sody will taste good
With atom sandwiches you bring;
But when love's lips get wet and woozeldy,
When my love shines its eyes on you;
Well, hmmm, that's one little thing the atom can't do. *(Chorus)*

Atom bells can ring my wedding;
Atom songs can fill my home;
Atom this and atom that,
My atom smile I can put on;
But when mommy and daddy nature
Teach you all the tricks they knew,
That's one little thing the atom can't do. *(Chorus)*

FROM *WOODY GUTHRIE FOLK SONGS* (LUDLOW) © 1963

THE WORD I WANT TO SAY

The word I want to say is easy to say, and yet is the hardest word I've tried to say.

It tries to make all of my feelings plain,

And what one word can I say that will say them all?

Most times I try to speak it, I never do get it said, and when I try to plan it, it always slips my plans and slips my tongue.

I am trying to be a singer singing without a dictionary, and a poet not bound down with shelves of books. My shelf of books is fairly high already, and many other words from out of other mouths are here and are ready for me to lay with and to play with, but I try to skip those books all that I can and say my words with my two freer hands.

The word I want to say is here, and close, and free and easy on my lip and tongue, but seldom said, like some slick water fish that jumps through net holes fast as I can knot and loop. I know what my word means. I know what my word says. I know its weight and measure, its name, label and trade mark. I know its shape and feel, its house and home, I know its taste and smell, its body touch. I know my unsaid word better than my unsaid word knows me. The same as I know you better than you will ever know me.

This one word I want to say would make all clear between my wife and myself, or, rather, would make me as clear as my wife is. She is always the clearest of the two of us. I am always the foggy and the mixed up one, and she is always the outspeaking, out thinking one. If I could just speak this one unsaid and unspoken word to her, things between us would be the limber and undanced dances they'd ought to be. Our house and our home is crippled and hurt just because of this one word I can't say nor speak.

This one word would make me know my children and would make my children know me. If I could just say this one word, my children's children would know that we are both just alike, that there is no difference in us big enough to separate and tear us apart. In our thoughts, I think, all of us could go around the

The note of hope is the only note that can help us or save us from falling to the bottom of the heap of evolution, because, largely, about all a human being is, anyway, is just a hoping machine, a working machine, and any song that says, the pleasures I have seen in all of my trouble, are the things I never can get—don't worry—the human race will sing this way as long as there is a human race.

world and know everybody on it if we could just find and speak this one same word.

It's not a secret word or a magic word. No word is secret. No word is magic. No word is hid. I've followed this one word now for several years, and around the house since I was born here. I've let it lead me by my finger out where the loose snow blows around these weedstems. I've climbed hand ladders of boxcars, shipsides, truck cabs, doors, fire excapes, wagons, and barnlofts. I've said it to cops, guards, vigilante men, soldier and to sailor, to farm women and farm girls, to housewomen and to house girls, to hotel women and to hotel girls, to street women and to street girls, to men and boys shingling roofs in southern states, driving nails in western mountains, digging dirt in eastern places, painting and welding in every state in the Union. I've said this one word in every tongue and language and unto every color of face, lips, ear and hair. To the brown, to the red, to the yellow, to the black skin and to the blankskin. You know this word when you heard it spoke, sung, motioned, signaled or danced.

The odd thing is about this word that it is no one certain word, but fits in the ring and tone sound of every word. It is the word inside of all of our other words, the word that gives our words a shape and a form, and a clearer sense. This is the free word that no jail can hold, no cell can keep, no chain drag down, no rope can lynch, no weapon can hurt or hinder. I say this word is that one word that makes all democracy clear, plain, and keeps democracy alive, the same as democracy keeps me alive, and I keep this one word alive. I will die as quick and as easy as I can to keep this one word living, because it keeps my whole race of people living, working, loving, and growing on to know more and to feel more. This is the word I want to say.

APPENDIX

AYD—American Youth for Democracy, youth group that succeeded the Young Communist League.

Almanac Singers—Singing group formed 1941 by Pete Seeger (Bowers), Lee Hays, and Millard Lampell. They often performed and recorded Woody's songs; he occasionally performed with them. The group later included Pete Hawes, Sis Cunningham, Arthur Stern, Gordon Friesen, and Bess Lomax Hawes.

Ambellans—Harold and Elizabeth Ambellan, with whom Woody lived in 1940 when he first came to New York City. Harold Ambellan, a sculptor, had a large studio with plenty of room for his hoboing friends from the folk music scene.

Arlo—Arlo Davy Guthrie, Woody and Marjorie Guthrie's second child (first son), born July 10, 1947.

American Youth Congress—Youth group of the Popular Front period (1935–1941). The Almanac Singers made their debut at an AYC gathering.

Bernie Asbel—Folk singer and songwriter with People's Songs.

Moe Asch—Head of Folkways Records and Asch Records, Woody's principal recording outlets after World War II. Son of noted Yiddish novelist Sholem Asch.

Richard Dyer-Bennett—English-born, Canadian-reared singer and lutist (1913–   ) who established a School of Minstrelsy, meant to revive the medieval art of the folk ballad, in Aspen, Colorado, in the late forties.

Bilbo—Theodore G. Bilbo, U.S. Senator from Mississippi, a synecdoche of racist populism.

Bina—Bina Rosenbaum, Cisco Houston's girlfriend in the mid-forties.

Bizerte—Tunisian port city.

The Boomchasers—Original title of *Bound for Glory*

Pete Bowers—Pseudonym used by Pete Seeger as a member of the Almanac Singers. He adopted it to protect his father's job in the Roosevelt Administration (the Almanacs were often harshly critical of Roosevelt), in the tradition of the revolutionary *nom de guerre.*

Harry Bridges—Australian-born leader of the West Coast International Longshoremen's Union, subject of frequent deportation attempts by the U.S. Government as a dangerous revolutionary.

Browder—Earl Browder, General Secretary of the U.S. Communist Party in the World War II period.

Bob Burns—Robert Burns (see below)

Burns—Robert Burns (1759–1796), the Scottish poet. Woody seems to have identified with Burns, as with Whitman, Sandburg, and Pushkin, because he, too, wrote in a version of his people's vernacular voice and because his work lent itself well to the sort of minstrelsy represented by "Auld Lang Syne" and "Comin' Through the Rye."

C.I.O.—Congress of Industrial Organizations, formed in 1935 by John L. Lewis's United Mineworkers and eight other unions as an explicitly radical alternative to the guild-style, class collaborationist policies of the American Federation of Labor (AFL). The C.I.O. wanted to organize the U.S. labor force in industrial groupings, rather than by individual job and craft categories. One of the early unofficial sponsors of the Almanac Singers, the C.I.O. and its member unions, including the United Auto Workers and United Electrical Workers, remained close to the cultural and political left through World War II. But in the Cold War climate thereafter, it retrenched, expelling all the Communist-led affiliates in 1949–50, and by 1955 it joined with the AFL in a merger that was more like a surrender.

John Cage—American avant-garde composer of "serious" music.

Cathy—Cathy Ann Guthrie (1943–1947), Woody and Marjorie's first child. Woody wrote "Letters to Railroad Pete" and the various pieces addressed to "Stackabones" for her. She died in a house fire caused by a radio with faulty wiring.

Charles Street—74 Charles Street, Woody's residence in 1941, just before his marriage to Marjorie. A dusty, dingy fourth-floor walkup, he called it El Rancho del Sol.

Cherbourg—French port city.

Cisco—Cisco Houston (1918–1961), one of Woody's chief singing partners, traveling companions, and Merchant Marine shipmates.

Crosby—Bing Crosby (1903–1977), premier Tin Pan Alley vocalist of the thirties and forties and, as such, the nemesis of folk song purism.

Jim Crow—The system of Southern segregation and its softer-spoken Northern counterpart. The name derives from a nineteenth-century minstrel show song.

Sis Cunningham—Agnes Cunningham, Oklahoma accordion player and singer. A member of the Red Dust Players in Oklahoma, she and her husband, Gordon Friesen, teamed with the Almanac Singers when they arrived in New York in 1941.

Joe Curran—Leader of the then-radical National Maritime Union, to which Woody, Cisco Houston, and other merchant seamen based on the East Coast belonged.

Dewey—Thomas Dewey, Republican governor of New York and that party's presidential candidate in 1944 and 1948. Widely regarded as the epitome of the stuffed-shirt conservative reformer. One of the pioneers of postwar Red-baiting.

Martin Dies—Texas congressman who chaired the House Un-American Activities Committee.

Marian Distler—Moe Asch's secretary and chief assistant.

Jane Dudley—Featured dancer in the Martha Graham Company.

Laura Duncan—Black folk, blues, and gospel singer, affiliated with People's Songs.

Dickie Flyer Dyer—Richard Dyer-Bennett (see above).

Elizabeth—probably Elizabeth Ambellan (see above).

William Floyd—Pretty Boy Floyd (see below).

Free Stone Tunnel—A part of the antislavery Underground Railroad.

Gordon Friesen—Husband of Sis Cunningham; a writer and cartoonist.

Jim Garland—Harlan County, Kentucky, singer, songwriter, and brother of Aunt Molly Jackson and Sarah Ogun Gunning.

Gates—John Gates, editor of the *Daily Worker*.

Will Geer—Actor (stage, screen, and TV). Geer recruited Woody to left politics in Los Angeles in the late thirties, brought him to New York, and put him on the stage and on radio in the early forties. They remained close friends to the end of Guthrie's life.

Jackie Gibson—Folk singer and Allan Lomax's sometime secretary.

Tom Glazier—(1914–   ), folk singer, multi-instrumentalist, occasional emcee and TV host.

Gordon—probably Gordon Friesen (see above).

Martha Graham—Modernist choreographer and dancer. She formed her own company in 1929 and by the late thirties began using folk sources as material. Marjorie Guthrie joined the Graham troupe, as student and then dancer, in 1935.

Greenblatts—Marjorie Guthrie's parents, Aliza and Isidore Greenblatt.

Aliza Greenblatt—Marjorie Guthrie's mother, a noted Yiddish literary figure in New York.

Bubby G., Bubby Greenblatt—Aliza Greenblatt.

"Bubby" is an Eastern European diminutive for "grandmother."

Izadore Greenblatt—Isidore Greenblatt, Marjorie Guthrie's father.

Harold—probably Harold Ambellan (see above).

Butch Hawes—Husband of Almanac Singer Bess Lomax, brother of Almanac Singer Pete Hawes.

Pete Hawes—One of the Almanac Singers.

Lee—Lee Hays (1914–1981), Arkansas-born singer, songwriter, sharecroppers' union organizer, and bass voice of the Almanac Singers and the Weavers.

Hearst—William Randolph Hearst (1863–1951), sensationalist, populist-reactionary American newspaper publisher.

Hereford, Clovis, Roswell, Las Cruces, Yuma, Riverside—Southwestern towns, all located along Route 66, the Okies' route to California.

J. P. Higgins—John Doe worker.

Hootenanny Hall of the Alamanac Singers—Undoubtedly a reference to the huge loft on New York's Fourth Avenue, near Union Square, where the group lived in its early days.

Hoover—Probably J. Edgar Hoover (1895–1972), head of the Federal Bureau of Investigation and one of the leading exponents of the postwar Reds-beneath-my-bed climate. Could also be Herbert Hoover (1874–1964), president from 1929 to 1933 and one of the architects of neoimperialism after World War II, but that's less likely.

Leo Hurwitz—Documentary film maker.

Burl Ives—Folk singer, broadcaster, actor, writer, who hoboed and sang with Woody, Leadbelly, and others in the late thirties. His best-known numbers were "Blue Tail Fly," "Foggy Foggy Dew," and "Big Rock Candy Mountain."

Aunt Molly Jackson (Aunt Molly)—Kentucky-born singer, songwriter, union organizer. Forced by anti-union government authorities to relocate to New York early in the Great Depression, she sang at labor meetings and, besides raising a family, running a restaurant, raising her family, and making several hundred records for the Library of Congress, became a fixture at union rallies and the Almanacs' early hootenannies.

Mary Jennings (Mary)—Woody's long-suffering first wife (1918?–   ), whom he married in her hometown, Pampa, Texas, in 1933, and lived with intermittently there, in California, and New York. They had three children—Gwendolyn (Teeny), Will, and Sue—before breaking up for good in 1940.

Jimmy—Jimmy Longhi, one of Woody's Merchant Marine partners.

Tom Joad—Protagonist of John Steinbeck's *The Grapes of Wrath* (1940), portrayed by Henry Fonda in John Ford's film (1941). Woody so loved—and identified with—the character that he not only wrote "The Ballad of Tom Joad" as a tribute but named his and Marjorie's second son Joady Ben.

Joady Ben, Old Man Joads—Joady Ben Guthrie (born 1948), Woody and Marjorie's third child, named after Tom Joad from *The Grapes of Wrath*.

Herb Kleinman—Popular music arranger.

Millard Lampell (Mill)—Member of the Almanac Singers and, with Pete Seeger, their chief songwriter. Lampell played college football at West Virginia, worked as a radical journalist, and later as a radio, television, and screen writer.

Pearl Lang—Martha Graham dancer on whom Woody developed a crush.

Leadbelly—The great blues and folk singer, born Huddie Ledbetter in Louisiana around 1889. Leadbelly was a huge, powerful man who served two terms for murder in Texas (around 1916) and Louisiana (around 1930). In the Louisiana prison farm, he was discovered and recorded by John and Alan Lomax, who also helped arrange his release from prison. They used him as their chauffeur, but by 1935 he was recording for small folk labels, and by 1937 he'd moved to New York City, performing on the college circuit and in theaters in the North, often with Woody and/or Pete Seeger. Reportedly, Leadbelly recorded more than 900 songs for Moe Asch alone. He was prolific, gregarious, a fine twelve-string guitarist and a singer of great force. His songs included "Goodnight Irene," "Alberta," "The Boll Weevil," "Cotton Fields," "The Midnight Special," "Rock Island Line," and "Pick a Bale of Cotton," almost all of them later hits for rock 'n' roll singers. Leadbelly died in 1949 of Lou Gehrig's disease (ALS).

Lefty Lou—Maxine Crissman, Woody's singing partner at radio station KFVD, Los Angeles, in the late thirties. The nickname wasn't political; he called her "Lefty Lou from Old Mizoo."

Liberty Ship—Prefab 10,000-ton steel freighters built at the start of World War II to carry supplies and cargo to the European theater.

Lindbergh—Charles Lindbergh (1902–1974), premier American aviator of the pre–World War II era. He made the first solo air crossing of the Atlantic in a flight from New York to Paris in 1927, becoming an international hero, a legend abetted by the kidnap and murder of his son several years later. By the early forties, however, he was notorious as the leading champion of "America First," the campaign to keep the United States out of World War II in order not to deter Hitler, with whom he associated.

Alan Lomax (Alan)—Folklorist, song collector, and archivist (1915–   ). Son of John Lomax, also a folklorist and song collector. Recorded many significant folk artists, including Muddy Waters, Leadbelly, and Woody. He was one of the first to introduce Woody to East Coast radicals.

McCormack—Patterson McCormack, owner of many right–wing newspapers and a particular Guthrie nemesis because he also owned New York City radio station WNEW, where Woody briefly had a show.

McCormick—Probably industrialist Cyrus McCormick (1809–1884), who invented the mechanized reaping machine and became one of the great robber barons of the nineteenth century.

Brownie McGhee—Blues singer and guitarist; polio-stricken partner of blues harpist Sonny Terry.

Uncle Dave Macon—Folk and bluegrass banjo player and singer (1870–1952).

Marcantino—Representative Vito Marcantino, progressive American Labor Party congressman, elected from New York City during the New Deal era.

Marion—Marian Distler (see above).

Marjorie—Marjorie Greenblatt Guthrie (1917–1986), Woody's second wife. A former leading member of Martha Graham's dance company, she also worked as a dance instructor and had her own dance studio in Brooklyn. In 1967 Marjorie founded the Committee to Combat Huntington's Disease and gave up her dance studio to give full time to the committee until her death.

Sophie Maslow—One of Martha Graham's featured dancers, later a choreographer in her own right. Maslow's 1941 *Folksay* featured Woody and was the occasion for his initial meeting with Marjorie Greenblatt Mazia.

Mazias—The family of Marjorie Guthrie's first husband.

N.M.U.—The National Maritime Union, the East Coast merchant seaman's union to which Woody belonged.

Nora Lee—(born 1950), Woody and Marjorie's fourth child and only surviving daughter.

Oakie, Okie—Somewhat derogatory term for the migrant farmworkers of the Great Depression. It originated in the fact that so many of those migrants (including Woody) came from Oklahoma, which was the center of the region known as the Dust Bowl.

Merle Oberon—(1911–1987), British-born Hollywood leading lady of the late thirties and forties.

Ohfuskee County, Rock Creek, Greenleaf Creek—Sites in Woody's native region of Oklahoma.

Oran—Algerian port city.

Ohta—Daddy Ohta, left-wing Japanese-American scene painter and Toshi Seeger's father.

PM—New York City's most liberal daily newspaper of the forties.

Pegler—Westbrook Pegler, nationally syndicated New York newspaper columnist; a devoted, skillful Red-baiter and reactionary.

Peter and Lee—Pete Seeger and Lee Hays.

Mr. Petrillo—James V. Petrillo, long-time president of the American Federation of Musicians, the musicians' trade union.

Pretty Boy (Floyd)—Notorious Depression-era gangster romantically immortalized in Woody's "Pretty Boy Floyd" and a host of subsequent songs, films, and legends, the best-known being Woody's ballad.

Pushkin—Aleksander Sergeevich Pushkin (1799–1837), Russian poet and nationalist hero.

William Clark Quantrill—Confederate guerilla captain who attacked Lawrence, Kansas, in August 1863 in one of the most atrocious assaults of the Civil War.

Railroad Pete—Woody's whimsical prebirth name for his first child with Marjorie. He obviously miscalculated her sex.

Louise Rainer—Luise Rainer, Austrian actress familiar to moviegoers of the thirties and early forties.

Rankin—John Rankin, Mississippi congressman. An outrageous racist.

Paul Robeson—Black American singer, actor, football star, and radical (1898–1976). Perhaps the most celebrated black man in the world from the mid-twenties through World War II. His recording of "Ballad for Americans" was to art song more or less what "This Land Is Your Land" is to folk song.

Earl Robinson—Singer, guitarist, composer, conductor, teacher (1910–   ). Wrote film scores and cantatas. Wrote Paul Robeson's "Ballad for Americans," Frank Sinatra's "House I Live In," and other pieces of radical patriotism. He and Woody were co-narrators of Maslow's *Folksay*.

Helen Robinson—Wife of Earl Robinson.

Roughnecks—Oil-field laborers; also used for workers in any job that involves more muscle than mind.

Roustabout—A laborer on the docks or in the oilfields, sometimes in a circus (there equivalent to a stagehand).

Sacco—Niccolo Sacco, early twentieth-century American anarchist executed in Boston for alleged insurrectionary bombings. Probably framed.

Sandburg—Carl Sandburg (1878–1976), poet, song-writer, author, and bombastic "Voice of the People."

Betty Sanders—Folk singer during People's Songs days.

Sue—Sue Guthrie (1937–1989), Woody and Mary's second daughter.

Sylvia Sidney—Movie star of the thirties and forties.

Stackabones (Stacky)—Pet name for Cathy Guthrie.

Belle Starr—Female outlaw of the Old West.

John Steinbeck—American novelist (1902–1968), author of *The Grapes of Wrath* (1940).

Susquehannah—Northeastern U.S. river, empties into Chesapeake Bay (not the Ohio, as Woody at one point mistakenly asserts).

Team skinners—Mule-drivers.

Teheran—Capital of Iran and site of 1945 meeting among Stalin, Roosevelt, and Churchill during which the Allies prepared for post-World War II conditions.

Blind Sonny Terry—Blues harmonica player and singer (1911–1986), partner of Brownie McGhee. Very popular from the thirties straight through the sixties folk revival. Occasionally worked with both Woody and Leadbelly.

Judge Thayer—Boston judge who sentenced Sacco and Vanzetti to die.

Tong buckers—Slang term for oil field worker.

Toshi—Toshi Ohta Seeger, daughter of "Daddy" Otah (see above), wife of Pete Seeger, and an offstage force in both People's Song and the Weavers.

Vanzetti—Bartolomo Vanzetti, early twentieth-century anarchist executed in Boston for alleged insurrectionary bombings. Probably framed.

Sam Wanamaker—American actor/director, mainly of stage plays but also of movies. After being blacklisted, he worked primarily in England.

R. P. Weatherald—R. C. Wetherald, RCA Victor executive in charge of recording Woody's *Dust Bowl Ballads*.

Joshua White—Josh White, blues and folk singer/guitarist (1908–1969), the slickest of the bunch, and the most readily popularized.

Mr. Whitman—Walt Whitman (1819–1892), American lyric poet, whose books include *Leaves of Grass*, among others.

Bob Younger, Cole Younger—The Younger gang, members of the infamous outlaw troop that ran with Jesse and Frank James in the late 1800s.

INDEX

Note: Page numbers appearing in boldface type denote illustrations; page numbers appearing in italics refer to song lyrics

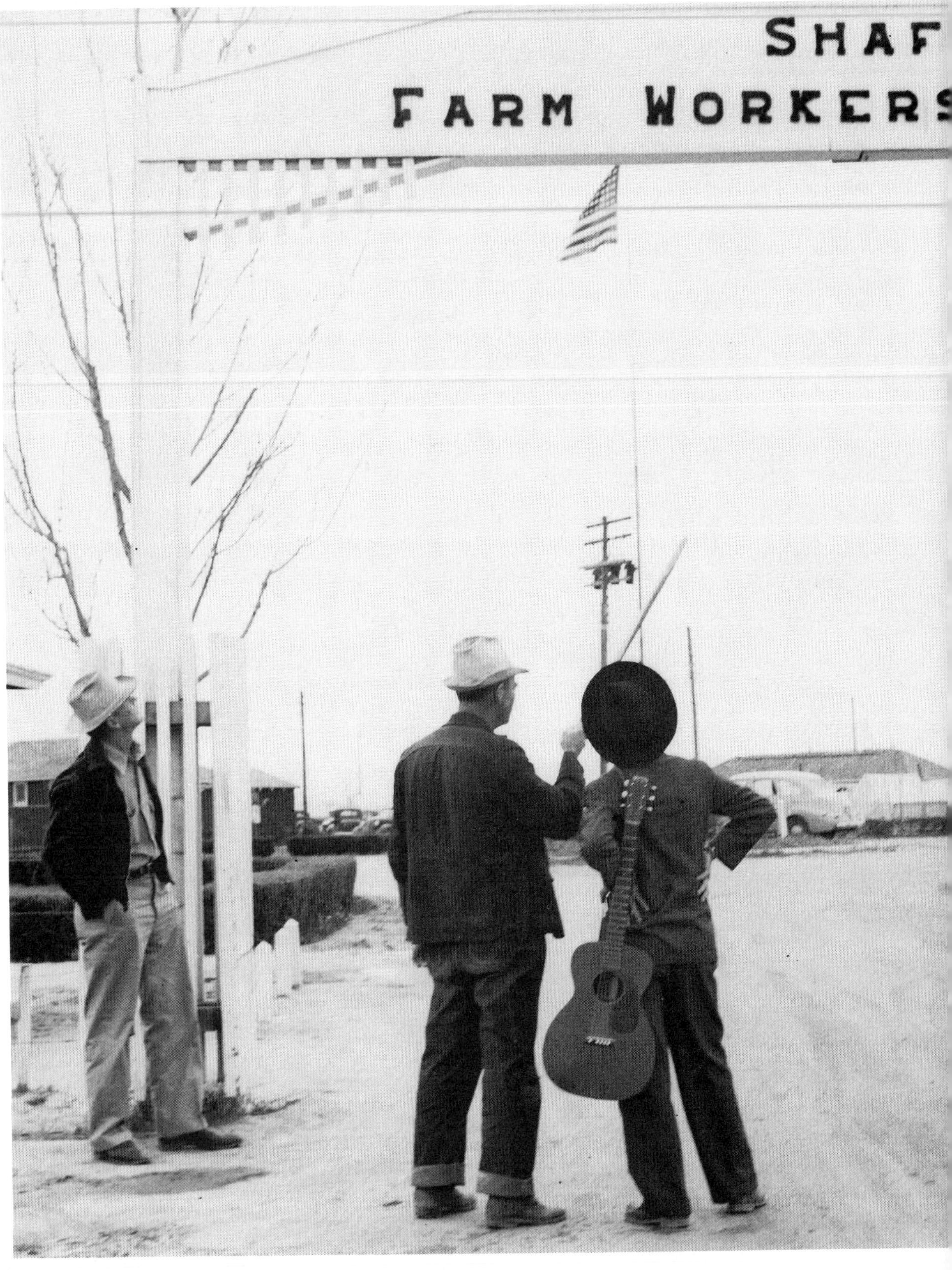
SHAF
FARM WORKERS

"This was the time when refugees from Oklahoma, Arkansas, and other areas of the Dust Bowl were streaming into California looking for work. Since there was none available, the government finally started to build housing developments to take care of their basic needs. This was done through the U.S. Department of Agriculture Farm Security Administration. One of these centers was in Arvin, California, near Bakersfield. Money was needed for everyday living so it was decided to throw a big fund-raising party at the C.I.O. headquarters in Los Angeles. The hall was rented, the program arranged, and of course the main attraction had to be Woody. As an added feature we wanted to get many of the dispossessed families from Arvin to come to the party. So Jack, Woody and I drove down there (it took approximately four to five hours). Woody sang his (and other) songs all the way with help from Jack, and I don't remember that he repeated himself either going or coming back. His repertoire was endless, and if he couldn't remember one song he would make up a new one as we went along.

"The particular center that we went to was called Shafter, and it was run in a very democratic way. Every adult had an equal voice and vote, including the government manager. Activities, classes, and recreation were organized for children and adults. The community buildings and grounds were kept spotless and discipline was enforced by the people's voice and vote. As usual, Woody reached everybody with his songs and guitar. Jack helped organize several carloads of people who came to the party, which turned out to be a big success." —Seema Weatherwax, 1988

Woody at the entrance to the Shafter Farmworkers Community, a California camp for Dust Bowl refugees, 1941. (Courtesy of Seema Weatherwax)